P9-CBR-968

Beyond Religious Freedom

For Terry --
With appreciation and
admiration,

Beth

beyond

religious

freedom

the NEW GLOBAL
POLITICS *of* RELIGION

ELIZABETH SHAKMAN HURD

Princeton University Press
Princeton and Oxford

Copyright © 2015 by Princeton University Press
Published by Princeton University Press, 41 William Street,
Princeton, New Jersey 08540
In the United Kingdom: Princeton University Press,
6 Oxford Street, Woodstock, Oxfordshire OX20 1TW
press.princeton.edu
Jacket art: An anti-landmine campaign "For Every Mine, a Flower"
(Por Cada Mina Una Flor) by Sahrawi artist Mohamed Moulud Yeslem,
with the berm separating the Polisario "Free Zone" from
Moroccan-controlled Western Sahara in the distance.
Jacket photograph © Samia Errazzouki.
All Rights Reserved
ISBN 978-0-691-16609-4
Library of Congress Control Number: 2015935299
British Library Cataloging-in-Publication Data is available
This book has been composed in Sabon Next LT Pro and ITC New Baskerville Std
Printed on acid-free paper ∞
Printed in the United States of America
1 3 5 7 9 10 8 6 4 2

For Ally, Sophie, and Audrey

Contents

100,000." She puzzles over whether these casualties can legitimately be described as "religious":

> The majority died in the civil war in the Democratic Republic of Congo. More than four million are estimated to have been killed in that war between 2000 and 2010, and CSGC counts 900,000 of them—or 20%—as martyrs. Over 10 years, that averages out at 90,000 per year. So when you hear that 100,000 Christians are dying for their faith, you need to keep in mind that the vast majority—90,000—are people who were killed in DR Congo. This means we can say right away that the internet rumours of Muslims being behind the killing of 100,000 Christian martyrs are nonsense. The DRC is a Christian country. In the civil war, Christians were killing Christians. In earlier estimates of martyrs, CSGC included killings that occurred in the Rwandan genocide. Again this is puzzling. It was not a conflict about religion—it was a case of Hutus killing Tutsis, and both sides were Christian. "The genocide in Rwanda was based on the systematic killing of an ethnic group in an attempt to completely wipe them out and it had nothing to do with the beliefs or the worship or the people who were killed," says Ian Linden, author of Church and Revolution in Rwanda, and associate professor in the study of religion at the School of Oriental and African Studies in London. "The civil wars in the DRC were the consequences of a failed state, disintegrated military force so that militias had almost full power because of the weapons they had. They were indiscriminately killing and raping and plundering and it's very difficult to describe any of that killing as creating martyrdom."

Alexander sought out a contrasting viewpoint in the work of John Allen, Vatican reporter and author of *The Global War on Christians: Dispatches from the Front Lines of Anti-Christian Persecution*.[6] In explaining that someone caught up in the DRC civil war could in fact have been martyred, Allen also alludes to the difficulty of securely identifying a particular act as "religious" in nature: "'A female catechist in Congo, who is having success persuading young people in her area not to sign up with the militias, and she is killed by one of those forces because they don't want to see the sources of recruits dry up. Now is that anti-Christian violence, or isn't it?'" Alexander then turns to CSGC director Todd Johnson to find out whether 20 percent is a realistic estimate of the number of individuals killed in the DRC because of their Christian faith. Johnson explains that "this figure was drawn from the 1982 edition of the World Christian Encyclopedia which estimated that on average 20% of African nations were actively practising Christians." "But surely," Alexander asks him, "it's not the case that all actively practicing Christians who are killed in a civil war, are killed because of their faith?" Johnson admits that CSGC had in fact "abandoned this statistic" in its more recent work, although the hundred thousand estimate remains in the 2013 Status of Global Mission. When Alexander points out that while violence continues in the DRC it is less extreme today than at its height, Johnson admits that this is a "weakness of this approach . . . even in the DRC things are not as intense as they were 10 years ago. Every year now it probably should go down. So it's probably decreasing year by year right now, but the method is not exact enough to [make those adjustments], so I've just kept it at 100,000 the last couple of years but I'm likely going to have to lower it unless something comes to our attention.' " Having concluded that "if you were to take away the 90,000 deaths in DR Congo from the CSGC's figure of 100,000, that would leave 10,000 martyrs per year," Alexander then poses the question of numbers of martyrs to Thomas Schirrmacher of the International Society for Human Rights, who concurs with Johnson that "'there is no scientific number at the moment. It has not been researched and all experts in this area are very hesitant to give a figure. . . . We are starting a research project with several universities worldwide on this topic and there we start with a guess of 7–8,000 Christians killed as martyrs each year.' " Alexander concludes that for these advocates number crunching is beside the point. John Allen appears to agree, observing that "'I think it would be good to have reliable figures on this issue, but I don't think it ultimately matters in terms of the point of my book, which is to break through the narrative that tends to dominate discussion in the West—that Christians can't be persecuted because they belong to the world's most powerful church.' "

This book reconsiders how we look at religious freedom and religious persecution. It explores the reasons for the persistent discomfort experienced by Alexander, myself, and perhaps others, when confronted with the increasingly common recourse in international public policy, human rights advocacy, and legal and foreign policy circles to "religion" as an explanatory category and a platform for policy innovation and implementation. Different aspects of politics are being collapsed too readily into the narrative of religious persecution, as evident in the account of the DRC civil war. In many cases, privileging religious difference as a causal factor in politics obscures the broader fields in which social tension, discrimination, and conflict take shape. This book seeks to bring global advocacy for religious freedom and religious rights into history, examining select aspects of the lives of these philosophical and political ideals as they materialize in particular contexts, shaping and transforming the lives of those they seek to redeem. It concludes that these efforts lead to a politics defined by religious difference, privilege forms of religion favored by those who write laws, control resources, and govern societies, and marginalize other modes of belief, being, and belonging.

In making this argument my intention is neither to judge individuals or local groups who choose to make political claims in the language of religious freedom, nor to undermine local groups working to oppose violence and discrimination. I do not seek to minimize the tragic effects of violence, discrimination, and inequality, whether they occur in Chicago or Cairo. At the same time, there is a larger story to be told about what is often rather hastily described as "religious" violence, persecution, freedom, and establishment. In exploring that story by bringing together the study of contemporary religion and the study of international politics in a new way, this book is intended to generate conversation among scholars, journalists, humanitarian relief and development experts, religious freedom and human rights advocates, and others working at the intersection of religion, law, politics, and policy. It pulls back from immediate pressures to locate a "solution" to better understand the world that is being created when the category of religion is privileged as a basis for developing foreign policy, protecting human rights, and designing interventions on behalf of imperiled individuals and communities. This larger story undermines the assumption that the solution to dilemmas of collective governance lies in the globalization of freedom of religion, government engagement with faith communities, and legal protections for religious minorities. These measures create political spaces and institutions in which state-sponsored religious distinctions not only are inevitable but become increasingly publically and politically salient. This book explores this emergent faith-based global political landscape, charting the blurred boundaries and complex power relations among expert religion, lived religion, and governed religion. In the process, it uncovers a different story about the contemporary global politics of religion.

Acknowledgments

This book would not have been possible without the support of colleagues in Political Science, Religious Studies, and Middle East & North African Studies at Northwestern University, where I have been fortunate to teach since 2004. I am also indebted to the Princeton Institute for International & Regional Studies, where I spent a sabbatical year in 2010–11 when this project was in its early stages. Thanks to Amaney Jamal for the hospitality in Princeton, and to Joan Scott and colleagues in her Secularism seminar at the Institute for Advanced Study.

I am especially grateful to Toby Volkman, Michael Gilligan, and the Henry R. Luce Initiative on Religion & International Affairs for their serious and sustained commitment to the study of religion and global politics, and generous support for the Politics of Religious Freedom project. That project afforded me a unique and valuable opportunity to develop my thinking on these issues over the past several years. To my three PRF co-organizers, Saba Mahmood, Winni Sullivan, and Peter Danchin, as well as the other project participants, thanks for your commitment to thinking through these questions collaboratively. Our discussions enriched this book immensely.

The arguments of this book were put to the test in lively discussions at lectures and workshops over the past few years at Arizona State, Brown, Columbia, European University Institute, Boston University, l'Institut d'Études Politiques, the India International Centre, George Washington University, the London School of Economics, Osgoode Hall Law School, New York University, Northern Illinois, Northwestern, Rice, Yale, the University of Chicago, the Université Libre de Bruxelles, the University of California, Berkeley, the University of Michigan, the University of Montréal, the University of Ottawa, and the University of Toronto. I am grateful to the organizers of these events and to the audience members, including many students, who thoughtfully engaged with my work in progress.

There are many colleagues and friends without whose encouragement, sense of humor, and sheer intellectual firepower this book would have been impossible. I am especially indebted to Benjamin Berger, Ian Hurd, Noah Salomon, Benjamin Schonthal, and Winni Sullivan for reading the manuscript so closely and offering critical feedback. I am also grateful to Helge Årsheim, Michael Barnett, Lori Beaman, Courtney Bender, Nathaniel Berman, Maria Birnbaum, Grant Brooke, Elizabeth Castelli, Nandini Chatterjee, Markus Dressler, Anver Emon, Alessandro Ferrari, François Foret, Phil Gorski, Ron Hassner, Robert Hefner, George Hoffman, Bonnie Honig, Yolande Jansen, Paul Johnson, Andrew Koppelman, Cécile Laborde, Thomas Lewis, Maleiha Malik, José Ciro Martínez, Nadia Marzouki, Toby Matthiesen, Melani McAlister, Jeremy Menchik, Rick Moore, Matthew Nelson, Mona Oraby, Robert Orsi, Mathijs Pelkmans, Chris Reus-Smit, Nukhet Sandal, Kathleen Sands, Evren Savci, Ariel Schwartz, Yvonne Sherwood, Sonia Sikka, Jack Snyder, Lars Tønder, Leslie Vinjamuri, Carolyn Warner, Erin Wilson, and Linda Woodhead. This book would not have been possible without Winni Sullivan's transformative contributions to the study of law and religion. Special thanks to Winni for setting the bar so high and for her unstinting support and encouragement.

I also want to thank E. J. Graff and the Op-Ed Project team, Jonathan VanAntwerpen and others at the *Immanent Frame*, David Johnson, Natalie Brender, and others who have helped at various moments to bring parts of this book to a wider audience. Erin Lockwood and Nazli Ozkan provided exceptional research assistance, Nicole Loring provided background and references on Burmese politics at a crucial moment, and Kerilyn Harkaway-Krieger, Mona Oraby and Joseph Dahm made critical editorial contributions in the final stages.

Eric Crahan's willingness upon joining Princeton University Press to dive in and encourage me to finish the manuscript came at just the right time. His quick grasp of the argument, helpful suggestions, and expert navigation of the final stages of the project were crucial. I also want to thank Chuck Myers, now at the University of Kansas Press, for helpful advice in the earlier stages of the project.

To Julia Paulk, Jessica Winegar, Joanna Grisinger, and my other book club friends, thanks for reading 1Q84 and other fun and diverting non-academic books with me. I'm lucky to have you as colleagues and friends.

To my parents, Steve and Susan, thanks for your tireless support of my career and the girls. And to Ian, Ally, Sophie, and Audrey: thanks for being there, and much love. This book is dedicated to you.

*   *   *

An earlier version of Chapter 5, "Minorities under Law," appears in the *Journal of Law and Religion* 29, no. 3 (2014) as "Alevis under Law: The Politics of Religious Freedom in Turkey" and is reproduced with permission. Parts of Chapter 2 appear in *Review of International Studies* 38, no. 5 (December 2012): 943–61. Parts of Chapter 3 appear in my essay "Believing in Religious Freedom," in *Politics of Religious Freedom*, ed. Winnifred Fallers Sullivan, Elizabeth Shakman Hurd, Saba Mahmood, and Peter G. Danchin (Chicago: University of Chicago Press, 2015). And excerpts from Chapter 6 appear in "Politics of Sectarianism: Rethinking Religion and Politics in the Middle East," special issue on Research and Methodology in a Post–Arab Spring Environment: Challenges for the Field, *Middle East Law and Governance* 7, no. 1 (2015).

We shall commit our self's [*sic*] to act and encourage the changes which are needed in our society by creating a network of those who have in mind tolerance and peace and exposure and expulsion of any kind of disrespect and extremism.

> —*US Agency for International Development–supported*
> *interreligious youth group, Inter-Religious Action for Tolerance*
> *and Co-Existence in the Balkans, Bosnia-Herzegovina (2005)*

The reinvention of government as the benign promoter of a new syncretistic public orthodoxy is only one step from oppression.

> —Julian Rivers, *The Law of Organized Religions:*
> *Between Establishment and Secularism*

CHAPTER 1

Introduction

In January 2014 an arsonist attacked the historic Maktabat al-Sa'eh (The Pilgrim's Bookshop) library in the old Serail neighborhood of Tripoli, Lebanon. The library burned to the ground, and seventy-five thousand books were destroyed. The motives of the perpetrators remain mysterious. Rumors had circulated that Father Ibrahim Srouj, the owner of the library and a Greek orthodox priest, had written an online article, or perhaps had a pamphlet in a book in his library, insulting Islam and the Prophet Muhammad.[1] Others suggested that a real estate dispute between Srouj and his landlord had led to tensions.[2] Prominent members of local civil society condemned the arson and emphasized long-standing, cross-cutting connections between various parts of the Tripoli community.[3] A representative of the Lebanese Internal Security Forces, a local MP, a local Salafi sheikh, and a former prime minister rushed to Srouj's defense, insisting that those seeking to incite intercommunal strife and violence would be shunned or imprisoned. In an interview stressing the relevance of the Syrian proxy war to the attack, Sheikh Salem al-Rafei told the *Daily Star* that "the Syrian regime seeks to show that Muslims in Tripoli are extremists and don't accept other people and that it [the Damascus regime] can [alone] protect minorities."[4] Civil society groups gathered outside the library, a former Ottoman police barracks, to collect donations to rebuild. Supporters created a Facebook page to collect books. Photos that circulated in the media showed ordinary people wearing face masks digging through the rubble attempting to salvage damaged books.

International religious freedom advocates responded differently to the library arson. Nina Shea, director of the Hudson Institute's Center for Religious Freedom and longtime activist, proclaimed that "flames of a violent hysteria against all perceived threats to Islam are spreading rapidly through the Muslim world today." Robert George, vice chair of the US Commission on International Religious Freedom (USCIRF), lamented that "the really bad news is that this is not out of the ordinary" and called for the promotion of religious freedom as a means of preventing future attacks.[5] While local residents rejected both the arson and representations of it as a harbinger of deepening religious divisions, Shea and George interpreted it as evidence of the coming apart of a community, region, and, perhaps, the world, along religious lines. Importantly, Shea and George also insisted on the equivalence between the Tripoli event and other episodes elsewhere in the world, all of which, in their view, could be reduced to episodes of religious violence and attributed to a lack of religious freedom.

These contrasting responses suggest a larger story waiting to be told about the politics of religious freedom. The responses of Shea and George are part of a powerful narrative circulating in global politics attributing acts of violence to religion or religious persecution and calling for the promotion of religious freedom in response. This book explores the politics of singling out religion as a basis from which to make foreign policy, international public policy, and conduct human rights advocacy. It historicizes the intense policy interest in religion that has taken hold in North American and European international public policy circles over the past two decades. Exploring the channels through which religion has been, and continues to be, "appropriated by worldly power holders,"[6] it draws to the surface and explores the tensions that emerge between the forms of religion that are produced and governed through these projects, and the broader fields of religious practice that they aspire to regulate and transform. What are the consequences when the category of religion becomes an object of international law and international public policy? What are the effects, on both religious and political practices, when religions are "granted intentionality and importance" and become "shadow players" in global politics?[7] What are the implications of construing religion as an isolable entity and causal powerhouse in international relations? How do these political interests and investments shape how individuals and groups live out and practice their religion? As Pamela Slotte asks of human rights law, how does this approach "regulate the space in which people are given the opportunity to live out their faith"?[8] Are there alternatives?

Though present in some form since the United States emerged as a global superpower in the mid-twentieth century, the current drive to "operationalize" religion through the promotion of religious freedom, interfaith understanding, toleration, and rights accelerated and became fully institutionalized after 9/11. The United States and key allies such as the United Kingdom and Canada have rallied around the notion that the flourishing of free and tolerant religion, increased dialogue between faith communities, and the legalization of minority rights are required to emancipate societies from intercommunal strife, economic deprivation, and gender and other forms of discrimination. A 2007 report by the center-right think tank Center for Strategic and International Studies, titled "Mixed Blessings: U.S. Government Engagement with Religion in Conflict-Prone Settings," registers the shift: "Parts of the intelligence community address religion as a transnational concern; the military services are increasingly developing doctrine and training on approaching religious leaders and communities in stability operations; USAID works with faith-based organizations and incorporates religious sensitivities into some development programming; and State Department officials promote international religious freedom and are focused on improving relations with the Muslim world."[9] The same report concludes that "the armed services are still determining how such knowledge should be used in practice. Much of the *strategic implementation of religious knowledge* today is occurring at the Joint Intelligence Operations Centers and the regionally focused Combatant Commands."[10] Coupled with the right forms of governance achieved through the "strategic implementation of religious knowledge," moderate religion is said to be capable of pushing back against, and ultimately triumphing over, its rivals. The right kind of religion, recognized and engaged by states and other public international authorities, has emancipatory potential. Moderate religion has the capacity to treat a variety of social ills, such as gender-based oppression and the exclusion of minorities, associated with retrograde forms of religion, fragile or failed states, and a lack of development. Tolerant religion, in this view, catalyzes democratization and political pluralism. It takes the wind out of the sails of extremist movements by offering a viable alternative to radicalization.

Of course state efforts to intervene in religious fields are not new, and various earlier moments could also be considered.[11] Noah Salomon discusses similar machinations in early twentieth-century British attempts to stamp out "Islamic fanaticism," whose main theater was Sudan, through an attempt to promote moderate scholastic Islam. In an interesting reversal of contemporary practice, at that time the categories of "fanatical" and "moderate" were mapped onto Sufism and "scholastic Islam," respectively.[12] Nandini Chatterjee has shown how religion was produced as a legal category in colonial India through a distinctly modern approach toward religious toleration that arbitrated between, rather than ignoring, religious difference. This engendered a novel species of political competition that consisted of collective claims asserted to be "religious" and accepted as such by the state: "Through the very fact of declaring a policy of religious 'neutrality' [the colonial state] committed itself to the identification of religious 'rights' borne by entities known as religious communities."[13] Going back further, Napoleon's efforts to integrate the Jewish population of France shaped and changed the practice of Judaism considerably. As Michael Goldfarb observes, "the practice of Judaism today would be unrecognizable to the recently emancipated Jews of Napoleon's time."[14]

Focusing on a contemporary international moment, the projects discussed in this book can be situated in this longer history of state efforts to define and shape forms of religiosity that are understood to be conducive to particular regimes of governance. This book does not trace these mechanisms of religious governance back to a single origin point but rather examines particular moments in which these forms of governance have become especially visible and influential in global politics. Today, spearheaded by the United States, the commitment to religious freedom and moderation has become global in scope, encompassing individual European states, the European Union, Canada, the United Nations, and many international and nongovernmental organizations, public and private. Leaders and decision makers have identified the cultivation of tolerant religion as a critical ingredient in addressing the ills that plague collective life in the early twenty-first century. Religion needs to be understood and it needs to be engaged. In the words of the US President's Advisory Council on Faith-Based and Neighborhood Partnerships, "We simply cannot understand our Nation or our world without understanding religion."[15] In Tony Blair's words, "the purpose should be to change the policy of governments, to start to treat this issue of religious extremism as an issue that is about religion as well as politics, to go to the roots of where a false view of religion is being promulgated and to make it a major item on the agenda of world leaders to combine effectively to combat it."[16] President Obama echoed these themes at the 2014 National Prayer Breakfast, stressing the connection between religious freedom and national security: "History shows that nations that uphold the rights of their people, including the freedom of religion, are ultimately more just and more peaceful and more successful. Nations that do not uphold these rights sow the bitter seeds of instability and violence and extremism. So freedom of religion matters to our national security."[17]

While there are rich histories to be mined in the context of the American project for global religious freedom, today these political forms for managing religion are being adopted and adapted globally. Their reach is impressive, and the American experience is far from exhaustive. Religious lives and possibilities are being legally tailored by a bevy of increasingly professionalized national and transnational actors to meet the global demand for tolerant religious subjects who enjoy freedom under law.[18] With the United States leading the charge, and others following suit, advocacy for religious freedom, tolerance, and protections for the rights of religious minorities has "gone viral." As a result, while being attentive to US foreign religious policy and programming, it is also important to consider how these political discourses materialize to shape legal and political fields in places such as Turkey absent explicit US religious interventionism. These discourses are being privileged in policy formulation in Canada, the United Kingdom, Italy, France, and the European Union, with the United States often cited as a model, yet without direct US political pressure. International organizations, state foreign policy establishments, nongovernmental organizations, development assistance agencies, and military establishments, to varying degrees and in different platforms, all have signed on to the project of promoting tolerant religion and moderate religious subjects. Communities around the world are increasingly understood as in need of varying degrees of social and religious engineering, ranging from a minor touch-up to an extreme makeover. Reformers seek to create the conditions in which secular states and their religious subjects become tolerant, believing or nonbelieving consumers of free religion and practitioners of faith-based solutions to collective problems. Religiously free states and subjects are said to naturally oppose terrorism, to support the free market, and to be inclined toward democracy. States marshal financial resources, gather information about religions, and train bureaucrats in departments and ministries on how to guarantee religious freedom, cultivate tolerant religious subjects, and protect religious minorities. New partnerships between state and international authorities and private actors are being created in pursuit of these objectives.[19] This goes beyond the American foreign policy establishment. Religious freedom, tolerance, and rights have become what Gerd Bauman describes as dominant discourses, in that each is "conceptually simple, enjoys a communicative monopoly, offers enormous flexibility of application, encompasses great ideological plasticity, and is serviceable for established institutional purposes."[20]

This book offers a focused discussion that brings together several questions and concerns that have not been considered together before to develop three related arguments about these political projects and the fields in which they are deployed. First, it shows how particular constructs of religious freedom, religious tolerance, and the rights of religious minorities are being packaged into political projects and delivered around the world by states and others. Second, it contributes to the literature on religion and international relations by historicizing and politicizing the attempt over the past two decades to incorporate a concern for religion into the study and practice of global politics. Much of this discourse treats religion as a self-evident category that motivates a host of actions, both good and bad. This book challenges such an approach. Religion is too unstable a category to be treated as an isolable entity, whether the objective is to attempt to separate religion from law and politics or design a political response to "it." Third, the book embeds the study of religion and politics in a series of broader social and interpretive fields by exploring the relation between these international projects and the social, religious, and political contexts in which they are deployed. Specifically, it focuses on the gaps created between the forms of religion that are sanctioned by expert knowledge and promoted through international advocacy for freedom, tolerance, and rights, and a diverse, shifting, and multiform field of lived religious practice. There is of course no strict dichotomy or sharp line to be drawn between these two categories. What I refer to as expert, official, and lived or everyday religions are all inextricably bound up with each other and with institutional religion. These distinctions are always to some extent arbitrary and porous and are themselves the product of law and governance. The challenge, then, is to signal an interest in a category, religion, which is legible to many, while also arguing for a different understanding of it.[21]

To this end, this book draws together and amplifies the findings of a broad and recent body of scholarship that pushes back in different ways against the received wisdom surrounding religious freedom.[22] It draws on a combination of my own primary research—government reports, meeting proceedings, legal decisions, media reports—and secondary research across several academic disciplines to propose a theoretical and conceptual step forward in the study of religion and world politics.

Distinguishing between religion and religious freedom as authorized by experts and governments and the broader fields in which these constructs are deployed reveals new possibilities for thinking about religion, law, and global politics. It opens new lines of sight onto political histories, struggles, and forms of religiosity that escape, defy, or are indifferent to efforts to govern religion "from above."[23] New interpretive possibilities emerge as a result of thinking differently about religion, of complicating and disaggregating the category. What if religion cannot be collapsed into a force for good or evil (or both)? What if it cannot simply stand in for whatever is considered to fall outside the secular?[24] Religion does not stand outside or prior to other histories and institutions. Religious practices unfold amid and are entangled in all domains of human life, forms of belonging, work, play, governance, violence, and exchange.[25] Religion cannot be singled out from these other aspects of human experience, and yet also cannot simply be identified with these either. In exploring what this understanding of religion entails for the study of global politics, this book works to "release the space of the political from the grasp of the secularization doctrine."[26] It is intended, in part, as a thought experiment that provides a glimpse of what the world would look like after religion is dethroned as a stable, coherent legal and policy category.

The argument unfolds as follows. Chapter 2 analyzes the understandings and assumptions about religion that authorize US-led global initiatives to govern religion through advocacy for freedom, tolerance, and rights. Chapters 3 through 5 follow an arc tracing how expert and official constructs of religious freedom (Chapter 3), religious tolerance and religious engagement (Chapter 4), and religious rights (Chapter 5) have been brought to life in sociopolitical and religious landscapes around the world. Though each chapter is differently structured, each explores a specific logic—freedom, tolerance, and rights—through which religion is overseen and governed globally. Each also draws attention to the gap between religion as construed by those in positions of power and the broader social, religious, economic, and political fields in which these authorized understandings are deployed. Taken together, these chapters are suggestive of the power and possibility, and also the limitations, that inhere in these political philosophical constructs (freedom, tolerance, rights) as they materialize in specific contexts. Rather than provide an exhaustive survey of these ideals in action, each chapter discusses select aspects of the work being done, and the religious and political worlds being realized, in their name.

There is variation in length and style in the empirical focal points that appear in this book, ranging from a detailed analysis of the situation of the Alevis to more focused discussions of the plight of the Sahrawi refugees in Algeria and the Rohingya in Myanmar and shorter descriptions of the politics of Guatemalan K'iche' land rights claims as they intersect with the politics of religious freedom. Two criteria governed the selection of these focal points. One is the extent to which the lives of particular individuals and groups have been, and continue to be, shaped by the social, political, and religious realities generated by these international efforts. The second is the extent to which a particular example illustrates the benefits of embedding the study of religion in a broader field of social and historical practice.

The balance of this chapter introduces three heuristics: expert religion, lived religion, and governed religion, each emphasizing a different set of themes and topics that are important to the argument as a whole. Briefly, *expert religion* is religion as construed by those who generate "policy-relevant" knowledge about religion in various contexts. In contemporary Europe and North America this field is dominated by the agenda of reassurance, which celebrates religion as a source of morality and cohesion, and, simultaneously, the agenda of surveillance, which fears religion as a potential danger to be contained and suppressed. As discussed in the next chapter these two "faces of faith" enjoy significant legal and political traction in contemporary international relations, having partially displaced among many scholars and practitioners a commitment to secularization understood as privatization. *Lived religion* is religion as practiced by everyday individuals and groups as they interact with a variety of religious authorities, rituals, texts, and institutions and seek to navigate and make sense of their lives, connections with others, and place in the world. It refers to a diverse field of human activity, relations, investments, beliefs, and practices that may or may not be captured in the set of human goings-on that are identified as "religion" for the purposes of law and governance. The latter is what I refer to as official or *governed religion*: religion as construed by those in positions of political and religious power. In today's world, this includes states, often through the law, but also other authorities such as supranational courts, governing entities such as the European Union, a variety of international and nongovernmental organizations, and churches and other religious organizations.

I am not the first to propose such distinctions. The sociologist Linda Woodhead has distinguished between what she calls strategic religion and tactical religion, or "Olympian" versus "non-Olympian" religion.[27] The former refers to the spaces created for religion by those in power—by purveyors of freedom, tolerance, and rights in the terms of this book—while the latter refers to the actions of those without power that are responding to the opportunities and constraints created by strategic religion.[28] Akeel Bilgrami contrasts between what he describes as "knowledges to live by" or "spiritual or learned ways of life," and "expertise to rule by." When the former is transformed into the latter, Bilgrami suggests, spiritual domains become impoverished, becoming the province of the few, rather than the many.[29] All of these distinctions have porous boundaries and blend into each other. While imperfect, they grant a certain critical distance from the oppositional pairs that loom large in the contemporary study of religion and politics, including secularism/postsecularism, establishment/ disestablishment, freedom/unfreedom, and separation/accommodation. They do so by interrogating the singular, stable understanding of religion that is often presupposed on both sides of these familiar binaries. More specifically for our purposes, distinguishing between expert, lived, and official religion allows for a focused examination of the effects of construing religion as a stable object of international law and public policy. As legal and political projects that rely on the category of religion take shape, they interact with broader fields of human activity, forms of collective belonging, and a variety of sociopolitical goods and goals. Disaggregating the category of religion makes these interactions and mutual transformations easier to see.

EXPERT RELIGION

In 2012 Wilton Park, an executive agency of the UK Foreign and Commonwealth Office published a report on religious freedom that observed that "in order to be effective, Foreign Service personnel need not only tools or toolkits but also knowledge to implement them."[30] The past two decades have witnessed the rise of an insatiable demand for knowledge about religion, religious leaders, and religious politics and practices. Experts have emerged to meet this demand, resulting in a flourishing of academic and public policy scholarship on the subject of religion in relation to global theory and practice. Academic journals and conferences are overrun with studies of religion and international policy and politics. Analyses of the effects of religious actors and belief systems on international political outcomes, peaceful or violent, are ubiquitous. Professional associations rush to create sections on "religion and" their particular field of expertise. Development experts and humanitarian groups hastily piece together their religion portfolios. White papers abound. Foundations and think tanks scramble to meet the demand for knowledge about religion in relation to every conceivable domain of human activity, from nuclear proliferation to environmental concerns, territorial expansion, asylum law, health care, and postwar reconciliation. Religion experts burnish their credentials. Universities create centers. Solutions for anxious policy makers are sought and found. The security industry, environmentalists, development experts, constitutional specialists, and democratization consultants are searching for ways to incorporate religion into their policies and programming. This is expert religion.

Chapter 2 explores the understandings of religion that underlie this outpouring of academic and public policy production. An impressive amount of scholarship over the past two decades has been presented, and received, as a corrective that is intended to remedy an alleged secularist bias permeating the academy and other elite institutions up until the so-called rediscovery of religion. This reparative and recuperative impulse vis-à-vis religion goes hand-in-hand with the denigration and marginalization of whatever and whomever is identified as "secular" or "secularist." It is presumed that religion had been excluded, and now that we have come to our senses, it needs to be "brought back in." Chapter 2 historicizes this narrative and one of its most influential variations, in which the world is said to be witnessing a battle between "two faces of faith": dangerous religion and peaceful religion. With some help from the domestic and international authorities, the story goes, the latter is destined to triumph over the former.[31] If governments and other stakeholders can be induced to shape religion effectively and engage religious actors properly through advocacy for religious rights and freedoms, religion will serve as what one analyst describes as a "force multiplier." It will contribute to international peace and security, economic growth, and human flourishing.

In this narrative "religion" appears as an aspect of social difference that is both a potential problem (a cause of violence and discord) and its own solution, inasmuch as interfaith cooperation can be institutionalized, extremists marginalized, and religion's benevolent tendencies harnessed for the public good.[32] This counterthesis has largely supplanted the secularization-as-privatization thesis among scholars and practitioners in international affairs. It fuels many of the initiatives discussed in this book. This partial displacement of the secularization thesis is the result of a shift in public and academic discourse in North America and Europe away from an understanding of religion as "private" and largely irrelevant to global governance, toward a different dispensation, and accompanying political agenda, in which religion is seen as public good *and* potential source of violence in need of domestication. Both dispensations could be described as secularist; as C. S. Adcock explains, and as I have shown in earlier work, "defining and contesting what counts as religious are practices internal to secular politics."[33] This book maintains a distance from the discussion and debate over secularism by focusing not so much on how that which is identified as religion becomes subject to particular forms of governance, but rather how, once established, these forms of law and governance relate to the broader political, social, and religious life worlds with which they interact. The intention is to open the field onto a more encompassing social and interpretive space than that afforded by an exclusive focus on religion as construed by secular power.

But we are not there yet. Religion defined as an isolable object has become a mode through which political power operates, in the sense described by Timothy Mitchell.[34] To the extent that religion has assumed importance as a legal and policy category in international law and politics, as I suggest it has, governments, courts, and other authorities are compelled to define it, and to distinguish between religious and nonreligious individuals, groups, and practices. This dilemma, as others have shown, is a—if not *the*—distinguishing feature of modern secular power.[35] Religion is conceived, to varying degrees, as an autonomous domain that is distinct from other parts of human life. Religion is construed as normative, singular, and prior to other human affiliations and forms of sociality. There are things in the world called "religions" that are interacting with each other. Martin Stringer describes the powerful grip of these assumptions in the disciplines of sociology and political science:

> From a more sociological, and increasingly from a political science-based perspective, the debate about religious diversity has assumed that there are things called "religions" out there that are interacting, and that that interaction needs to be either studied or managed. When we explore in more detail what these "things" called religions are, then in most cases the assumption being made is that a "religion" is primarily a group of people, more or less organized, who share a common belief system and who engage in a common set of rituals. It is also assumed that these people see their "religion" as a

central element of their own identity and so can define themselves relatively unproblematically as "Christian," "Buddhist," "Muslim" or whatever. . . . Almost all authors working in this field assume that "religions" are a social fact and that the real question is "how do they, or how should they, interact?"[36]

Stringer's description is important. In contemporary international affairs, and I refer here both to the production of knowledge in the social sciences and to its application in policy circles, religions are portrayed as unproblematic social facts comprised of bounded entities and faith communities that need to be studied, engaged, and, perhaps, reformed. As Pamela Klassen and Courtney Bender observe, "modern secular fields encourage frequent appeals to the epistemological autonomy of religion and locate that autonomy in particular, recognized historically constituted traditions."[37] Robert Orsi notes similarly that "a politics free of religion has come to seem naïve and old-fashioned, and with this has come an insistence on the singular, coherent and authoritative nature of religious traditions."[38] This is particularly the case when it comes to the religion of the "other." As discussed in Chapter 6, the religious lives of social scientists are often understood to be more intentional and unbounded as compared to the religious lives of those they study.[39]

That many scholars and decision makers understand "religions" as singular and coherent entities that motivate particular forms of politics is important for at least three reasons. First, when religion is taken as a plausible explanation for political action it sets the stage for—and arguably requires—political intervention to engage and shape it, to tap into its benevolent and transformative powers. Second, to declare religion the cause of particular political conflicts reduces complex questions of causation and obscures the broader economic, historical, and political contexts in which discrimination and violence occur. Basic categories of social conflict and coexistence are framed in religious terms. Social tensions and conflicts with multiple contributing factors are depoliticized, their causes explained away through reference to intractable religious difference. As Samuli Schielke has argued, "there is good reason to be cautious about a question that reinforces, instead of investigating, the growing imagination of a world religion as an entity with agency."[40] Finally, privileging religion as an entity with agency also shapes the lives of the individuals and groups who live under these designations. The concept of lived religion offers a point of entry into these histories and experiences.

LIVED RELIGION

There is a complex and unstable relation between the "religion" that is authorized for legal and political purposes and a broader, messier world of religious belonging, belief, and practice. Many forms of affiliation and experience fit uncomfortably, if at all, into an understanding of religion as a singular, bounded "cause" of political behavior. Many operate outside of the understanding of religion presupposed by its secular legal and administrative "management." Many fail to conform to orthodox understandings of what religion is or should be. In the process of engaging religion and promoting religious freedom, specific forms of religion, certain religious leaders, and particular religious traditions are inevitably singled out from a more expansive field. That which is singled out is privileged and consecrated through legal and political advocacy and guarantees for freedom, rights, and toleration. It often does not align with—and may sideline or crush—disparate, improvised forms of religious belonging and practice. Dissidents, doubters, and those who identify with nonorthodox versions of protected traditions struggle for representation.

The category of lived religion is meant to draw attention to the practices that fall outside the confines of religion as construed for purposes of law and governance. And yet to distinguish between official and lived religion in this way is to risk reifying and romanticizing lived religious practice. There is tension between the claim that religion is too unstable a category for government management and the simultaneous insistence on the importance of lived religion as standing apart from official religion or expert religion. This book emphasizes the mutual interactions and blurred boundaries between these fields. Lived religion does not exist in a vacuum separate from institutional or organized religion. There are no clean lines. There is no autochthonous religion that stands independent of "elite," "orthodox," or "legal" religion. The challenge, then, is to constantly problematize a clean juxtaposition between everyday and official religion even while relying on these distinctions as heuristic devices that allow us to ask new kinds of questions, pressing the field in new directions. Inhabiting this productive paradox forces us to consider forms of sociality and religiosity that escape the field of vision of scholars and practitioners who are trained to study legally and academically authorized definitions of religion. The life worlds "beyond" religious freedom otherwise tend to fall between the cracks because when scholars and practitioners look for religion they seek out religious leaders and institutions, recognizable texts and defined orthodoxies, and religious authorities in fancy robes and impressive hats. These authorities matter, but they do not exhaust the field; rather, organized or institutionalized religion occupies a series of spaces that overlaps and interacts with both "governed" and "lived" religion. Some conceptual imprecision is warranted, even necessary, in these circumstances, as Cécile Laborde has pointed out.[41]

While acknowledging the importance of religious authorities and institutions, and the contributions of scholars and practitioners who have been socialized to look in particular places when they are told to find "religion," this book seeks to open the study of religion and global politics up to a broader social and interpretive field. Lived religion is part of this field but does not exhaust it, as Robert Orsi, Winnifred Fallers Sullivan, and others who have complicated the study of contemporary religion have shown. Orsi invented the term "everyday religion" to describe "not solely or primarily what happens in specially designated and consecrated sacred spaces, under the authority of religious elites, but in streets and alleys, in the souvenir stalls outside shrines, and in bedrooms and kitchens; 'everyday religion' does not happen at times determined by sacred calendars or official celestial computations, but by the circumstances and exigencies of people's lives. The everyday religious is not performed by rote or in accordance with authority; it is improvised and situational." This lends itself to the study of not specific religious traditions per se but rather the "manifold paths of daily life." It does not exist apart from either religious tradition or religious authorities but is in constant interaction with and constituted by them.[42] Sullivan's *The Impossibility of Religious Freedom* illustrates the ways in which the legal process forcibly elicits the hierarchical definition and juxtaposition of "legal" versus "outlaw" or "anarchic" religion. Her argument develops through a close reading of a 1999 trial, *Warner v. Boca Raton*, which hinged on the legality of regulations at a municipal cemetery in Boca Raton that placed limitations on how mourners could materially commemorate loved ones at their gravesites. The legal point of contention involved whether vertical commemorative statues and shrines were protected under Florida law as forms of religious expression (the plaintiffs' argument) or should be interpreted as "optional" personal preferences that could be legally removed by cemetery groundskeepers (the city's argument). The plaintiffs lost the case.[43] Sullivan, who served as an expert witness at the trial, documents in her book the always-particular understandings of religion that underlie attempts to guarantee religious freedom and illuminates the dissonance between these understandings and the broader fields of religious practice that they shape and constrain.

This book explores these concerns in a different context, uncovering the tensions between the religion promoted and provided for through expert religion and official advocacy for freedom, tolerance, and rights, and the improvised, situational practices that often take place outside of churches, synagogues, and mosques. When states and other international authorities privilege religion in law and international public policy it often comes at the expense of these practices to the point of rendering them invisible, illegible, or unrecognizable as religion. Privileging religion in law and international public policy also creates religion through discourse about it, forcing practices into the category of "religion" that might not have been considered religious before. To fix religion in law— to give it over to expert and official religion—effaces the indeterminacy of evolving and contested sets of traditions that are not reducible to whatever the authorities count as religion.

Bringing lived religion into our field of vision as scholars of global politics also highlights a disconnect between the actual religious lives of most Americans, including those who advocate most fervently for international religious freedom, and the version of the American myth of religious freedom that is projected abroad by the US government. "Curiously," as Sullivan explains, "a gap has opened between the version of the myth we are offering for export, and the religious lives of most Americans. Freed from the domestic constraints of the Constitution and of politics, as in so many other areas Americans are promoting a version of the rule of law that establishes authority abroad, religious and otherwise, in ways unacceptable, even incomprehensible, at home, where antinomian religion continues to flourish in new guises, whether in city squares, sweat lodges, or prisons."[44] These forms of extraterritorial establishment—and the extent to which they would be considered unacceptable or even unconstitutional in the states that are sponsoring reforms—are a recurring theme of this book and the subject of Chapter 4.

GOVERNING RELIGION

Chapters 3, 4, and 5 explore different aspects of governed religion, the religion that is privileged through advocacy for international religious freedom, religious toleration and interfaith understanding, and guarantees for the rights of religious minorities. A novel combination of global political will, shifting patterns of religious governance, accelerating legal globalization, unparalleled financial resources, and historical contingencies such as 9/11 and the rise of counterterrorism have led to a global field of religious and social engineering that is unprecedented in size, scope, and reach. Several factors account for the acceleration and intensification of this programming in recent decades. Stringer is right that the American-led "war on terror" and the securitization of Islam are important drivers of the new religious policy imperative,[45] but the traction enjoyed by these projects is also attributable to longer-term shifts in how the role of government is understood in relation to religion in Europe and North America. In the United States, for example, as Sullivan argues, religion and spirituality are increasingly understood to be natural parts of the human experience, and government at all levels as a partner whose job it is to ensure the conditions of its flourishing.[46] Religion is being "naturalized," and as a result the "American government speaks of its citizens as being naturally spiritual and in need of spiritual care."[47] This naturalization of religion and spirituality is among the enabling conditions for the current full-court press for global spiritual reform. Government efforts to legally remake religion, craft religiously tolerant global subjects, and guarantee religiously free citizenries and polities appear as natural, or even to be expected, in a world in which the government's job is understood to include particular forms of religious stewardship. The phenomena described in this book, then, are part of a larger story that involves a shift in the United States and, to varying degrees in Europe and elsewhere, away from the preeminence of a hard-edged separationism—distinguished by the attempt to extract religion from governmental affairs and government from religious affairs—and toward a different dispensation in which government is seen as a handmaiden and governor of tolerant, democracy-friendly, legally supervised religion—at home and abroad. In this model, the government's job is to support and engender the conditions in which tolerant, nonestablished religion can flourish.

The three core chapters of this book explore the politics of international advocacy for religious freedom, tolerance, and the rights of religious minorities, situating these efforts in the broader fields in which they are deployed. Chapter 3 examines the politics of protecting and promoting an international right to religious freedom. Describing three consequences of framing social difference through religious rights and freedoms, it shows that these efforts single out groups for legal protection as religious groups, mold religions into discrete faith communities with clean boundaries, clearly defined orthodoxies, and senior leaders who speak on their behalf, and privilege a modern liberal understanding of faith. Drawing on examples from Myanmar, South Sudan, Guatemala, and India, this chapter repositions religious freedom as one among many possible modes of governing social difference in contemporary international relations. Rather than a stable norm or social fact that stands above the fray, the deployment of religious rights is a technique of governance that authorizes particular forms of politics and regulates the spaces in which people live out their religion. Also running through this chapter is a concern for the politics of nonrecognition: specifically, the forms of political struggle and modes of collective belonging that are obscured by talk of international religious freedom.[48] Many violations of human dignity fail to register as religious freedom concerns, thus remaining outside an international spotlight that is trained on "persecuted religious minorities." Examples discussed in the chapter include the predicament of the K'iche' people in Guatemala, caste oppression in India, and women imprisoned for witchcraft in the Central African Republic. None of these groups conform to the persecuted religious minority framework because violations of their ritual practices do not register as religious.

Chapter 4 turns to the history and politics of US religious engagement. Religious engagement and efforts to promote religious freedom are part of a decades-long project in which the promotion of American-friendly "free" religion in other countries is understood to benefit not only Americans but also the rest of the world by saving them from religious and political tyranny. These religious reform projects are sustained by a powerful myth of American exceptionalism that posits the United States as not only the home of religious freedom, but also the place where both religion and freedom have been perfected. Contemporary religious engagement programs are the latest in a series of American attempts to position the United States as the global guardian of free religion, and freedom in general. These include US attempts to promote "global spiritual health" during the Cold War, a USAID project intended to promote religious tolerance in Albania in the early 2000s, and contemporary religious outreach and liaison activities of US military chaplains stationed overseas. The debate over religious engagement, the chapter concludes, is not a question of whether religion can be separate from government, ignored or contained—as many separationists would have it. The debate over religious engagement is also not about whether "persons of faith" should be included in public life to help achieve collective goals. The question is how these entanglements between the US government and authorities abroad take shape when religion is privileged as a political and legal category: who gets chosen and why, which version of which religion is supported, which authorities are heard, and whose voices are silenced. To access these dynamics it is helpful to distinguish between the "governed" religion that is engaged and supported through these programs, and the broader field of practice in which they operate. Government-sponsored religious outreach requires that the government decide which groups count as "religious" and to discriminate among vying sects and denominations, privileging some at the expense of others. In the case of US foreign policy this leads to support not only for American-friendly leaders and institutions, but also for religions that conform to an American understanding of what it means for religion to be free.

Chapter 5 turns away from US foreign policy and toward international political and legal attempts to constitute and govern groups as religious minorities. Proponents of minority rights have called for urgent measures to protect the Copts in Egypt, the Ahmadis in Pakistan, and the Bahá'í in Iran, Egypt, and elsewhere as a means of securing religious diversity, shielding minority populations from discriminatory practices, and preventing religious violence. State governments, international organizations, international tribunals, and human rights advocates promote religious liberalization as the antidote to the violence and discord that is often attributed to these divisions. Enshrined in international agreements and promoted by a small army of global experts and authorities, legal protections for religious minorities are heralded as the solution to the challenges of living with religious diversity. Chapter 5 documents the risks of adopting religion as a category to draw together individuals and communities as corporate bodies that are depicted as in need of legal protection to achieve their freedom. Who defines orthodoxy? Who is transformed through such definitions into a "minority" or a "sect," and with what social consequences? How are the complexities and ambivalences of everyday religious belonging translated and reconfigured through the process of becoming legalized and governmentalized? What is lost in the process? These questions are addressed in a case study of the legal status of the Alevis, a community and a category formally constituted as a single whole relatively recently as part of the Turkish nation-building project. Two legal constructions of Alevism, by the Turkish state and the European Court of Human Rights, anchor the discussion. While premised on differing assumptions, both of these legal construals of Alevism are examples of "governed religion" that downplay the indeterminacy surrounding Alevism as a lived tradition embedded in a broader field of social and cultural practices, while bolstering the role of the state in overseeing religiosities in the service of Turkish nationalism. To classify the Alevis as a collective subject of religious rights and freedoms guaranteed by the state and backed up by international legal instruments reinforces a tradition of Turkish secularism in which an implicit Sunni-majority state serves as the arbiter of religious identity and practice.

CONCLUSION

The construct of religion brings together a vast, diverse, and shifting set of social and cultural phenomena. The category has a long genealogy, emerging in the contentious history of church-state religions in Europe at the time of the founding of the modern state system and forged through the histories of colonialism, state building, and other processes associated with political modernity.[49] As Helge Årsheim has observed it is only with the rise of religion as a generic category following the Protestant Reformation that religion became legally available as a stand-alone category, both domestically and internationally.[50] Religion never "left" politics or international relations but has assumed different forms and occupied different spaces under modern regimes of governance, which are often understood to be secular. Neither religions nor religious actors are singular, agentive forces that can be analyzed, quantified, engaged, celebrated, or condemned—and divided between good and bad. To rely for policy purposes on the category of religious actor is, rather, to presume a certain form of actorship motivated by religion that is neither intellectually coherent nor sociologically defensible.[51] It is something that is claimed about a particular group by a particular authority in a specific context.[52] There is often no agreement within any religious tradition on who speaks authoritatively on behalf of that tradition, who is in and who is out, which texts and practices represent the core of the tradition, and so forth. There is no single Judaism or Christianity. There are many. There are no neat lines between believers and nonbelievers, or between the world of the sacred and everyday life. As Robert Orsi shows in his ethnography of Italian Harlem, "the world of the sacred was not entered only, or even mainly, in churches: it was encountered and celebrated through family life, hospitality, and friendship, as well as in the daily trials of the people."[53] This "theology of the streets" or popular spirituality is not "merely a corruption or a poor assimilation of Catholic doctrine," but expresses a Catholic sensibility that is "woven deep into the fabric" of people's lives.[54] The complexity and ambivalence of religion and religious belonging, its embeddedness in other forms of human sociality and activity, and its persistent failure to conform to modern binaries such as belief/unbelief, good/bad, and faith/reason suggest the need for a more nuanced and context-specific approach to religion, law, and governance, domestically and internationally.

And yet the pressure for normative closure, for a definitive metalanguage in which to define and discuss religion and develop policy solutions, remains strong. Powerful forces, including the law, incentivize individuals and groups to make claims for rights, dignity, and justice in the languages of religious rights and freedoms. Political and material rewards await individuals and groups who can convincingly frame identities and specify collective needs as religious actors, religious minorities, and religious communities in search of their freedom. If being a persecuted religionist makes it more likely that one's life chances will be improved, then we should expect to see a rise in persecuted religionists. If legalizing religious freedom makes it more likely that development assistance, trade deals, or accession to the European Union will be forthcoming, we should not be surprised to see legislative, executive, and judicial action at all levels privileging the category of religion.

Those in search of a policy prescription for how religion should be governed by the modern liberal state or the international community may be disappointed in this book. The category of religion does not lend itself to such prescriptions.[55] Instead this book historicizes and politicizes the new global politics of religion, turning the prism in a new way to catch sight of the possibilities of a world beyond religious freedom. It is a cautionary tale, inviting scholars and practitioners to step back and consider the work being done by the modifier "religious" when it is deployed to describe situations, actions, and decisions—and prescribe solutions. Situating religion in a series of broader social and interpretive fields allows us to see beyond sectarianism and beyond religious freedom, both of which, I suggest, are discourses of religion authorized by those in positions of power.

In conducting research for this project among scholars, policy makers, and politically active religious leaders, I was often reminded of a comment made by an eminent anthropologist in the context of a discussion of policy-relevant knowledge about religion. "Ordinary people don't have policies," she suggested, "they respond to and submit to policies."[56] If there is a prescriptive thread running through the book, it is to highlight the "objects" of the proliferating number of projects being undertaken in the name of religious freedom, including those who may be indifferent to or chafe against their seemingly limitless aspirations and ambitions.

CHAPTER 2

Two Faces of Faith

Henceforth we can do no more than keep insisting (somewhat anxiously) that true religion always believes in the rough equivalence of the voice of the gods and basic principles of civil obedience. We hope and pray for this and manipulate true religion in this direction, even as we betray our fears by anxiously reiterating to religion and all adherents what true religion ought to be, will be, must be (in truth always has been).

—*Yvonne Sherwood*

All over the world, this battle between the two faces of faith is being played out.

—*Tony Blair*

The "two faces of faith" is a discourse that shapes the contemporary global governance of religious diversity.[1] It organizes and structures expert knowledge about religion and international affairs. It is a form of expert religion. This chapter introduces this discourse, explains how it shapes contemporary international politics and policy, and illustrates its impact on the politics of transnational humanitarian assistance in North Africa. The North African example demonstrates how the "two faces" framework shapes the lives of the Sahrawi refugees in southwestern Algeria, one of many contexts in which the global dynamics of good religion–bad religion have materialized. This discussion also develops the distinction that is central to the argument of this book between religion as construed by those in positions of power—expert religion and governed religion, of which the "two faces" is an example, and a broader field of cultural and religious practice. Viewing the Sahrawi experience through this lens uncovers the mixed political consequences of representations of the camps as "ideal spaces" occupied by tolerant refugees who support religious freedom and interfaith dialogue. It allows us to access a broader social and interpretive landscape, beyond religious freedom.

RELIGION AS INTERNATIONAL PUBLIC GOOD

In recent years religion has shifted from a marginal factor in the study of international relations to a place of prominence in the discipline. Among international relations theorists, it was conventional to assume that states dealt with religion internally, if at all. That assumption began to crumble before 9/11, accelerated by Huntington's clash of civilizations thesis in the 1990s, and gathered decisive momentum after 9/11 as experts turned to religion as a central problem to be solved (the agenda of surveillance), or as its own solution (the agenda of reassurance).[2] This agenda, in which religion appears as simultaneously a problem and its own solution, corresponds to what Tony Blair describes as the "two faces of faith."

The first "face" is bad religion, which is said to require discipline and surveillance. One side of the new conventional wisdom is that religion is perceived as relevant to global politics when dangerous forms of it escape the control of the state and are understood to be in need of discipline. At that point religion becomes an object of securitization and a target of legitimate violence or reform. States are expected to work with other states and the international authorities to contain or suppress dangerous and intolerant manifestations of politicized religion. Such fearful restive religion is associated with the violent history of Europe's past and much of the rest of the world's religious present, thus including both the sectarian violence of the wars of religion during the European Reformation and afterward, and the intolerance and fanaticism associated with certain forms of what is often described today as religious extremism or religious fundamentalism. Bad religion is understood to slip easily into violence. Bad religion is sectarian. It is understood to be divisive and associated with the failure of the state to properly domesticate it—or, in some cases, of religion to properly domesticate itself. Contemporary notions of religious violence, as Brian Goldstone argues, are anchored in the opposition between a terrifying figure of the premodern past, on one hand, and an enlightened believer at home in the world on the other: "While the latter is rendered normative, the former has to be subject to correction or made extinct. The discourse of [bad] religion is what makes this project work."[3]

At the same time, and as part of the same discursive framework, religion has come to be seen as relevant to international affairs as a means of promoting the common international good through humanitarian relief and development assistance programming, human rights campaigns, transitional justice efforts, and so on. Good religion has work to do, and it is the job of the government and other public authorities to facilitate it.[4] Public authorities are expected to recognize and empower conciliatory religious actors and institutions, while reforming or marginalizing their sectarian and extremist rivals. International tribunals and organizations are primed to guarantee religious freedom, protect religious rights, and incorporate a "religious dimension" into their decisions and programming. Humanitarian intervention and foreign assistance programs, nation building and democratization initiatives, counterterrorism and counterextremism programs, and other public international projects are committed to the "strategic implementation of religious knowledge."[5] The Center for Strategic and International Studies "Mixed Blessings" report mentioned earlier bemoans the fact that "efforts to operationalize religion are still limited to boutique programs and discrete job functions."[6] Irenic religion, in this narrative, enhances international public order by providing moral sustenance and support for international human rights, facilitating the spread of freedom, and promoting human flourishing through advocacy for religious tolerance and interfaith understanding.

These two "sides" of religion—dangerous religion and peaceful religion, good religion and bad religion—are what Tony Blair describes as the two faces of faith: "There are two faces of faith in our world today. One is seen not just in acts of religious extremism, but also in the desire of religious people to wear their faith as a badge of identity in opposition to those who are different. The other face is defined by extraordinary acts of sacrifice and compassion—for example, in caring for the sick, disabled or destitute. . . . All over the world, this battle between the two faces of faith is being played out."[7] Put simply, according to this narrative good religion is to be restored to international relations and bad religion is to be reformed or disciplined through new partnerships for the public good. Tolerant faith-based leaders and "authentic" religious content—theologies, texts, institutional forms—are seen as waiting patiently in the wings, biding their time, standing by to be tapped by states and public international authorities who recognize the need for religious voices and actors to assume their proper place in international public life. Religious goods and religious actors are heralded as contributors to global justice campaigns, engineers of peace building, agents of postconflict reconcilia-tion, and a countervailing force to terrorism.[8] With a little help from the authorities, peaceful religion will triumph over its intolerant rivals. As one observer concludes, summarizing this approach, "the role of religion in global affairs cannot be reduced to conflict, mistrust, and stagnation, but includes cooperation, creativity, and reconciliation."[9]

In these accounts peaceful religion appears as a long overdue correc-tive to secularist attempts to quarantine benevolent religious actors and voices, a view expressed by the first ambassador to the Canadian Office of Religious Freedom, Andrew Bennett: "In Canada and I'd say the liberal western democracies, we've pushed any expression of faith so far into the private sphere in the last half-century or so that we've sometimes forgot-ten how to have that faith-based discourse, and engage faith."[10] Propo-nents insist "faith-based" actors are relevant to politics, especially interna-tional politics, because they are particularly well equipped to contribute to global relief efforts, nation building, development, and peace building. Religion enhances the moral foundations of international public life. It is an agent of transformation. It is necessary for politics and public life to unfold democratically and religious freedom to flourish globally. Robert Joustra explains, "The good news is that religious actors, when permitted autonomy—some call it religious freedom—can serve as a force multi-plier for important social and political goods, including democratization, peacemaking, and reconciliation. In short, religion is a public good. Or it can be, if embedded into a political system which recognizes it as a voice to be heard, both in public and in private."[11] Religion "done right" is not only good for the individual but also indispensable to international pub-lic life. It is a public good, a force multiplier.

This approach to religion and international relations dominates in US foreign policy circles, and is reflected in the rationale for the US invasion of Afghanistan in 2001. Among other objectives, the US justified the war as an attempt to rescue Muslim women from their (overly religious) male oppressors through moral and religious reform.[12] Religion was construed as both the problem and the solution. The United States sought to liber-ate Afghan women by transforming them into *correctly* religious (tolerant, free, Muslim or post-Muslim) women active in the public sphere, shop-ping, wearing lipstick, and removing their headscarves.[13] The objective was not to exclude religion from public life—after all, the war to liberate Afghan women from the Taliban took place even as the Bush administra-tion was advocating more conservative positions for women in the United

States in the name of Christian morality. It was, rather, religious and social reform. Afghan women were to be brought "into the present" by transforming them into tolerant religious subjects and modern consumers of goods and mass media.[14] Eric Fassin describes this impetus to reform as an exercise of "civilizing power," observing that "in the United States, the sexual clash of civilizations is meant to bring legitimacy to military operations abroad: it is less about borders and more about expansion. The point is not to keep other civilizations out but, on the contrary, to go out and civilize them."[15]

The "two faces of faith" has provided the discursive scaffolding for the so-called return of religion to international affairs among the Western powers over the past several decades. It is an exercise of civilizing power. It occupies the field in which many scholars and decision makers, primarily but not exclusively in Europe and North America, frame and respond to questions involving religion and international public life. It structures scholarly inquiry, media conversations, and policy debates. In many international legal and public policy circles, as mentioned earlier, the two faces framework has partially displaced the secularization thesis, understood as the privatization, marginalization, or disappearance of religion in modernity. This partial displacement is the result of a shift in public and academic discourse away from an understanding of religion as "private" and largely irrelevant to global governance and toward a different dispensation, and accompanying political agenda, in which religion is seen as a public good, agent of transformation, and potential source of violence in need of domestication. While these two approaches to religion—secularization as privatization and religion as international public good—are both present in American and European academic and policy discussions, the latter has come to dominate the former. This book is about the effects of this shift on both politics and religion. I do not give a complete history of these developments—there is no linear story to be told that precisely accounts for when the tipping point was reached and a new way of talking about religion and global politics became normalized. Instead, I examine key episodes that illustrate these shifts in the collective episteme away from the presumption of the privatization of religion and its alleged irrelevance to global governance and toward the "two faces" regime. The latter may also be considered secularist in the sense described by Hussein Agrama, in that it both relies on and generates a preoccupation with drawing lines between religious and secular, good religion and bad religion, religion and politics.[16] Of course on the surface the "two faces" discourse disavows any association with secularism, insisting rather that we have forgotten how to "engage faith," in Bennett's words, and must work to remember how to more fully inhabit a "faith-based discourse."[17]

This narrative enjoys impressive political traction, drawing support from across the political spectrum in Europe and North America. The simultaneous attraction to religion as a public international good, and fear of it as a potential source of discord and violence, has broad appeal in societies in which there is otherwise little agreement, and often significant confusion, at the intersection of religion, politics, law, and public life.[18] The two faces model also has generated new demands for knowledge about religion, religious leaders, and religious politics and practices. A range of experts has willingly presented itself to meet this demand, generating what is described in this book as "expert religion." This knowledge is being put to work in the service of a variety of collective aims of governments, international organizations, and the international community, aims that include the prevention of terrorism, constitution writing, postconflict stabilization, and efforts to guarantee political rights for religious minorities. Across these diverse contexts and constituencies, the right kind of religion is understood as a benevolent agent of political transformation in need of legal protection. The wrong kind of religion is an object of reform and discipline.

The impetus to marginalize or reform dangerous religion while empowering peaceful religion serves as a common point of departure for state and international public policy and unites a disparate set of actors and authorities. It animates discussions not only in the US government but also in the Chinese Communist Party (CCP), the British and French governments, the Council on Foreign Relations, and at academic centers and programs around the world. As André Laliberté has described the CCP's position, "the views of the Party on religion, as can be inferred from policies and actions of the last ten years, can be schematically divided in two approaches: religion as a 'threat' and religion as 'social capital.'"[19] Discussing the UK Foreign and Commonwealth Office's activities, Peter Edge observes that "alongside support for particular theological stances within the UK, the government also looks beyond its own borders to encourage particular forms of Islam through Foreign and Commonwealth Office's projects under CONTEST which 'challenge extremist ideologies and support mainstream voices.'"[20] In 2009 the French government established a *pôle religions* in the Ministry of Foreign Affairs, staffed by six and headed by

Joseph Maïla, a sociologist and former rector of the Institut Catholique de Paris. The office is tasked with "the observation and analysis of major tendencies and movements that affect religion throughout the world."[21]

Scholars of international relations have responded in different ways to this collective turn to religion as a policy tool, the elevation of religious actors as purveyors of the public good, and the demand for new forms of expertise about religion. Many remain indifferent, still committed to the inevitability or desirability of secularization. Some incorporate religious actors, traditions, and institutions more explicitly into the study of international theory, politics, and history.[22] Others seek to excavate the moral and ethical resources of various traditions and apply them to contemporary dilemmas in international public life.[23] Still others seek to import the insights of religious leaders and traditions into international public policy decision-making processes, from diplomacy to conflict management to development assistance.[24] For some, religion is a variable that explains international outcomes, such as the frequency and longevity of violent conflict.[25] Each of these approaches seeks to restore (that which is defined as) religion, religious ideas and traditions, and religious actors to their proper place in international theory and practice.[26] Doing so, it is argued, will help to solve the myriad problems posed by religion—and by having ignored religion—in international politics. The connection between these various forms of expert knowledge about religion and practices of governance is of course complex, full of feedback loops that disrupt the notions of efficient causality favored by many political scientists.[27]

There is a sense in which the two faces paradigm reproduces a number of familiar conventions for conceptualizing religion that have been problematized in recent years in scholarship cutting across academic disciplines.[28] Yet there is also a twist, because religion is not only no longer private, along the lines of José Casanova's influential argument (or never was private, as Bruno Latour persuasively argues), but it takes on specific new forms of publicity.[29] New partnerships with government are being created, new mandates for moral and spiritual reform are being drafted, and new centers for interfaith understanding are being built. The Saudi-supported King Abdullah Bin Abdulaziz International Centre for Inter-religious and Intercultural Dialogue (KAICIID), located in Vienna, is an example. According to its website, KAICIID "was founded to enable, empower and encourage dialogue among followers of different religions and cultures around the world."[30] It is not only the Saudis. A small army of states and international public authorities with financial means and unflagging political will are posing this question: what can be done to locate and promote (that which the authorities define as) tolerant, free religion?[31] Purveyors of the "two faces" narrative have an answer that has proven compelling: certain religions, and certain forms of certain religions, need to be recognized, reorganized, and rescued from secularist condemnation and marginalization. Religious inputs and actors need to be identified and propelled into the international spotlight to serve as global problem solvers. The international community and state foreign policy establishments need to open the door to religious representatives, insights, and voices in domestic and international public life. This narrative resonates powerfully across international public policy domains and is reflected in political projects of striking reach and variety including transitional justice,[32] human rights advocacy, development assistance,[33] nation and public-capacity building efforts, the UN Alliance of Civilizations, religious engagement initiatives, interfaith dialogue, humanitarian and emergency relief efforts, and foreign policy legislation and administration, including the 1998 US International Religious Freedom Act. New forms of horizontal collaboration and cooperation among academic experts, domestic and international public authorities, and religious actors and institutions propel these initiatives forward.

Underlying this emergent faith-based consensus is a very particular understanding of religion. In this view—and this becomes important in later chapters—religions and religious actors are identifiable. It is obvious who they are. They are inherently different and distinguishable from secular actors. And, most significantly, they have allegedly been heretofore excluded. Thomas Banchoff and Robert Wuthnow, for example, call for a "more inclusive approach to the religious politics of human rights" because "religious actors" provide "vital resources—most centrally the belief in the transcendent equality and dignity of all human beings" which provide "emotional foundations" for an increasingly desiccated secular rational global rights discourse.[34] The two faces framework enacts a discursive and political logic that produces its own object ("religion") and then assigns it causal powers and significance. It treats religion as a self-evident category that exists prior to the social fields in which it is enfolded, making it possible for something called "religion" to be represented as motivating a host of actions, both good and bad.

This book challenges this treatment of religion as an isolable entity, whether the objective is to attempt to separate "it" from law and politics, bring "it" back in, or design a political response to "it." There are a number of things that could be said about this treatment of religion, but my interest lies in the fact that the production of "religion" as an object for the purposes of law and governance appears to bear only a limited relation to the complex varieties of contemporary religious practice described by many actual scholars of religion. This gap tends to be overlooked or disregarded in the literature on religion and politics. Indeed, the discursive logic of the "two faces" narrative begins to unravel quickly once one begins to explore the gaps between the forms of good religion that are sanctioned by expert knowledge and promoted through governmental advocacy for freedom, tolerance, and rights, and the messier, multiform fields of religious practice, tradition, belonging, and belief in which they are confidently deployed. Disaggregating religion along these lines makes it possible to isolate the "two faces" as a particular form of expert religion, a civilizing discourse authorized by those in positions of power, including not only government authorities but also a wide range of self-appointed public experts on religion. It also makes it possible to track its social consequences in the broader fields in which it is deployed. It allows us to historicize the agenda of reassurance, which celebrates good religion as a source of morality and cohesion, and the agenda of surveillance, which fears bad religion as a potential danger to be contained and suppressed. These are particular, deeply politicized understandings of religion. To return to a point made in the introduction, there is no unmarked, "authentic" religion that stands apart from politics, law, and other forms of collective governance. It does not make sense to talk about the essence of Islam—or of any other religion, in these terms.[35] As Helge Årsheim explains, "where religion begins and ends, and which competencies, rights and duties should arise from its identification is continuously contested across differing social, political and legal arenas."[36]

North American and European conceptions of good and bad religion, religious freedom, religious outreach, and interfaith understanding do not stand apart from the world but inform actions and decisions, shaping individual and collective lives. Elena Fiddian-Qasmiyeh's account of the Sahrawi refugee experience in Algeria illustrates these dynamics.[37] The Sahrawis, as we will see, live under specific designations of religious freedom, tolerance, and interfaith understanding that are authorized jointly by transnational donors and local Polisario leaders. The Sahrawi experience points to the fuzzy boundaries and complex interactions between "tolerant religion" as construed by transnational donors and advocates, "good religion" as construed by local leaders and represented to international audiences, and the actual religious practices and traditions of the Sahrawi people. These distinctions—this triangle of expert, official, and everyday religion—and the fluid relations between them, are conditioned by local history, state power, economic realities, regional politics, and local geography. The predicament of the Sahrawis suggests that religious freedom and religious tolerance cannot be taken as self-evident categories but rather are entangled in and shaped by specific sociohistorical, economic, and political contexts.

THE GOOD SAHRAWI AND THE POLITICS OF TOLERANCE

Located in Tindouf province in southwestern Algeria, the Sahrawi refugee camps were established in the mid-1970s for refugees fleeing Moroccan forces during the Western Sahara War. Situated on a flood-prone desert plane known as the "Devil's Garden" with limited access to water and scarce vegetation, the camps depend almost entirely on foreign aid. The nationalist, leftist Polisario Front (Frente Popular para la Liberación de Saguiat El Hamra y de Rio de Oro), which claims to represent the Sahrawi people, has governed the camps since its official establishment in 1973. European and North American constructs of good and bad religion, progressive Muslims, religious freedom, and interfaith dialogue—all constructs associated with the two faces of faith—have shaped transnational and intra-Sahrawi politics in the camps for years. Fiddian-Qasmiyeh reports that the Polisario has "successfully projected the Sahrawi camps as 'ideal' spaces inhabited by 'good' refugees, in part by reflecting mainstream European and North American normative preferences for the development of a 'good' and 'progressive' Islam."[38] In interactions with non-Sahrawi audiences and potential donors, particularly those from Europe and North America, Polisario leaders make reference to notions of secularism and religious tolerance in an effort to substantiate the "ideal" nature of the camps and their inhabitants to audiences presumably primed to react positively to these discourses. Yet this projection is only one among many different representations of the refugees in the Polisario leadership's repertoire; which representation is tapped in any given interaction varies according to audience. This strategy enables the Polisario leadership to draw from a substantial and diverse array of both "secular" and "religious" international political and financial support, both inside and outside the camps.

These supporters not only provide material aid to the refugees but also engage in lobbying campaigns in their home countries on behalf of the

Polisario's political objectives. The latter include most prominently an attempt by the Polisario to reclaim a degree of sovereign authority over Western Sahara from the Moroccan government, which has controlled the disputed territory for four decades. From the late 1800s until the mid-1970s, when the Polisario launched an armed rebellion, the territory was occupied by Spain and known as the Spanish Sahara. Under pressure from Morocco, and increasingly the United States, Spain reneged on its promise of independence and in 1975 agreed to a joint Moroccan and Mauritanian occupation, which later become exclusively Moroccan. Half the Sahrawi population subsequently fled into Algeria and became the refugees they remain today. The United States continues to support Morocco's refusal to hold a referendum on independence, while the UN formally recognizes Western Sahara as a non-self-governing territory— Africa's last colony.[39] Armed conflict continued between the parties until a UN-brokered ceasefire was negotiated in 1991.

Held up to the argument of this book, the strength of Fiddian-Qasmiyeh's work lies in her focus on the triangular set of relationships that evolved among evangelical humanitarian groups including the Defense Forum Foundation, Wisconsin-based Christ the Rock Community Church, and Christian Solidarity Worldwide–USA, the Polisario leaders, and the Sahrawi people.[40] There is a particularly close connection between the Polisario and the evangelical humanitarians that are active in the camps. As Fiddian-Qasmiyeh explains, "the Polisario's determination to activate not only evangelists' humanitarian assistance but also their political support is arguably, at least in part, as a result of these organizations' proven dedication and efficiency in so prominently lobbying on behalf of 'the Sahrawi people.'"[41] The Sahrawi's purported "religious tolerance" is critical to this alliance. As Fiddian-Qasmiyeh explains, Defense Forum Foundation representative and pro-Sahrawi activist Suzanne Scholte "has widely transmitted accounts of the Sahrawi's receptivity to Christianity and overarching religious tolerance in the international arena, including before the US Congress and the UN Decolonization Committee on numerous occasions since 2002. In addition to Scholte, several other evangelists have lobbied for the Polisario on Capitol Hill and before the UN Decolonization Committee, including (in October 2009) Dan Stanley, senior pastor from RockFish Church, who reportedly led the first prayer session in the camps, and Cheryl Banda and Janet Lenz from Christ the Rock Community Church."[42]

Equally significant for our purposes is Fiddian-Qasmiyeh's account of the *intra*-Sahrawi politics that resulted from the cooperative relationship between the Polisario and their foreign humanitarian supporters. As she explains, "the international celebration of the Sahrawi refugee camps' success is . . . directly associated with and even dependent upon the concealment, or discursive minimization, of everyday Muslim identity, practice, and institutions."[43] Maintaining the appearance of religious tolerance depends upon what Fiddian-Qasmiyeh describes as a "tyranny of tolerance," or "a system of *repress*-entation which purposefully centralizes certain groups, identifiers, and dynamics whilst simultaneously displacing and marginalizing those which challenge official accounts of the camps."[44] The journalist Timothy Kustusch, who attended an interfaith dialogue session in the camps in 2008, elaborates on these dynamics: "To avoid potential tension, only a few political leaders from the Polisario Front (the independence movement of the Sahrawi people), local religious leaders, and volunteers from Christ The Rock were invited."[45] Fiddian-Qasmiyeh explains that "the Sahrawi 'audience' was restricted to those who had already officially demonstrated their allegiance to the official script of 'tolerance.'" Dissenting, unofficial scripts were inexpressible and inadmissible in this arena. Reporting on the same session, Janet Lenz, founder of Christ the Rock's Sahrawi project, noted that "'while a few of the attendees at the inaugural session did attempt to debate, the proceedings were for the most part peaceful and cordial.'" For Lenz, the achievement of tolerance and peacefulness hinges on what Fiddian-Qasmiyeh identifies as "the repression of 'debate' or contestation on-stage, recreating the camps as spaces of unequivocal acceptance of the religious Other."

There is tension between the construal of "religious tolerance" and "religious freedom" by the Polisario-evangelical axis of cooperation, on the one hand, and on the other those Sahrawis whose "individual, familial and collective priorities and concerns may be irrevocably different from those of Polisario and evangelical actors alike."[46] The Polisario/foreign humanitarian axis of cooperation crowds out dissenting Sahrawi voices, which go unheard not only by non-Sahrawi audiences but also, and crucially, within the Sahrawi community itself:

> Although the Polisario has the potential to "ingratiate themselves" with their supporters through representations of the camps as unique spaces of religious freedom and tolerance and of "the Sahrawi people" as inherently welcoming of evangelical groups, these performances equally have the potential to create an irreconcilable rupture not only with other, non-evangelical donors (including "secular" Spanish "Friends of the Sahrawi"), but also between the Polisario and the

very refugees which this organization purports to represent. The enactment of such debates and contestations, however, is suppressed in
the camps via strategies of *repress*-entation which limit the audibility,
visibility and very presence of those actors whose individual, familial
and collective priorities and concerns may be diametrically opposed
to those of key donors and the Polisario alike.[47]

Fiddian-Qasmiyeh's description of the dissenting Sahrawi refugees' lack
of voice and agency illustrates who and what are excluded when religious
freedom, tolerance, and interfaith dialogue—and the material benefits
that follow in their wake for those in a position to claim them—capture
the field of emancipatory possibility as unchallengeable political and social goods.[48] These dynamics are central to the politics of the "return"
of religion to international affairs. The complex field of power relations
in the Sahrawi camps attests to the value of differentiating between religion and religious freedom as authorized by those in positions of power,
including both the religious and political authorities, and the religious
practices of the individuals and groups who are subjected to these forms
of governance and control. It points to the gap between expert religion
and governed religion, which often support each other, and the practices
and experiences of everyday people who have complex and shifting relationships to the institutions, orthodoxies, and authorities that allegedly
represent them, from which they may have fallen away, or to whom they
may have never fully subscribed. Claims to secularism, religious tolerance, or interfaith understanding cannot be disentangled from these specific histories of the construal and management of "religion" as a matter
of difference and governance.

CONCLUSION

In contemporary international relations a proliferating number of well-
funded projects and programs, both public and private, strive to discern
and defend peaceful religion and project it internationally through states,
international tribunals, and international and nongovernmental organizations. Other projects, and sometimes the same ones, are consumed by
equally pressing efforts to reform or suppress intolerant religion and ensure that it is not projected internationally. Both rely on the persuasive
authority, and, if necessary, the use of force, by states and other actors to
realize these objectives.[49]

These "two faces of faith" offer a compelling framework. It will not be easily displaced. It provides structure and simplicity for scholars, government officials, journalists, and practitioners with little background or interest in religion. It reduces complex and shifting social fields and religious landscapes into a two-step prescription: identify and empower peaceful moderates, and marginalize or reform intolerant fundamentalists with the latter including "religious practitioners of whatever faith who [are] at odds with liberal modernity generally and specifically with its religious and political expectations."[50] The good religion–bad religion mandate has become an industry. There is an international political economy of good religion, generating stable careers for many, and considerable wealth and status for a few. Think tanks, foundations, foreign policy pundits, and religion experts have reaped the benefits. In the US foreign policy establishment, experts on all things religious have produced an avalanche of scholarship, offering up for public and official consumption what Samuel Moyn described in another context as "theoretical rationales for the American policy shop that they sometimes directly serve."[51] The unifying theme of this flood of white papers, reports, and memos is that when religious moderates are identified, engaged, and empowered—and fundamentalists identified, sidelined, and reformed—the problems posed by extremist forms of religion will fade, and (religious) freedom, rights, and toleration will spread unimpeded across the globe. The US State Department's Office of Religion and Global Affairs, launched in 2013, institutionalizes this logic. These efforts are not entirely new; as discussed in Chapter 4, they are reminiscent of US Cold War attempts to combat communism by promoting global spiritual health. At that time, the United States intervened in other countries to identify and bolster the religion that aligned with US interests. That religion was either "freed" or co-opted.

This book casts doubt on the assumption that academic experts, government officials, and diplomats (and especially "religious" ones) know what religion is, where it is located, who speaks in its name, and how to incorporate it in foreign policy and international public policy decision matrices. This presumption has enabled scholars, practitioners, and pundits to leap straight into the business of quantifying religion's effects, adapting religion's insights to international problem-solving efforts, and incorporating religion's official representatives into international political decision making, public policy, and institutions. If religious actors and practices are incorporated and engaged in the right way, the argument goes, the problems associated with extremism will be mitigated and the potential for religion to contribute to the betterment of the world more fully realized.[52] Good religion blends seamlessly into support for the international authorities, while fractious or seditious religion contravenes them. Good religion is presented as the "clean, enlightened alternative to a messy, primitivistic cosmology."[53]

The notion that something called "religion" can be engaged and liberated generates an endless stream of bland statements "anxiously reiterating to religion and all adherents what true religion ought to be, will be, must be (in truth always has been)," returning to Sherwood's statement in the epigraph to this chapter. This new global politics of religion elicits constant, anxiety-ridden attempts on the part of governments and other public authorities to discriminate between good and bad religion, to select who is entitled to speak for a community and who is not, and to find ways to convince and cajole those who are at risk of moving "into the very sharp end"[54] to come around and reject a "false view of religion."[55] It authorizes particular understandings of what it means to be a tolerant, rights-bearing consumer of free religion. It endows particular actors with the capacity to serve as the arbiters of orthodoxy, in the case of the Sahrawi, the Polisario and their American supporters. It creates the conditions in which states and international authorities feel compelled to identify and protect "their" religious minorities. The next three chapters explore each of these dynamics in turn, beginning with the politics of promoting international religious freedom.

CHAPTER 3

International Religious Freedom

"Ah, my friend, my friend," he said, drawing back and thumping his chest, "I have a heavy feeling in here. I feel as if I have a stone in my heart. I wonder what'll become of us all."

"I think we'll be divided," said Mehmetçik sadly. "Suddenly it matters that I am a Christian, where it mattered only a little before."

—*Louis de Bernières, Birds Without Wings*[1]

G overnment-sponsored programs to promote international religious freedom have gathered momentum in recent years. Passed in 1998, the US International Religious Freedom Act (IRFA) established an Office on International Religious Freedom in the State Department headed by an ambassador-at-large. The office prepares an annual report on the status of religious freedom in every country in the world except the United States, and advises the president on which countries should be designated as "Countries of Particular Concern."[2] IRFA also created an independent watchdog agency, the US Commission on International Religious Freedom (USCIRF). Canada, several European states, and the European Union are also institutionalizing external religious freedom promotion.[3] The British and the EU promote religious freedom through the Foreign and Commonwealth Office (FCO) and European External Action Service, respectively.[4] Italy and Germany are exploring bilateral arrangements to make advocacy for faith communities integral to their foreign policy agendas.[5] In 2012 the French government launched a public-private partnership, the Pharos Observatory (Observatoire Pharos), poised to pursue a similar agenda.[6] These programs tap into diverse constituencies, including liberal legal internationalists who support international human rights, advocacy groups for whom some form of Christianity serves as the foundation of democracy and freedom, American nationalists for whom the "city on a hill" narrative resonates with long-standing ideals of American exceptionalism, European rights advocates concerned with the fate of persecuted Christians, and missionaries for whom religious liberalization signals an openness to their missions that may not have existed or was felt and framed differently in an earlier era. It is this combination of forces—and not only evangelical lobbying—that propels this programming forward.

Despite certain differences, these initiatives share a benign view of religious freedom as a stable and fundamental human right,[7] legal standard, and/or international norm that can be measured and achieved by all political collectivities.[8] It is a matter of persuading citizens and governments to understand and comply with a universal norm.[9] States and societies are positioned on a spectrum of progress, either inclined toward the achievement of religious freedom as a social fact, or slipping backward into religious persecution and violence, caused allegedly by religious hatred or persecution.[10] This chapter departs from such an approach to religious freedom. Human rights advocacy is a particular mode of governing social difference that implicates religion in complex and variable ways. Advocacy for religious freedom is a specific, historically situated form of governance. The historical specificity of the promotion of religious freedom and its authorization of particular forms of politics and religion, and not others, allows us to see these efforts in a new light. Guarantees for religious freedom are neither the instantiation of a stable and universal norm, nor the realization of any particular religious tradition in a secular world.[11] Instead, these projects stabilize and amplify particular forms of religious and religious-secular difference, obscure other contributors to social tension and conflict, and favor historically specific understandings of religion, religious subjectivity, and freedom itself. Guarantees for religious freedom are a modern technique of governance, authorizing particular forms of politics and regulating the spaces in which people live out their religion in specific ways.[12]

This chapter develops three interrelated claims about the politics of governing social difference through religious rights and freedoms. First, conceiving and governing social difference through religious rights singles out individuals and groups for legal protection as religious individuals and collectivities. The discourse of religious freedom describes, and legally defines, individuals and groups in religious or sectarian terms rather than on the basis of other affinities and relations—for example, as groups based on political affinities, historical or geographical ties, neighborhood or occupational affiliations, kinship networks, generational ties, or socioeconomic status. In positing religion as prior to these other identities and affiliations, the religious rights model heightens the sociopolitical salience of whatever the national or international authorities designate as religion. This accentuates religious-religious and religious-secular differences, leading to what historian Sarah Shields describes as a particular "ecology of affiliation."[13] It is an ecology based on religious difference. Other factors that contribute to social tension, discrimination, conflict, and coexistence are lost from sight.

Second, governing through religious rights shapes how states and other political authorities distinguish groups from each other, often in law. It singles out groups and authorities as "religions" and locates them on a playing field in which they are presumed to represent a common type— "religious groups"—and to operate as equals. It consecrates groups as discrete faith communities with identifiable leaders and neatly bounded orthodoxies. These groups are both presupposed and produced as static bodies of tradition and convention that lend themselves to becoming objects of state and transnational legal regulation, and, as discussed below, government engagement and reform. Official spokespersons are called forth to represent these faith communities, strengthening faith leaders that enjoy friendly relations with political authorities seeking engagement and empowering groups that "look like" religions to those in power. On a religious landscape populated by faith communities, not only are particular hierarchies and orthodoxies reinforced, but dissenters, doubters, those who practice multiple traditions, and those on the margins of community are rendered illegible or invisible. On a political landscape governed through religious rights and freedoms, many violations of human dignity fail to register at all, languishing beneath the threshold of national and international recognition as limited resources are devoted to rescuing persecuted religionists and defending faith communities that have achieved legal and political legibility and legitimacy. These selection dynamics inhere in the process and politics of enforcing a right to religious freedom and cannot be remedied through a more sophisticated understanding of religion or religious community. Certain questions recur: Which religions to protect? Which leaders to engage?

Third, contemporary international religious freedom advocacy emphasizes belief as the core of religion. The right to religious freedom is widely understood to refer to a right to choose to believe or not to believe. To be religious is to believe in one of a few major belief systems, often skewed toward Christianity and token "unbelief." This reflects a particular understanding of religion and the religious subject that emerged out of European Christianity and is not universal. To treat belief as the core of religion is to sanctify a particular religious psychology that relies on the notion of an autonomous subject who chooses beliefs and then enacts them. It presupposes and produces subjects for whom believing is taken as the defining characteristic of what it means to be religious, and the right to choose one's belief as the essence of what it means to be free. Governing social difference through this designation—enforcing the right to believe or not to believe—protects and privileges individuals and communities who subscribe to a modern liberal understanding of faith and those who are willing and able to reform their religion to conform to this understanding, excluding other ways of relating to communities beyond the self.

The chapter unfolds in three parts, each elaborating on various aspects of these claims through a combination of empirical illustrations and theoretical discussion. Two criteria govern the selection of the empirical focal points, as discussed earlier. The first is the extent to which the lives of individuals and groups have been, and continue to be, shaped by the social, political, and religious possibilities and realities that are produced through efforts to globalize and legalize a right to religious freedom. The second is the degree to which a particular case illustrates the analytical significance of distinguishing between discourses on religion as authorized by those in power and a broader field of social and religious practice and modes of coexistence. The first section on the global political production of religious difference draws on an extended discussion of the Rohingya in Myanmar. The second section on the creation of a landscape populated by faith communities and the effects on those excluded from such designations incorporates examples from the Central African Republic, Guatemala, India, and South Sudan. A final section on the mutually supportive relations between religious freedom advocacy, the creation of a believing religious subject, and the ideology of the free religious marketplace builds on the work of anthropologists and religious studies scholars who complicate the notion of belief as the core of religion.

Scholars of religion and politics are often asked "what is the best way to guarantee religious freedom and reduce religious violence?" This chapter explores the grounds for my skepticism concerning the intellectual viability and political advisability of posing or responding to these kinds of questions. Neither religion nor religious freedom is a stable, fixed quantity that can be used as a dependent or independent variable. Stabilizing a definition of religion or religious for the purposes of assigning causal significance and drawing generalizable conclusions is impossible. Instead, one might ask, as this chapter does, what is accomplished in specific contexts when social difference is conceived and governed by those in positions of authority through religious rights and freedoms? What does it entail to govern religion as a right? What political practices, social relations, and religious possibilities are enabled, or disabled, through such an approach? Or, as in Chapter 6, what are the political stakes when those in positions of authority identify acts of violence or discrimination as having religious causes, and therefore, presumably, religious solutions? The global promotion of religious rights and freedoms, like sectarianism, is a discourse of expert religion and governed religion, defined and authorized by those in power. It both presupposes and produces the very divides that it is meant to soften or transcend, creating in the process new forms of social friction defined by religious difference.[14]

THE RELIGIOUS RIGHTS IMPERATIVE

Privileging the category of religion as an aspect of social difference for the purposes of law and governance has at least three consequences. First, lodged within a religious rights regime is the imperative to define identity in religious terms: "are you this or are you that?" You need to know what you are to know how you fit in. Individuals with multiple affiliations, mixed backgrounds, and dissenters from legally protected religions are uneasily accommodated in the rubrics of strict religious-secular identity and difference demanded by the logic of religious rights. Those who do not identify with orthodox versions of protected religions or beliefs fall between the cracks. Families that include multiple traditions under the same roof must choose a side. Such "in-between" individuals and groups find themselves in an impossible position: either they must make political claims on religious grounds, or they have no ground from which to speak.[15] This occurred in Bosnia in the 1990s, when people who described themselves as atheists before the war woke up to find themselves identified—and divided—publically and politically, by a newly salient religious identity.[16] Governing social difference through religious rights singles out individuals and groups for legal protection as religious individuals and collectivities.

Second, privileging religion as an official marker of difference engenders an "ecology of affiliation" that presupposes and produces hard and fast religious identities that trump other modes of belonging. Singling out religion from among the many different given and chosen human affiliations naturalizes religious-religious and religious-secular divides. It identifies individuals and groups along these lines rather than on the basis of other ties—whether socioeconomic, geographic, familial, professional, generational, or political. Positing discrete religious communities as defining features on the political landscape lends agency and authenticity to groups designated as religions, helping to create the world that this discourse purports to describe. These groups come to occupy what Elizabeth Castelli describes as "the full terrain of the thinkable vis-à-vis freedom."[17] Religions are transformed into tractable, alienable commodities, in the sense described by Jean and John Comaroff in their work on the commodification of ethnicity and Samuli Schielke in his discussion of world religions as entities with agency.[18] Governing citizens as Christians, Muslims, or Hindus conjures a collective imagining of fixed, stable categories of religious affiliation and confers upon them social and political currency. This diminishes the possibility of crosscutting, nonsectarian forms of politics.

Third, governing social difference through religious rights reduces complex social, historical, and political histories and inequalities to a problem of religion. As Michael Peletz has argued in reference to the notion of "Islamization," the promotion of religious freedom "discourages recognition of the complexity of the phenomena to which it is purportedly relevant."[19] It collapses a diverse array of social, economic, historical, political, and geographical considerations into an emphasis on religion, obscuring other causes of discrimination and social tension and deflecting attention away from caste, class, colonial history, economic justice, land rights, and other factors.

The debate over how the international community should respond to the plight of the Rohingya people in Myanmar illustrates these dynamics. A population of roughly eight hundred thousand people living primarily in northwestern Burma bordering Bangladesh, the Rohingya claim Burmese citizenship but are effectively stateless, having been denied citizenship by the Burmese state, classified by the government as "Bengali immigrants" and subjected to "persecution, discrimination and intrusive restriction on their rights to marry and have families."[20] Though many have lived in Rakhine (formerly Arakan) state for generations,[21] the

Burmese state does not recognize them as one of the country's 135 ethnic groups, and the Rohingya have suffered a long history of exclusion and government-sponsored oppression. As journalist Kate Hodal explains, "Large-scale Burmese government crackdowns on the Rohingya—including Operation Dragon King in 1978, and Operation Clean and Beautiful Nation in 1991—forced hundreds of thousands to flee to Bangladesh. Thousands of others have left for Thailand, Malaysia, and Indonesia, many of them by boat."[22] State-sanctioned violence has worsened in recent years, with many Rohingya driven out of their villages, separated from their families, and confined to squalid refugee camps. Those who remain in their villages cannot leave, even to go to the hospital.[23] The capital of Rakhine state, Sittwe, had a population of about seventy-three thousand Rohingya, which as of 2014 had dwindled to five thousand confined in one heavily guarded neighborhood. According to anthropologist Elliott Prasse-Freeman, referring to the Rakhine (or Arakanese) majority population in Rakhine state, "local media, citizen bloggers, Buddhist monks all rallied around the Rakhine. Or more accurately, rallied *against* the Rohingya," describing them as illegal immigrants, a threat to Buddhism, a threat to security, and "simply aesthetically unpleasant." A refrain heard often from Prasse-Freeman's Burmese acquaintances was " 'they are not like us; we cannot accept them.' "[24]

Most international commentators describe the Rohingya as a persecuted Muslim minority.[25] In 2012 USCIRF called for religious freedom for the Rohingya, identifying them as persecuted Muslims, and many journalists and academics rely on a religious persecution narrative to describe their situation. Yet the Rohingya are not excluded from Burmese society exclusively with religious slurs, but also with racist and other dehumanizing terms. Prominent monks leading the charge to democratize Myanmar have turned against the Rohingya, blocking humanitarian assistance and calling for their social and political exclusion along the lines of what some have compared to apartheid in South Africa or segregation in the southern United States.[26] A leaflet distributed by a monks' organization described the Rohingya as "cruel by nature." Ko Ko Gyi, a democracy activist and former political prisoner, has stated that the Rohingya are not Burmese. A loosely organized Buddhist activist group composed of monks and laity called "969," and its most prominent spokesperson, a Mandalay-based monk named U Wirathu, call for the social and economic exclusion of the Rohingya from Burmese society.[27] Claiming to work on behalf of the "religious rights and freedoms" of the majority

Buddhist population of Myanmar, 969 reportedly "enjoys support from senior government officials, establishment monks and even some members of the opposition National League for Democracy (NLD), the political party of Nobel peace laureate Aung San Suu Kyi."[28] A representative of the Burmese Muslim Association compared the movement to the Ku Klux Klan.[29] Another 969 affiliate, the Organization for the Protection of Nation, Race and Religion—or, in the Burmese acronym, Ma Ba Tha, is also led by well-known Buddhist monks and oriented around pro-Buddhist, pro-Burman activism.

Understanding attempts to exclude the Rohingya from the Burmese state, society, and economy requires situating them in a more encompassing analytical field that includes, but is not reduced to, religion or religious difference. Three factors are particularly salient. The first combines colonial history, geographical considerations, and elite political competition. Rakhine (Arakan) state, where many Rohingya live, was independent from Rangoon and Mandalay until the Burman conquest in 1785, and a strong sense of territorial identity distinguishing the region from the rest of Burma persists today. Muslim-Buddhist "divide and rule" policy in that area dates to the British colonial era (1824–1948) and was further exacerbated at a number of critical moments throughout the twentieth century and into the present. During the Japanese occupation for example, which began with the Imperial Army's invasion in 1942, the British armed Rohingya "Force V" militias while the Japanese armed a variety of Buddhist-led groups, with the two sides pitted against each other in a proxy struggle.[30] In March 1962, the Burmese military seized power in a coup and sought to impose ethnic purity by marginalizing minorities and non-Buddhists, again increasing tensions considerably.[31] In 2013, as Burmese dissident Aung Zaw explains, the conflict with the Rohingya and the Kachin, another ethnic group in Burma, diverted attention away from power struggles within the governing elite in a time of transition:

> The violence suggests a power struggle within the elite. Infighting between hard-line and moderate forces in the government, which took power two summers ago under the moderate general Thein Sein, is no secret. His cabinet, Parliament and the army remain dominated by holdovers from the regime of the former dictator Gen. Than Shwe. Many are resisting President Thein Sein's reforms. The generals who ruled the country for five decades control much of the nation's wealth, and some are close to Chinese interests that stand to be eclipsed if Myanmar deepens economic ties to the West.

The anti-Muslim violence is a useful distraction from Burmese grievances against China.[32]

A second factor is the intensification of economic competition due to the relaxation of military rule in recent years and heightened competition for jobs and scarce natural resources. The Rohingya are easily marginalized in tense economic times, scapegoated as illegal immigrants and potential threats to job or rent seekers in an increasingly competitive economic environment. These tensions are exacerbated by state economic interest and the resultant securitization of Burmese borders areas. The Burmese government oversees security for a new multibillion-dollar China-Burma oil and gas pipeline that stretches over fifteen hundred miles from the Indian Ocean through Burma to the southwestern Chinese city of Kunming. The new pipeline, which brings gas from the Shwe fields off the coast of Arakan state, allows China to bypass the Malacca Strait, one of the world's busiest shipping lanes. With many other large-scale energy, trade, and infrastructure projects under development located in what are known as "ethnic minority borderlands," Martin Smith has argued that "Myanmar could be moving toward economic restructuring where the geopolitical consequences will have an epoch-shaping impact on internal affairs."[33] After decades of conflict, Smith foresees a heightened securitization of Myanmar's borders and border areas as neighbors seek trade and other economic opportunities that require both "constructive engagement" and "borderland stability." He cites as precedents efforts in 2009 to tighten security on the Chinese, Bangladeshi, and Indian borders, "with the Indian authorities especially concerned that insurgent groups from northeast India were using borderline sanctuaries to continue their struggles."[34]

A third contributing factor is the rise of a generalized exclusionary politics in Burma, including linguistic violence and dehumanization campaigns against the Rohingya. As these politics have intensified the Rohingya have been stripped of their name, and are increasingly referred to by government authorities and others as "Bengalis." This is significant in that the name "Rooinga" had been recognized as early as 1799, before the First Anglo-Burmese War, and was recognized by the Burmese state on several previous occasions. Yet a 2013 government report refers to the Rohingya as "Bengalis," emphasizing their status as outsiders. Security forces compel Rohingya to refer to themselves as Bengalis,[35] and to qualify for the government's resettlement plan Rohingya are required to self-identify formally as Bengalis. As Jared Ferrie recounts, "when officials tried to survey displaced people in camps around Theak Kae Pyin village, protests broke out with women and children chanting, 'We are Rohingya.'"[36] This "casting out" of the Rohingya extends beyond government circles. According to Smith, "while most borderland opposition groups recognize the rights of Muslim communities in the northern Rakhine state, some do not accept 'Rohingya' as a term of identity—a position also taken by the [regime's] SLORC-SPDC."[37] A day after his release from prison, one camp resident, Fious Ahmad, explained in an interview outside Nga Pon Shay's mosque, "I don't know why the police seized me. The police said to me, 'Say you're Bengali.' I told them, 'Yes, I'm Bengali.' But the police beat me anyway."[38]

Discrimination against the Rohingya is complex and multifaceted: it is ethnic, racial, economic, political, postcolonial, and national. There are other factors as well. It is impossible to isolate any one of these as the definitive cause of a particular act of violence or discrimination. To speak of the Rohingya as a persecuted religious minority is to single out religious identity from the vast web of discriminatory forces in which the Rohingya are suspended. Identifying religious difference as motivating the violence misrepresents the complexity of the situation and deflects attention away from the Rohingya's comprehensive exclusion from Burmese state and society historically and in the present. It masks the economic and political interests that profit from their subordination and repression. It deflects attention away from state-sponsored violence, political and economic disagreements among the governing elite concerning the speed and content of proposed reforms, the anti-immigrant and xenophobic basis of the discrimination, and economic insecurities and regional power dynamics accompanying Burma's tentative opening to global trade and foreign investment.

But the problem also runs deeper. To depict the violence as fundamentally religious in nature not only absolves the governing elite from their complicity in it but also serves to reinforce 969's narrative that these particular lines of difference are indeed the most salient aspect of this profound societal and human crisis. Promoting religious rights, in this case, effectively strengthens the hand of a violently exclusionary set of nationalist movements that depend for their existence on perpetuating the perception of hard-and-fast lines of Muslim-Buddhist difference and immutable ties among majoritarian (Buddhist) religion, race, and Burmese national identity. In other words, the logic of religious rights fortifies those who are most committed to excluding the Rohingya from

Burmese society. For them the Rohingya are subhuman. As Prasse-Freeman puts it, "those who are killed are arguably not even killed *as* an identity group, but rather as so much detritus falling outside of a group, and hence outside of the political community entirely."[39] By reinforcing their status as Muslims rather than as Burmese citizens or as human beings, lobbying for the religious rights of the Rohingya makes it less likely that the Burmese government—or the democratizing monks—will include the Rohingya in Burmese state and society as citizens and humans, rather than as Muslims. To complicate matters further, not all Burmese Muslims are Rohingya, and those that are not have a different relationship to the state. These details are lost from sight in a focus on religious persecution as the problem, and religious freedom as the solution.

In a speech in 2013, the former US ambassador to Nigeria John Campbell urged his audience at the Council on Foreign Relations not to describe recent violence in Nigeria as religious violence. "Are people [in Nigeria] being killed because they're Muslim, herders, or Hausa? It is often very hard to say."[40] Are the Rohingya being killed because they're Muslim, because they're immigrants, or because they're perceived as an economic or political threat to the former junta or other national or regional economic interests? Are Syrians being killed because they are Christian, regime supporters, or had been employed by or are related to a particular leader of the resistance? It is hard to say. Many factors lead to discrimination and violence: local histories, class disparities, disputes over natural resources, immigration status, urban-rural tensions, family grievances, oppressive governance, outside interventions, colonial legacies, land disputes, and economic rivalries. When social tension, discrimination, and violence are reduced to a problem of religious intolerance or religious persecution, the complex and multidimensional tapestry of human sociality and history is lost from sight, and the multifaceted problems faced by persecuted groups become more difficult to address. In the case of the Rohingya and other imperiled groups, imposing a religious rights framework heightens the sociopolitical salience of whatever the authorities designate as religion: in this case, Muslim-Buddhist difference. Rather than defanging 969 and its allies, it reinforces religious divides while deferring and subduing the potential of alternative, cross-cutting movements that might challenge the array of entrenched political and economic interests that profit from the Rohingya's exclusion.

The rise to prominence of a global imperative to identify groups as religious minorities and religious communities engenders particular forms of politics. Though the specific dynamics vary depending on context, the religious rights imperative presupposes and produces lines of difference between discrete religions, eclipses other axes of being and belonging, and, in some cases, contributes to the very tensions that it is intended to mitigate or transcend. These dynamics are not unique to Burma. As we will see in Chapter 5 the global rights imperative is transforming the situation of the Alevis in Turkey who, like groups everywhere, are subject to increasing pressure to constitute themselves legally as a discrete faith community with clear boundaries, identifiable leaders, and neatly defined orthodoxies. The next section examines some of the consequences of these designations for those living under them.

EMPOWERMENT AND EXCLUSION

Under the logic of religious rights, becoming and being a "religion" bestows certain benefits. Governing religion as right funnels individuals into discrete faith communities, empowers those communities and their spokespersons, and marginalizes other modes of solidarity. It hones in on religious identity as stable and singular, compelling those who identify with several traditions to choose one above the others. Boundaries solidify. Lines between groups become more salient—a process described by political theorist William Connolly as a modern drive to "overcode" the boundaries between groups.[41] Governing through religious rights overcodes the boundaries between religions, and naturalizes the line between religion and nonreligion. It relies on and produces discrete faith communities, perpetuating the assumption that such communities are, as Martin Stringer observes, "coherent enough that individuals and leaders within [them] could more easily influence others within the community than those outside." It endows these communities with agency and authenticity. As Stringer explains, the "assumption of strong boundaries and clear identities within the community" means that "rather than breaking down these boundaries the policy aims to work within them and to build on the assumed solidarity of the community itself."[42]

On such a political landscape, faith communities are expected to have representatives. A religious rights framework elicits individuals authorized by themselves or others to speak in the name of these communities. Their representatives meet with governments, nongovernmental organizations, international organizations, and other authorities, becoming the objects of religious engagement that are the subject of the next chapter.

Governments and other authorities expect and encourage leaders to step forward. The USAID Program Guide on Religion, Conflict and Peacebuilding informs practitioners, "Engagement with top religious leadership is critical to engagement at the local level. Without buy-in at this level, leaders at the local level may be reluctant to participate in the program even if they are interested and personally supportive of the program. As a result, *organizing at the community level requires a great deal of groundwork and relationship building with senior leaders.*"[43] The United States relies on religious leaders to secure access to local populations and garner support for American political and strategic objectives in conflict and postconflict situations, as seen in Chapter 4. In 2005 a Pentagon contractor paid Sunni religious scholars in Iraq $144,000 to assist in its public relations campaign. The contractor, the Lincoln Group, was paid to "identify religious leaders who could help produce messages that would persuade Sunnis in violence-ridden Anbar Province to participate in national elections and reject the insurgency."[44] Such programs would likely violate the Establishment Clause if undertaken domestically because they are sect-preferential. As Jessica Hayden explains, "these programs are differentiated from domestic faith-based initiatives in that beneficiaries of U.S. funds are not chosen in spite of their religious affiliations, but rather *because* of their ties to a specific religious group."[45] The British Foreign and Commonwealth Office (FCO) also pursues outreach to religious leaders as part of its external religious freedom programming, encouraging its 270 diplomatic posts to "consult local religious leaders" to determine whether "religious believers [are] able to publicise their religious information and promotional materials without unreasonable interference by the authorities."[46]

The point is neither to condemn nor to celebrate these activities but to understand the assumptions about religion, religious community, and religious authority that underlie them. In this case, as Stringer points out, religions are presumed to be entities with agency, strong boundaries, and clear identities within the community, occluding the processes through which particular authorities become constituted and publically and politically recognized as "religions." In an interesting reversal of these selection dynamics, governing religion as right also leads to a politics of *non*recognition for individuals and groups that fail to qualify as religions. While empowering those who qualify as faith communities and their authorized spokespersons, the logic of religious rights renders politically invisible less established religions, collective ways of life, and modes of being and belonging that do not qualify as "religious." Nontraditional religions, unprotected religions, and nonreligions are pushed into the wings. Violations of human dignity that fail to register as religious infringements languish beneath the threshold of national and international recognition as the international community dedicates limited resources to rescuing persecuted religionists. These dynamics of nonrecognition are evident in contexts as diverse as Central America, South Asia, and Africa. To see them however requires expanding our field of vision beyond authorized legal and political constructions of religion and religious freedom to include a broader field of religiosities, histories, and forms of sociality. This means approaching local practices and histories on their own terms, even or especially to the extent that they appear as unintelligible or illegible, rather than seeking to domesticate or assimilate them into conventional legal or normative frames. To fail to do so is to miss or misconstrue a broader field of contentious politics.

The K'iche', a Maya ethnic group living in the western highlands of Guatemala, represent a case in point. Perhaps the most well-known K'iche' is indigenous rights activist Rigoberta Menchú, who won the Nobel Peace Prize in 1992. In 2009, the Newberry Library in Chicago announced the digitization of the most studied indigenous document of Mesoamerica, the mid-sixteenth-century Popol Vuh, or "book of events," a mytho-historical narrative based on pre-Colombian oral traditions that recounts the creation of the universe, the origins of the K'iche' people, and the history of their dynasties until the arrival of the Spanish in 1524.[47] Tensions between the K'iche' community and the Guatemalan state have increased in recent years as eighty-seven Maya communities in the department of El Quiché, represented by the K'iche' People's Council (KPC), unanimously rejected the mining and hydroelectric projects proposed for Guatemala in the wake of the North American Free Trade Agreement and other treaties. Foreign commercial companies responded to those rejections with offers to reward the KPC with a higher percentage of profits, failing to understand that, as Dianne Post observes, "the reason these projects were rejected is not monetary but is linked to the refusal to allow destruction of the earth for religious and cultural reasons."[48] The KPC's refusal to acquiesce in these projects has led to discrimination and violence, including massive violations of K'iche' cultural heritage and land rights facilitated by collusion among multinational mining corporations, the police, and the Guatemalan state.

The K'iche are unable to portray these abuses as violations of religious freedom. As described by scholars of indigenous religion in other contexts,[49] K'iche' attachment to the land does not register legally as religious, making it difficult or impossible for them to avail themselves of national or international legal protections for religion, religious rights, or religious freedom. Their claims are invisible to organizations, actors, and legal instruments focused on the legal realization of religious freedom, because, in some sense, they are perceived as having no (recognizable) religion.[50] The 2012 State Department International Religious Freedom Report for Guatemala confirms that there were "no reports of abuses of religious freedom" in the country. When they are cast in terms of religion understood as the right to believe or not, violations of K'iche' religio-cultural heritage fall below the threshold of political and juridical legibility.

Similar dynamics of nonrecognition have emerged in the Central African Republic (CAR), where, in 2010, the US State Department's Religious Freedom Report observed that as many as 60 percent of the imprisoned women in the country had been charged with "witchcraft," which is considered a criminal offense by the government. The State Department concluded that the CAR government "generally respected religious freedom in practice," and gave the CAR a good ranking overall. Discrimination against African traditional religion does not count as religious discrimination. Women imprisoned for witchcraft cannot suffer from violations of religious freedom because, in the eyes of the government and the authors of the religious freedom report, they have no religion. Like the K'iche', the imprisoned women in the CAR fail to appear on the persecuted religious minority radar screen because abuses of their religion, culture, and tradition do not count as violations of the right to believe or not to believe that are protected by international instruments and advocates for religious freedom. As discussed below, these instruments are indebted to a religious economies model that favors consumers of religion for whom believing is taken as the defining characteristic of what it means to be religious, and the right to believe (or not) as the essence of what it means to be free.

Individuals who identify with multiple religions also find themselves in a legally precarious position under a religious rights regime that privileges recognized confessional identities and faith communities. While the new state of South Sudan guarantees a list of religious rights for its minority citizens, including its Muslim population, the government has struggled with the question of religious representation because there, as elsewhere, it is often difficult to classify citizens as believers (or nonbelievers) in a single faith tradition.[51] As is the case in many African countries, numerous South Sudanese practice both African traditional religions and Christianity or Islam, and do not distinguish sharply between these and other traditional practices.[52] As Noah Salomon explains, "to think of such 'traditional' practices as distinct confessions does not represent the reality of South Sudanese who may identify as Christians and at the same time see no contradiction in maintaining these rites and rituals."[53] Under a regime of religious rights and freedoms, those who identify with several traditions either are compelled to choose between (now, suddenly different and discrete) religious traditions and their appointed faith leaders or are rendered religiously invisible—even as officially recognized religions gain newfound political standing. This contributes to a striated political field organized by and through religious difference. The South Sudanese government's Bureau of Religious Affairs, for example, registers faith-based organizations, rejecting Christian organizations whose constitutions "do not line up with Biblical chapters or verses," according to one inspector in the bureau interviewed by Salomon. In this scenario, as Rosalind Hackett explains, "African indigenous or traditional religions are hampered by being part of a generalized and heterogeneous category with no clear designation or centralized leadership." Though indigenous religions are therefore what Hackett aptly describes as "religious freedom misfits," the solution is not to assimilate them into international protections because, as she explains, "recent moves to grant institutional, protective space to indigenous expressions of 'spirituality' not only essentialize and objectify traditional forms of belief and practice but also translate and recast them to appeal to cultural outsiders who formally or informally adjudge these rights' claims."[54]

As C. S. Adcock has shown in recent work on early twentieth-century India, and as Hackett's research also suggests, translating particular actions and forms of political struggle into the language of religion or religious freedom and the politics of representative "faith communities" obscures and silences alternative political projects and possibilities. In *The Limits of Tolerance*, Adcock explores the history and politics of *shuddhi*, a ritual form of purification in India that was treated as religious but signified more broadly within a ritual politics of caste. Broadening the canvas, she demonstrates that the identification of shuddhi as religious proselytizing and conversion was not inevitable and carried significant implications for the politics of caste. By delinking debates over Indian secularism from the politics of caste, the translation of shuddhi into the language of religion deflected attention from its central role in the struggle against the micropolitics of exclusion by low caste groups of all religious backgrounds. Designating shuddhi as religious conversion, or as "making Hindus," thus effaced the complex politics of caste, erased the political complicity of the Gandhian ideal of Tolerance in these forms of exclusion, and, in deflecting attention away from the uncertainties surrounding Untouchables' religious identity, helped to establish a representative politics structured around a Hindu constitutional "majority" and Muslim "minority," laying the groundwork for current tensions.[55]

Acknowledging the historical specificity and limits of "religious freedom" as authorized by particular authorities in particular contexts, and coming to terms with the politics of privileging faith communities and their spokespersons, suggests that religious freedom is a specific, historically located technique of modern governance. It is located within and not outside of history. Guarantees for religious freedom require the authorities, including religion experts, judges and lawmakers, religious authorities, and government officials, to make determinations about what constitutes religion and nonreligion, who counts as a legitimate religious subject or association, and who is authorized to represent these communities.[56] These processes entrench religious-religious and religious-secular lines of difference and division by enforcing the interests and identities of groups that are defined and delimited in religious terms. They strengthen the hand of those in a position to determine what counts as religion, and whose religion counts most. They participate in what Olivier Roy, Pasquale Annicchino, Nadia Marzouki, and the ReligioWest research team describe as the "formatting" of religion,[57] as states and other authorities mold religions into static bodies of tradition and convention, transforming them into objects of regulation and reform. Practices that fall outside or defy the tradition as defined by the religious freedom-defining authorities are pushed aside.[58] Forms of religion that have "little to do with the Church," do not "look like religion," or are deemed politically undesirable or unorthodox for whatever reason—perhaps they challenge caste hierarchies, threaten entrenched material interests, or cast doubt on the legitimacy of social order in new ways—are cast out as "pagan and primitive."[59] Those who do not choose to speak or act as Christians, as Hindus, as Jews, or as unbelievers are rendered inaudible. As the anthropologist Amahl Bishara explains, to identify Christian Palestinians *as* Christians is "not inviting to those Christian Palestinians who do not choose to speak or act as Christians."[60]

These dynamics of empowerment and exclusion inhere in the logic and practice of recognition and cannot be transcended by adopting a more informed understanding of contemporary religion or a more effective regime of rights implementation. Critics of the politics of liberal multicultural recognition have developed these insights in other contexts.[61] Patchen Markell diagnoses the binding quality of recognition and challenges the equation of recognition with justice by asserting that the conception of justice employed by recognition obscures the dynamics of subordination.[62] The politics of recognizing faith communities and their leaders correspondingly contributes to fixing particular politically authorized religious differences while constraining and subduing alternative forms of subjectivity and agency. Analyzing the legal and affective practices and social effects of liberal multiculturalism in Australian indigenous communities, Elizabeth Povinelli has shown that the liberal insistence, in the name of cultural or religious diversity, that colonized subjects identify not with the colonizer but with authentic traditional culture serves to reinforce liberal regimes of governance rather than opening them up to difference.[63] In the case at hand, individuals or groups who resist or subvert the clean taxonomies and hierarchies of the secular-religious and religious-religious divides instantiated through regimes of religious freedom are marginalized, falling between the cracks. Exploring the contentious politics and diverse political possibilities in play in the lead up to the establishment and recognition of Pakistan and Israel as a "Muslim Homeland" and a "Jewish National Home," respectively, Maria Birnbaum tracks the ways in which "Muslim" and "Jewish" references became differentiable and politically recognizable—in the process subsuming and suppressing a multitude of ambiguous, and sometimes contradictory, political possibilities. In uncovering the reifying tendencies of recognition that sidelined these alternatives, Birnbaum seeks to gesture toward, and perhaps recover, alternative religiopolitical sensibilities that animated debates over partition and national identity in these contexts.[64] Finally, in a discussion of the politics of international attempts to protect the rights of sexual minorities, Joseph Massad has shown that the "Gay International"[65] movement reifies boundaries and risks imposing Western sexual ontologies and categorizations in diverse contexts.[66] Adapting Massad's terms, one could say that "Religious Freedom International" authorizes and grants legal personality to "religions" in the terms described in this chapter while rendering invisible diverse and multiform religious practices that cannot or refuse to be assimilated into its normative frame. The next section looks more closely at the forms of social and religious being and belonging that are sidelined through the focus in these projects on protecting individuals and groups for whom belief is presumed to be the essence of religion.

THE SUBJECT OF (RELIGIOUS) FREEDOM

Contemporary expert and official international religious freedom discourse presupposes a particular understanding of religion and the religious subject that emerged out of European Christianity and is not universal.[67] Governing difference through rights—the right to believe or not to believe—regulates religious activity along particular lines, in accordance with the logic of the free religious marketplace.[68] Privileging some forms of religion over others, it excludes modes of living in the world, and ways that people are beholden to communities beyond the self, that do not take belief as the essence of religiosity.[69] The commitment to religion as belief—and believers as religious—also shapes the spaces in which people live out their religion.

International authorities and experts have attempted to define religion or belief for the purposes of legally guaranteeing religious freedom. For the UN Human Rights Committee, charged with monitoring the implementation of the International Covenant on Civil and Political Rights, religion or belief includes "theistic, non-theistic and atheistic beliefs, as well as the right not to profess any religion or belief." For legal scholar and religious freedom advocate Malcolm Evans, "it is the freedom to believe and to manifest beliefs, subject only to those limitations strictly necessary to protect the rights and interests of others, which is the subject of human rights protection, and not the beliefs themselves." For the UK Foreign and Commonwealth Office, whether a belief is protected depends on its "cogency, seriousness, cohesion and importance": "The word 'religion' is commonly, but not always, associated with belief in a transcendent deity or deities, i.e. a superhuman power or powers with an interest in human destiny. The term 'belief' does not necessarily involve a divine being; it denotes a certain level of cogency, seriousness, cohesion and importance. So not all beliefs are covered by this protection. For example, if someone believed that the moon was made of cheese, this belief would not be likely to meet the test above."[70] There is tension between these anguished expert and official attempts to define religion as reasonable belief for the purposes of international legal regulation, and the fact that most scholars of religion departed some time ago from an exclusive focus on belief as the essence of religion. As Constance Furey observes, in the past three decades "attention to body and society corrected the Protestant-style tendency to equate religion with interiority and belief." This course correction in the study of religion has led to a "fundamental change in the way many religionists now think about the religious subject . . . this scholarly trend in religious studies strongly undermined the assumption that the object of the religionist's inquiry is (and should be) a freely volitional subject." [71] Yvonne Sherwood echoes Furey in noting that religion scholars "have spent most of their energy in the last thirty years decoupling religion from belief," which has been "kicked into the sidelines as a Christian/colonial imposition." [72] With this shift in orientation, scholars of religion appear to be catching up with the lived realities of religious practice and experience.

Religious affiliation in an everyday, lived sense has always involved more than a choice between belief and disbelief. Citing a colonial American minister from the Carolina backwoods named Charles Woodmason, historian Jon Butler recounts that he "observed religious bewilderment, fascination, repulsion, confusion, and a distanced evasion, including indifference, rather than unbelief or a choice between belief and unbelief, or atheism." [73] The difficulty with equating belief and religion, Butler explains, is that "the laity have seldom phrased their own views about religion in such dichotomous and essentially exclusive ways." [74] T. M. Luhrmann echoes this point in her observations on contemporary American evangelicalism:

> Secular Americans often think that the most important thing to understand about religion is why people believe in God, because we think that belief precedes action and explains choice. That's part of our folk model of the mind: that belief comes first. And that was not really what I saw after my years spending time in evangelical churches. I saw that people went to church to experience joy and to learn how to have more of it. These days I find that it is more helpful to think about faith as the questions people choose to focus on, rather than the propositions observers think they must hold. [75]

Robert Orsi reaches a similar conclusion, noting that "the word *belief* bears heavy weight in public talk about religion in contemporary America: to 'believe in' a religion means that one has deliberated over and then assented to its propositional truths, has chosen this religion over other available options, a personal choice unfettered by authority, tradition, or society. What matters about religion from this perspective are its ideas and not its things, practices, or presences. This is not necessarily how Americans actually are religious, of course, but this account of religion carries real normative force."[76]

Viewed skeptically today by most of those who study religion both past and present, the arguably nonexistent freely volitional subject who chooses to believe (or not) persists, and, strangely, carries normative force in the world of international religious freedom advocacy.[77] The expert definition and official protection of international religious freedom as a universal norm hinges upon, and sanctifies, a religious psychology that relies on the notion of an autonomous subject who chooses beliefs, and then enacts them freely. This understanding of religion normalizes (religious) subjects for whom "believing" is taken as the universal defining characteristic of what it means to be religious, and the right to choose one's belief as the essence of what it means to be free. Anchoring this approach to religion is a specific, historically located figure of faith, and a particular, historically contingent notion of belief.

Talal Asad's account of the shifting and lived experience of belief helpfully calls into question the universality of the liberal democratic requirement that it is belief or conscience that properly defines the individual, thereby representing, for many liberals, the essence of religiosity.[78] Asad dates this concept of belief to a new religious psychology and a new concept of the state that began to emerge in seventeenth-century Europe. In that religious psychology, which is also at the core of John Locke's theory of toleration, belief should not be coerced because it affronts the dignity of the individual, and cannot be coerced because it is located in the private space of the individual mind. Authenticity, according to many liberal philosophers, "consists in the subject's ability *to choose* his or her beliefs and act on them."[79] Donald Lopez, Jr. has described this seventeenth-century notion as "an ideology of belief, that is, an assumption deriving from the history of Christianity that religion is above all an interior state of assent to certain truths."[80] This discourse of belief was accompanied by a particular understanding of the secular state, as Asad explains: "Although the insistence that beliefs cannot be changed from outside appeared to be saying something empirical about 'personal belief' (its singular, autonomous, and inaccessible-to-others location), it was really part of a political discourse about 'privacy,' a claim to civil immunity with regard to religious faith that reinforced the idea of a secular state and a particular conception of religion."[81]

Like Butler, Asad draws our attention toward the shifting, lived experience of "belief." Experiences now translated as "belief" (*croyance*) were always embedded in distinctive social and political relationships and sensibilities. This is illustrated, as Asad explains, in Dorothea Weltecke's description of a young peasant woman named Aude Fauré who was brought before the Inquisition:

> She was unable, she said, to *credere in Deum*. What she meant by this, Weltecke points out, emerges from the detailed context. Aude Fauré took the existence of a God for granted. It was because, in her desperation, she could not see in the Eucharist anything but bread and because she found herself struggling with disturbing thoughts about Incarnation that she had no hope of God's mercy. It is not clear that the *doctrine* of God's body appearing in the form of bread is being challenged here; what is certainly being expressed is the woman's *anguished relationship* to God as a consequence of her own incapacity to see anything but bread. In short, it is not that our present concept of belief (*that* something is true) was absent in pre-modern society, but that the words translated as such were usually embedded in distinctive social and political relationships and articulated distinctive sensibilities. They were first of all lived and only occasionally theorized.[82]

Like Furey, Butler, Sherwood, Lopez, Luhrmann, and others, Asad's discussion of belief complicates the notion of a universal right to religious freedom understood as the freedom to believe (or not). Inasmuch as the official protection of religious freedom hinges upon and sanctifies a religious psychology that relies on a particular notion of an autonomous subject who chooses and enacts beliefs, and a particular notion of the secular state that does not (and cannot) coerce such beliefs, these projects privilege and elevate—often in law—particular forms of religious subjectivity, while disabling and depriviliging others. This excludes other modes of living in the world, as bodies in communities and in relationships to which they are obliged, without attention to or concern for individual belief.

But belief itself is also limited. It is not free. Religion or belief, as Sherwood argues, is a limited membership club. "There is no place at the table for purely political beliefs (known as 'opinions')—that is, beliefs that cannot aggregate in official and large collectives, or beliefs that lack the institutional edifices and props of antiquity to assert their status and make their case."[83] The promotion of international religious freedom, then, is part of a larger story involving the costs and consequences of mistaking, in William Cavanaugh's words, "a contingent power arrangement of the modern West for a universal and timeless feature of human existence."[84]

The momentum behind the legal globalization of the rights of believers and nonbelievers is formidable. Calls for an international convention to protect the freedom of religious (non)believers are urgently made. Many prominent scholars have joined a chorus of experts warning that legal protection for religious freedom should be seen no longer as "only an option" as "it is fast becoming a necessity in order to prevent the further erosion of the position of religious believers in many countries."[85] The international community has been charged by Malcolm Evans and others with "developing a more precise understanding of what the freedom of religion as a human right actually entails, and to do so in a coherent and transparent fashion to which all interested parties can contribute" so that "we might then be better placed to develop the means by which it can be realized." There is a powerful drive to settle on the norm, agree on a definition, and fix it in a convention as a remedy for a host of societal ills, from poverty and oppression to violence and discrimination. An international convention, according to this argument, would breathe new life into an anemic global consensus that has "done little to combat the rising tide of restriction, hostility and violence experienced by many religious believers." It would tackle head-on "the overriding problem, which is how to hold States to account for their own failure to respect and protect the rights of all believers." The reference to religion or belief, at least outside the United States, includes nonreligious belief as well. It is not only religionists but also nonreligionists that are defined by belief. It is said to include everyone.

Yet the historical particularities of the rise of a certain economy of belief, and its close ties and constitutive relationship to modern, post-Protestant notions of religion, subvert the promise of freedom implicit in Evans's and others' international legal ambitions. Contemporary international religious freedom advocacy not only protects particular kinds of religious subjects, but also helps to create individuals and faith communities for whom choosing and believing, in the sense historicized by Asad and lionized by Evans, are seen as the defining characteristics of what it is to be religious, and the right to choose to believe (or not) as the essence of what it means to be free. To achieve this unity in freedom of belief—belief in belief, as it were—across communities of belief (and nonbelief) is what it means to have achieved religious freedom. There are no exceptions. As Evans insists, "Faith communities must reject the superficial attractions of claiming or accepting such freedoms for themselves alone, and unhesitatingly support the freedom of religion or belief for all. Unless or until religious communities are prepared to champion for everyone the freedoms that they wish their own followers to enjoy, there is likely to be little opportunity for seriously furthering the freedom of religion or belief at all."[86]

The official identification of religion and faith communities with a right to freedom of belief leaves little room for alternatives in which religion is attained through practice and lived relationally as ethics, culture, and even politics but without, necessarily, belief and, perhaps, as a matter of command or presence, and not freedom. As Orsi explains, "belief has always struck me as the wrong question . . . the saints, gods, demons, ancestors, and so on are real in experience and practice, in relationships between heaven and earth, in the circumstances of people's lives and histories, and in the stories people tell about them."[87] It is not that belief is necessarily absent or irrelevant to religious experience, but rather that we need to destabilize its privilege and question its naturalness for the religious subject. It is not to deny the presence of belief but to posit its contingency on certain political, legal, and historical processes, and its complex relation to affective and corporeal practices in ways that destabilize the Cartesian divide and the dichotomy between ethics and theology.[88] The foreclosure on religion without and beyond belief shuts out dissenters, doubters, and those on the margins of or just outside those "faith communities" celebrated by many religious freedom advocates, whose voices are subsumed or submerged by the institutions and authorities that are presumed to speak in their name. It endows those authorities with the power to pronounce on which beliefs deserve special protection or sanction. It occludes the fundamental instability of the notion of religious belief. Who decides what counts as a *religious* belief deserving of special protection and legal exemption rather than as some other form of belief?[89]

Of course certain ways of life are protected under contemporary regimes of religious freedom. As Pamela Slotte observes, "as human rights are interpreted at the moment, they seem quite able to protect certain forms of belief, the sort of faith-based life that accords with a modern liberal understanding of faith."[90] Protected belief includes a few major belief systems, skewed toward Christianity and token "unbelief."[91] Religious freedom advocacy is built around a particular notion of the free believing or nonbelieving human that is disseminated through secular international institutions and instruments. This freely choosing, believing, or nonbelieving subject is, like Lila Abu-Lughod's human subject of secular liberalism, "everywhere—translated, resisted, vernacularized, invoked in political struggles, and made the standard language enforced by power."[92] The subject of religious freedom is an autonomous individual defined by his or her freedom to choose to believe or not. In the words of Suzan Johnson Cook, former US ambassador-at-large for international religious freedom, "anyone who identifies as a believer (though religious freedom is for believers and nonbelievers) can come to our roundtable."[93]

Sherwood explains the politics of this attempt to protect believers and nonbelievers: "by giving a place at the table to humanist societies as, effectively, an 'extra' world religion, and allowing them to function as an official 'lack of religion,' a state can appear to do justice to all the sites where the gods may have gone while in truth only protecting all the gods and the non-god (or rather their believers and adherents)."[94] This believing/nonbelieving subject is being protected and normalized not only through US foreign religious engagement but also through a proliferating series of non-American public international legal regimes and administrative initiatives that have adopted this template and have as their objective to promote a right to religious freedom. These initiatives promote a particular notion of (free) religion understood as a set of propositions to which believers assent (or nonbelievers do not),[95] making religion, as Webb Keane has observed, "a matter not of material disciplines or of ritual practices . . . but of subjective beliefs."[96] Part of the strength and appeal of international religious freedom advocacy is drawn from its imbrication with the powerful political doctrine of freedom. Religiously liberated subjects are not brought into a particular American or capitalist normative system. They are brought into freedom itself.

RELIGIOUS FREEDOM AND THE POLITICS OF RELIGIOUS DIFFERENCE

From China to the United States, from South Sudan to the European Union, guarantees for religious freedom and the rights of religious minorities—and programs to ensure their social and legal promotion—are often defended as the answer to the question of how to coexist peacefully, prosper economically, and thrive politically.[97] Celebrated as the key to emancipating individuals and minority communities from violence, poverty, and oppression, religious freedom is heralded as the solution to political and economic backwardness, the tyranny of immoderate and archaic forms of religion, and the violence and despair associated with a host of societal ills from women's oppression to economic desperation to environmental degradation. Communities around the world are seen as in need of transformative social engineering to create the conditions in which secular states and their religious subjects become tolerant, believing or nonbelieving consumers of free religion, willing practitioners of faith-based solutions to collective problems, and, as is often the case, compliant defenders of American or international security as discussed in the next chapter.[98] Guaranteeing a right to religious freedom is said to ensure an ideal balance between allegiance to the state and to (reformed) religion under law.

Today scholars and practitioners working on religion, law, human rights, and international relations are subject to considerable pressure to offer a prescription for how to live together peacefully amid social and religious diversity. For many the discourse of religious rights and freedoms has persuasively presented itself as the solution. Powerful forces, including the law, incentivize individuals and groups to articulate demands in the languages of religious freedom and religious rights. Some may perceive that they have no alternative but to seek protections on these grounds. This is understandable. If being a persecuted religionist makes it more likely that development aid will be forthcoming or asylum will be granted, then we should not be surprised to see a rise in persecuted religionists. As mentioned earlier, my intention is neither to judge individuals and groups who find themselves in difficult circumstances nor to undermine local groups working to assist them. Many local legal aid organizations are doing important work in this field at significant risk. But there is also a larger story to be told. Privileging the category of religion in developing foreign policy, writing constitutions, protecting human rights, and designing development and humanitarian interventions creates a particular kind of world, as described in this chapter, leaving other possibilities for coexistence behind.[99]

Are there alternatives? Can religious freedom be refashioned? Can it be otherwise? Is it possible, as Lars Tønder asks of the modern construct of tolerance, to reorient the discussion "if the very terms of this reorientation are defined by a discourse that either disavows the plurality intrinsic to the history of this practice or limits the plurality to a linear progression toward something like reasonableness and recognition as the primary, if not sole, goal of democratic politics?"[100] Can we "activate the concept's plurality" to "pluralize our divergent images" of what religious freedom has or could mean? I think not. Before concluding that religious persecution is the culprit—and religious freedom the solution—it is worth calculating the costs of locking into this narrative by protecting religion in law, positing religion as a stable and coherent category in political and policy analysis, and privileging religion as a basis for making foreign policy and protecting human flourishing. This chapter has shown that debates over religious freedom always participate in broader complexes of contentious politics. Pulling back to view these conflicts through a wider lens reveals that governing social difference through religious rights and freedoms authorizes particular forms of politics and shapes the spaces in which people live out their religions in specific ways. Governing through religious rights presupposes and elicits an emphasis on religion and religious difference as exceptionally threatening forms of social difference that need to be kept in check by the authorities (the logic of sectarianism) while obscuring complex social, economic, and political histories and inequalities, as well as alternative religiosities. It empowers established voices and institutions of protected groups that enjoy good relations with state and transnational authorities, while marginalizing individuals and groups that fall into the gray areas between contemporary formations of the secular and the religious (the logic of empowering faith communities). It privileges and protects a particular understanding of religion as the right to choose and enact one's belief or nonbelief (the logic of the free religious marketplace).

There is no single prescription that emerges from this discussion. Inventing a more inclusive mechanism of protection by increasing the number or diversity of groups represented, or by exchanging a focus on religion as belief for a more inclusive model of religion as communal practice or ethics, does not offer a solution. A more encompassing, new and improved "International Religious Freedom 2.0" will serve to (re)enact a modified version of the same exclusionary logic. This diagnosis may not sit well with many liberal internationalists and others for whom human rights have come to represent the last best hope for humankind. Political efforts to promote religious rights and freedoms are likely to retain their appeal for some time, across the political spectrum. Yet those interested in thinking critically and historically about the politics of international human rights need to avoid reproducing, in the guise of protecting human flourishing, those normative distinctions and discourses that stand most in need of interrogation and politicization. Religious rights and religious freedom fall in this category. Governing difference through religious rights and freedoms authorizes particular understandings of what it means to be religious, and what it means for religion to be free. Naturalizing the very lines of difference they are intended to tame, these projects risk exacerbating the social tensions, forms of discrimination, and intercommunal discord that they claim to be uniquely equipped to transcend. In its strongest versions, religious freedom "usurps the entire universe of moral discourse,"[101] capturing the field of emancipatory possibility and effacing the distinction between law and justice.

CHAPTER 4

Religious Engagement

If the threat of Communism is to be met effectively, a moral and spiritual offensive is necessary.

—*US Information and Education Exchange, 1951*

For the first time since World War II, Albanian young people are coming of age in an environment that allows open religious practice. The religious beliefs that they embrace, whether traditional Albanian pluralism or less moderate ideologies, will set the tone for Albania's future of tolerance.

—*USAID RelHarmony Final Report, 2007*

In the summer of 2013 the US State Department launched an Office of Faith-Based Community Initiatives to engage with faith communities outside the United States.[1] Speaking at the launch of the office, now called Religion and Global Affairs, Melissa Rogers, director of the White House Office of Faith-Based and Neighborhood Partnerships, observed that "strategic engagement with religious leaders can help us to break cycles of violent conflict."[2] In the lead-up to the creation of the office, President Obama assembled an Interagency Working Group on Religion and Global Affairs, cochaired by the Office of Faith-Based and Neighborhood Partnerships and the White House National Security Staff, to develop "a comprehensive map of how our government currently engages religious actors in foreign affairs through USAID Missions, Embassies, and Departments across government from the Department of Defense to the Department of Health and Human Services."[3] The United States has a Strategy on Religious Leader and Faith Community Engagement.[4] The US Department of Homeland Security has a Faith-Based Security and

Communications Advisory Committee.[5] The list is long: from environmental policy to development to counterterrorism, from constitution writing to nation building to the provision of health care, government-sponsored religious outreach is being heralded as the solution to dilemmas of modern governance, domestic and international. In this "new era of partnerships," in the title of one government report,[6] state and religious authorities cooperate to advance shared interests, promote tolerant religion, and redress the strategic errors made by ignoring the "missing dimension of statecraft" discussed in Chapter 2.[7] "Religious believers," according to USAID, "are on the front lines of the world's greatest challenges."[8]

This chapter explores the politics of US foreign religious engagement. It situates contemporary programs to engage religious leaders and communities abroad on a longer historical timeline and as part of a larger American project. Since World War II, the promotion of American-friendly "free" religion abroad has been understood to benefit the rest of the world by saving it from religious and political tyranny. For decades, the United States has designed and sponsored religious reform projects to instruct religious individuals and groups abroad on how to be free, or at least freer, versions of themselves.[9] While many of these activities would likely raise constitutional questions if pursued domestically in the United States, as foreign policy initiatives they are buoyed by a powerful myth of American exceptionalism that posits the United States as the inventor of religious freedom, as the place where both religion and freedom have been perfected. The United States is where religion goes to become free. Contemporary US religious engagement programming is the latest iteration of a series of attempts to position the United States as the global guardian of free religion, and of freedom in general.[10] In this view, "religious freedom" is achieved through the cultivation and establishment of forms of religion abroad that conform to American standards of what it means to be free, both religiously and politically. So while religious engagement does involve an attempt to strengthen US-friendly religious authorities and communities abroad, it is, at the same time, and more fundamentally, a project of religious reform, of transforming religions into what is understood to be better versions of themselves.

A focused discussion of three empirical focal points in the history of US foreign relations illustrates this argument, beginning with American efforts to promote "global spiritual health" during the early Cold War. A crucial element in anticommunist propaganda, the promotion

of spiritual health was seen as an obligation owed by a privileged subset of the world's population to citizens abroad who risked falling prey
to communism. During the 1950s, the United States established alliances with anticommunist religious leaders throughout Southeast Asia
to promote forms of Buddhism that conformed to American conceptions of political and religious freedom. Moving forward in time to the
early 2000s, a second example reveals that similar objectives motivated
USAID-sponsored efforts to promote religious tolerance in Albania. Like
the Cold War campaign for spiritual health, the RelHarmony project
was designed to transform Albanian religions and religious subjects into
freer and more tolerant versions of themselves, rendering them less susceptible to the lure of extremism and more amenable to US and European control. Most recently, US-sponsored overseas religious reform has
been pursued through the expanded duties of US military chaplains
stationed abroad, whose responsibilities include religious outreach and
liaison activities in local communities. As the lines between combat, stabilization, and development operations have become more porous, chaplains have been asked to serve as cultural consultants, sources of "human
terrain intelligence,"[11] and liaisons with local religious leaders, in addition to meeting the religious needs of service members and their families abroad.

All of these US foreign religious engagement activities are understood
in First Amendment terms to secure the possibility of the free exercise
of religion, and not to promote its establishment. This chapter argues
that government-sponsored religious outreach activities are not, and cannot be, evenhanded efforts to "bring religion back in" to international
relations to compensate for its alleged exclusion or to secure its free exercise.[12] The category of religion is too unstable to bear the weight of
such political definition and legal regulation. Rather, to privilege religion as a platform from which to conduct foreign policy and engage
overseas counterparts puts the onus on the government to define who
is a religious actor and who is not, who counts as a religious authority
and who does not, and which religions are considered legitimate partners for engagement and which are not. In requiring that such choices
be made, religious engagement foments intracommunal conflict over the
politics of representation and the distribution of scarce resources, while
marginalizing or excluding dissenters, doubters, and those on the fringes
of the communities that are selected for engagement. This becomes evident in distinguishing between the "official" religions that are supported

through religious outreach projects and the broader fields of practice, belonging, and belief in which they are deployed. Disaggregating the religious field in this way also allows us to interrogate the assumptions about "religion" that underlie legal debates over the constitutionality of US overseas activities in this domain. Such debates often reveal more about the limits—some would say the irrelevance—of the religion clauses than they do about the actual history and politics of US overseas religious reform efforts.

THE RELIGIOUS OFFENSIVE

US-sponsored religious reform initiatives are not new, and various earlier moments could also be considered.[13] Since the founding, the United States has seen itself as exceptionally committed to religious freedom, and at least since the mid-twentieth century, as uniquely qualified to export it.[14] In past decades the United States has sought to cultivate moderate foreign religious subjects and marginalize those defined as political (i.e., communist) or religious (i.e., radical Islamist) threats to American interests. In earlier centuries, the US government sponsored Protestant missions around the world, forced conversion of Native Americans at home, and sought to civilize and Christianize the Philippines.[15] The provision of religious freedom, tolerance, and rights is often understood as an obligation owed by a privileged subset of the world's population to individuals and groups awaiting their freedom.[16]

During the early Cold War, the US government developed a series of programs intended to cultivate a "spiritually healthy world" and weaken the appeal of communism for "susceptible subjects" abroad. It was widely believed that godless secularist-communist parties would lose their appeal and wither on the vine in such a world.[17] During this period, it was not religious extremism but communist secularism that was seen as the chief impediment to bolstering America's reputation as the global guardian of free religion, and of freedom in general.[18] In pursuit of these objectives, American officials undertook a "religious offensive," as it was called at the time, which involved measures to foil communist designs on global spiritual health through religious reform at home and abroad. In April 1951, President Truman created the Psychological Strategy Board (PSB) to pursue psychological (defined as nonmilitary) warfare against communism, in a "winning hearts and minds" effort of that era.[19] Both Truman and Eisenhower sought to strengthen US diplomatic ties with the Vatican to work together to oppose communism.[20] Also in 1951, the United States Information and Educational Exchange (USIE, an initiative created in 1948 to cultivate a favorable image of the United States abroad) established a three-person council of religious leaders charged with investigating the "moral and religious factors" of psychological warfare.[21] In language presaging more recent US international religious freedom advocacy, a 1951 USIE panel report recommended that the United States pursue a healthy balance between material might and spiritual conviction: "To build this 'balance of spirit,' three things are necessary: (a) we must convince others of our own moral and spiritual stamina and dependability, (b) we must arouse others to the defense of their own right to moral and spiritual freedom, and (c) we must use the interest which we share with others in the preservation of moral and spiritual values to cement friendship and understanding among all peoples who cherish those values."[22] In the early 1950s the State Department distributed Bibles and religious periodicals, including *Christian Century, Commonweal,* and *Commentary,* in 165 information centers abroad. As historian Jonathan Herzog recounts, the *Voice of America*'s director of religious programming, Roger Lyons, sought to create "in the minds of foreigners an image of a righteous American state driven by religious zealotry. In this ideation the United States seems the perfect foil for Communist designs—a nation ready to martyr itself so that others could worship God."[23] In 1953, Eisenhower established the US Information Agency and replaced the PSB with the Operations Coordinating Board (OCB), a national security committee reporting to the NSC and including an "Ideological Subcommittee on the Religious Factor."

On the home front, the campaign for global spiritual health extended beyond government circles to include prominent religious, business, entertainment, and academic figures. Between 1952 and 1957, fifty-six overseers including entertainers Ronald Reagan, Bing Crosby, Walt Disney, and Cecil B. DeMille, and business leaders J. C. Penney, Fred Maytag II, and Conrad Hilton, alongside the presidents of Brown University and the University of California, ran the Committee to Proclaim Liberty (CPL). The CPL lobbied for the Fourth of July to be observed as "a day of solemn religious observation when church leaders would expound upon the connection between religion and Americanism."[24] The American Political Science Association took up the call, joining the Foundation for Religious Action in Social and Civil Order (FRASCO), in order to "energize our accepted institutions in the present, global war of ideas and spiritual powers."[25] FRASCO, created by Eisenhower's minister, Edward Elson, working with the White House, was designed to be "a more inclusive and politically congenial alternative to the National Council of Churches," because, as explained by Mark Hulsether, the latter had been "unwilling to fight communism with the enthusiasm the White House desired."[26]

FRASCO proposed an overseas "spiritual offensive movement against [Vietnamese] communism in which the active agents will be native Buddhists, Cao-Daiists, Catholics, and other men and women of conviction."[27] The United States sent a Buddhist advisor to Cambodia and cultivated a religious alliance with a Thai police general, who founded the Society for the Promotion of Buddhism in 1954. According to Jonathan Herzog, "soon 'instruction teams' funded with American dollars were traveling through villages in Thailand with colorful bands of dancers, comedians, puppeteers, and soldiers who taught peasants 'The Seven Bad Things about Communism.'" By May 1956 an estimated three million Thais had witnessed these presentations. That spring, the OCB formed the Committee on Buddhism to coordinate the religious offensive into 1957.[28] With representatives from the State Department, the CIA, and USIE, the Committee on Buddhism "was charged with studying the 'effectiveness of Buddhist organizations' in several Southeast Asian countries so as to discover 'ways and means to ensure that the influence of Buddhist monks and lay leaders is exerted in favor of U.S. interests.'"[29] US-supported campaigns in Laos and Cambodia sought to encourage Buddhists to combat the antireligious forces of communism. In Laos, this involved support for the Royal Lao government in its effort to portray the Pathet Lao as anti-Buddhist, while in Cambodia it involved support for Lon Nol in his "religious war" against Vietcong and Khmer Rouge.[30]

David Kaplan has suggested that early twenty-first century US religious reform efforts are modeled on US anticommunist strategies during the early Cold War: "One of the era's great successes was how Washington helped break off moderate socialists from hard-core Communists overseas. 'That's how we're thinking. . . . It's something we talk about all the time,' says Peter Rodman, a longtime aide to Henry Kissinger and now the Pentagon's assistant secretary of defense for international security affairs. 'In those days, it was covert. Now, it's more open.'"[31] Whether or not contemporary foreign religious engagement is explicitly modeled on the Cold War experience, all of these projects are at the center of American efforts to break off US-friendly "moderate religionists" from US-hostile "hard-core extremists," as illustrated in the discussion of RelHarmony and military chaplains' duties below. Taking a longer-range perspective on US foreign religious engagement upends the assumption that religion was absent from foreign policy until recently due to a deeply institutionalized commitment to an antireligious form of secularism. To the contrary, even a brief excursion into this history suggests that American foreign relations have been replete with attempts to cultivate forms of religiosity in other countries and at home that not only align with American strategic interests but also conform to specific and historically contingent conceptions of what it means to be religious and to be free. These efforts would continue in new forms in the post–Cold War era.

EXPORTING MODERATE RELIGION AT USAID

Sponsored by USAID and launched in the early 2000s, Fostering Religious Harmony in Albania (RelHarmony) was a development project designed to promote religious pluralism and to prevent the emergence of religious conflict and extremism in Southeastern Europe.[32] The project was focused on four Albanian religious communities, Catholic Christians, Orthodox Christians, Sunni Muslims, and Shi'a Bektashi, in seven cities: Shkoder, Lezha, Librazhd, Elbasan, Durrës, Kavaja, and Tirana. According to the project's Final Report, RelHarmony reached "over 250 religious leaders and over 1,200 believers" as well as "thousands more Albanians through national broadcast of roundtables and documentary films that addressed religious issues."[33] The Final Report describes the program's rationale: "Although Albania has not experienced religious conflict, concerns about the possibility of a conflict are growing. In June 2003 an informal survey of 2,110 people in 14 Albanian cities hinted that extremist religious views were growing in the country. Concerns over entry into the European Union and the possibility of destabilization in the Balkans led USAID to develop RelHarmony."[34] Like other US foreign religious engagement efforts, RelHarmony sought to strengthen local religious authorities and institutions that shared American concerns about the rise of "foreign extremism" in Southeastern Europe, to transform Albanian religions and religious subjects into what the Americans considered to be freer versions of themselves, and to establish modes of state religious governance that would support these objectives through legal reform, interreligious dialogue, and educational programming. In other words, it supported specific forms of governed religion. In the process, USAID and its partners and contractors were forced to discriminate between local groups, selecting for engagement those that represented the potential for Albanian "religious pluralism" rather than "foreign extremism." This soft establishment of US-friendly religion was meant to empower and educate the former while taming or marginalizing the latter.[35]

RelHarmony pursued these objectives through several channels. It organized training and exchanges to equip "religious leaders and institutions with the skills they need to be serious stakeholders in interfaith activities." It awarded a grant to the State Committee on Cults (Komiteti Shteteror I Kulteve) called "Drafting Agreements between the State and Religious Communities" designed to regularize and rationalize relations between Albanian religious communities and the state.[36] It funded the development of religion-related databases, including "a database of religious institutions and leaders in Albania; a database of governmental and non-governmental international and local institutions that deal with religious affairs and conflict prevention; a database of experts, researchers, and trainers of potential interest to the project; a database of local and international media institutions that work in Albania; and a bibliography of Albanian and international literature on religious affairs." It sponsored an interfaith youth summer camp that was featured among USAID's online "Success Stories," produced a film extolling Albanian religious diversity called *Living Together* (which aired forty-five times on national television channels), and produced a second film describing "the story of four young believers in their own words" titled *What Do I Believe* (which was not distributed due to the "sensitivity" of the content of the film).[37] Another youth initiative informed young Albanian activists about, in the words of the Final Report, "religions' basic beliefs, interfaith harmony as a key element for progressive development, the role of youth religious communities, and the need for greater engagement in interfaith initiatives to promote peace and tolerance."[38]

According to project documents, RelHarmony sought to engender "long-term changes in values and tolerance"[39] by bolstering "religious moderates" and encouraging "positive change" *internal to* Albanian religious traditions. As Courtney Bender argues, "these plans do more than alter and transform the relationships between religions and 'build' on what is already present in a nascent and natural state. They *actively seek to reshape religion* into something new, in relation to the new Albanian state."[40] Given these ambitious objectives, the specific religious content—the theologies, hermeneutics, and institutional forms—that were privileged in the RelHarmony project remain vague and shrouded in mystery, perhaps even to those who implemented it. By all appearances RelHarmony seems to have favored established, institutionalized religions and their adult male leaders.[41] In terms of religious content, it is likely that program leaders never thought of their jobs in these terms because, like the other initiatives discussed in this chapter, Americans running the program would have understood the commitment to enhance "traditional Albanian pluralism" through "positive change" in local traditions as promoting the free exercise of religion, and not its establishment. In this context it is taken for granted, as Bender observes of the religious economies model and recent sociological analyses of American religious pluralism, that "a plurality of religious groups is needed to indicate a thriving religious freedom, and that the American example presents a clear case of actually free religion."[42] Religions abroad need to become more like American religions: freer and more tolerant. This assumption and this logic help to explain the apparent legitimacy of USAID's self-appointed role as theological authority and executive director of religious reform, uniquely equipped to decide which religions, and which versions of which religions, count as "traditional pluralism" and which appear suspect as "non-Albanian," "foreign," or "less moderate." It also helps to explain how it was possible for RelHarmony to support a roundtable discussion on "Media Coverage of Religion," which concluded that the media should collaborate with religious communities in order to "avoid unwarranted involvement of politics in religious affairs."[43] In this logic, either USAID's activities in Albania including the roundtable qualified as "warranted" government involvement in religious affairs, or USAID did not in those moments represent the government, standing above politics as the neutral purveyor of religious liberalization and religious freedom. Or both.

Cited as "a model for fostering interfaith harmony," RelHarmony is one of many US-sponsored religious engagement and education projects dedicated to overseas religious reform. Initiated in 2003, the USAID-funded KEDEM: Voices for Religious Reconciliation "brought together Israeli Jewish, Arab Christian, and Arab Muslim religious leaders to learn to work together."[44] The Legal Education (or "Street Law") Program in Kyrgyzstan offered "classes in madrasas on democratic practice and religious freedom" to teach Kyrgyz religious communities about their legal rights vis-à-vis the state and to foster "better integration of religious communities into secular society in order to prevent them from becoming marginalized and susceptible to recruitment by extremist groups."[45] The Islam and Civil Society Program was a collaboration between USAID, the Asia Foundation's Islam and Civil Society program, and Indonesian Muslim leaders and organizations to encourage "the development of a politically secular Indonesia, based on values of freedom, religious tolerance, and pluralism."[46] USAID's Inter-Religious Action for Tolerance and Co-Existence in the Balkans, launched in 2004, also sought to "make religion part of the solution."[47] Among other activities, this project supported the Inter-religious Council of Bosnia-Herzegovina to "lead the way to peaceful change and religious tolerance" by establishing a regional network of interreligious leaders to promote peace, reconciliation, and conflict prevention, to strengthen religious women, and to support an interreligious youth group.[48]

These projects are motivated by a perceived need to promote religious leaders and forms of governed religion that are amenable to US strategic and political interests. But perhaps more powerfully, they are also driven by a desire to promote forms of religion that conform to American understandings of what it means to be free, religiously and politically. This understanding is particular to the American experience, and is not universal. As Bender explains, it is informed by a background assumption in which "free-church Protestantism is the norm against which all other religious groups are measured as capable of being free, and capable of forming the kind of religious actors who can defend 'religious freedom.'"[49] Lori Beaman and Winnifred Sullivan observe that the free-church model of religion has become "largely naturalized in the US, even for Catholics and many non-Christian communities."[50] In light of these and other peculiarities of US religious history, it is not surprising that certain religions and religious leaders would appear as more fit for US engagement than others. Some conform to the model better than others. Some groups don't qualify as religions, in the eyes of the authorities. Choices have to be made.

A similar set of conditions shapes how the Albanians respond to the invitation to interfaith dialogue. Local Albanian religious leaders participating in RelHarmony opposed including nontraditional religions in project activities. According to the Final Report, "religious leaders from Albania's four traditional religious groups were, with few exceptions, supportive of interfaith initiatives, which included all traditional religions, however their views differed on the question of including members of non-traditional religious groups in RelHarmony activities. Elbasan's Project Advisory Committee, for example, supported an inclusive approach and even hired a member of a non-traditional religious group to manage the Interfaith Community Center. However some leaders in other cities did not support this inclusive approach, raising the prospect that they and their followers would not participate in activities that included members from non-traditional religious communities."[51] Nontraditional religions and unorthodox versions of protected religions were absent from that interfaith table.

Many Albanians reacted with skepticism to RelHarmony, as USAID's "Religion, Conflict and Peacebuilding" report concluded: "Developing conflict programming in a country without conflict can create skepticism ... many people did not understand the need for the program since there was no conflict or visible signs of a possible conflict. They raised concerns that implementing a project like this could draw attention to the possibility of conflict and thought it would be better to leave the situation alone."[52] The same report acknowledged that "efforts to build trust must ... remain a top priority to ensure religious actors do not view the program as a covert attempt to interfere with religious institutions, communities, or beliefs."[53] The RelHarmony Final Report conceded that patience is required because "religious communities often have a long history and established traditions. As a result, a shift in community consciousness can be slow. Patience is key, as is a focus on the small incremental steps that can build the path for positive change." The report concluded that while "some USAID programs stray into entanglement with religion that result in the appearance of programs favoring certain religious groups or in the propagation of theological positions ... critical analysis and consultations with local partners and community members will ensure USAID programs are strategic and build religious considerations into programming where necessary, and exclude them when not necessary."[54] RelHarmony's objective in Albania, like other US religious reform initiatives, is the establishment of religious freedom, American-style.[55] "Straying into entanglement" and the "propagation of theological positions" are unavoidable.

CHAPLAINS ABROAD: CULTURAL INTELLIGENCE AND MULLAH ENGAGEMENT

Since the founding of the US Army Chaplain Corps in 1775, military chaplains have served the religious needs of military personnel and their dependents overseas.[56] The US Joint Chiefs of Staff describes this as the "delivery of religious support."[57] According to the US Navy, chaplains may also "minister (when authorized and directed) to captives, evacuees, detainees, migrants, refugees, and EPWs [enemy prisoners of war]."[58] According to the Chief of Chaplains personnel office, the US Army has 1,300 chaplains in the active Army, of whom 1,243 are Protestant, 113 are Catholic, 6 are Orthodox Christian, 10 are Jewish, and 6 are Muslim. There are also several Buddhist chaplains, and at least one Hindu chaplain. An equal number of chaplains serve in the Reserves and National Guard.

Legal challenges to the US military chaplaincy on establishment grounds have been unsuccessful. Like their counterparts at USAID, military chaplains are understood to secure the possibility of the free exercise of religion, and not to promote its establishment.[59] In 1986, in *Baz v. Walters*, the Seventh Circuit Court of Appeals affirmed that the Department of Veterans Affairs had not established religion by employing chaplains and having rules and regulations regarding their conduct. The court concluded that "a V.A. chaplain is hired to conduct a ministry in a V.A. facility and is provided with detailed instructions as to his duties and as to the prohibitions that apply to his actions. He is not simply a preacher but a secular employee hired to perform duties for which he has, by dint of his religious calling and pastoral experience, a special aptitude."[60] In *Larsen v. US Navy* (2007), a US district court in Washington rejected a challenge to the Navy's chaplain selection criteria and held that the criteria were constitutional because the Navy has "broad discretion to determine how to accommodate the religious needs of its service members."[61]

Beginning in 2009, US military doctrine formalized an expanded religious liaison and religious advisement role for military chaplains, requiring that they "participate in operational planning and advise the command and staff on matters related to religion" and "provide assistance in liaison with local religious leaders in a given area of operation."[62] (There is also a well-developed religious liaison role for chaplains involved in stability operations in the Canadian, Australian, Norwegian, and South African armed forces,[63] and there are chaplains affiliated with international organizations, with the first NATO chaplain post created on the SFOR, or stabilization force, staff in Bosnia in the 1990s.) As Stacey Gutkowski and George Wilkes explain, under the new US military regulations, "in addition to liaising with the local population, the chaplain is tasked with acting 'as the principal adviser to the commander on religious affairs . . . [as] a member of the commander's personal staff. . . .' Such action is authorized where a chaplain 'meets with a leader on matters of religion to ameliorate suffering and to promote peace and the benevolent expression of religion.'"[64]

American military chaplains in Iraq and Afghanistan have established religious councils, coordinated mosque renovations, and attempted to reconcile with the families of civilians killed by US forces. They have organized community religious celebrations and trained local security forces to serve as chaplains.[65] In a report for the US Institute of Peace, chaplain Larry Adams-Thompson describes a "mullah engagement strategy," a program he designed to systematize interactions between chaplains and local Afghan mullahs.[66] Adams-Thompson obtained one million dollars in CERP (commander's emergency response program) funds to work through provincial reconstruction team commanders to arrange meetings between chaplains and mullahs.[67] Through the program, chaplains "coordinated with mullahs for the renovation of religious structures and the provision of such items as carpets and sound systems for mosques, generators for orphanages, and educational supplies for schools."[68]

US military chaplains have become a conduit of religious engagement and reform. These activities take different forms, ranging from supervising Koran lessons to providing tolerance training for counterparts abroad. In 2011, Navy Chaplain Lieutenant Commander Nathan Solomon found himself in "the unexpected role of counterinsurgent" (and an authority on the Koran) when he and his colleagues in Afghanistan were ordered to find ways to "counter the Taliban's message." Solomon and his Afghan liaison started Koran lessons for local citizens that were delivered weekly by radio, and invited area elders and mullahs for a *shura* where influential local tribesmen explained "Islam's true nature."[69] In a related effort, also in 2011, the Marines sent forty-five elders and politicians from Helmand province in Afghanistan to Amman, Jordan on a "collaborative influence program" called Voices of Religious Tolerance, where the Afghans toured mosques, parks, and shopping malls to learn about life in a "religiously tolerant" country. US military chaplains also provide tolerance and religious support training for their overseas counterparts. In 2012, US Army Africa chaplain John McGraw traveled to Kinshasa to provide resiliency training to the Democratic Republic of the Congo's (DRC) Armed Forces chaplains. As McGraw explains, "the Congolese are very spiritual people . . . DRC chaplains are great pastors and preachers, yet they want to know more about improving their ministry with soldiers and the areas of pastoral care." Follow-on training with DRC chaplains focused on training in combat stress prevention, family life skills counseling, and other "religious support" missions. Africa Command chaplain Jerry Lewis, who accompanied McGraw to Kinshasa, stressed that "the roles of chaplains can have big connections to peace and stability of this nation, and there are great contributions that our chaplains can make here in the future."⁷⁰

The expanding remit of chaplains' duties to include religious engagement and tolerance training reflects a broader imperative discussed in this book involving the "operationalization" of religion as a platform from which to conduct foreign policy. These new duties reflect a revitalized commitment to religious leaders and communities as strategic resources with the potential to serve US nation-building and stabilization objectives, not unlike during the early Cold War. Religious leaders are depicted as sources of cultural intelligence that, if properly engaged, will yield positive outcomes for US interests. Citing Major Laura Geldhof and her coauthors writing in *Special Warfare* in 2006, the Center for Strategic and International Studies's Danan explains, "In response to recent military operations that include close contact with local populations and a mixture of traditional and counterinsurgency tactics, a growing literature on the utility of 'ethnographic intelligence (EI),' 'cultural intelligence,' and 'human terrain intelligence' for the battlefield has emerged. This new group of cultural intelligence advocates considers *religious groups to be a critical empowered network*, with 'key personnel and groups [that] have become the new key terrain. These may comprise religious clerics . . . or anyone with influence over a large or important constituency.'"⁷¹

Cultural information about host populations, including information about religious sites, leaders, and practices, carries operational relevance. The Army describes "operationally relevant cultural knowledge" as most pertinent for stability ("phase four") operations involving peacekeeping, counterinsurgency, and counterterrorism.⁷² As the military has received an increasing proportion of the overall development budget and the lines between combat, stabilization, and development operations have become more porous or disappeared, military personnel have been expected to perform tasks that had previously been associated with the provision of development assistance, emergency relief, and humanitarian aid.⁷³ Chaplains are expected to serve as cultural consultants, sources of "human terrain intelligence," religious educators, and liaisons with local religious leaders, in addition to meeting the religious needs of American service members and their families. In this context, an increasingly important part of the chaplain's job is to promote what the United States identifies as benevolent religion and to marginalize forms of religion deemed threatening to American interests and incompatible with American understandings of what it means for religion to be free. This requires making decisions about which individuals and groups count as religions, which leaders are eligible to speak on behalf of particular communities, and which religious groups are best suited to fulfill these objectives. Like their predecessors on the Committee on Buddhism and their contemporaries at USAID, military chaplains are expected to identify and promote US-friendly religious authorities and communities abroad, in a context in which the government is increasingly understood as the handmaiden and governor of tolerant, nonsectarian religion.

In this nonseparationist landscape of overseas religious engagement and reform, legal controversies over which US-funded activities abroad are "inherently religious" and which promote a "secular purpose" may seem out of place, even anachronistic.[74] Yet policy makers continue to rely on these unstable categories despite the fact that the realities on the ground have undermined their relevance. A 2009 USAID inspector general's audit raised concerns about $325,000 in expenditures to rehabilitate four mosques in a Fallujah compound, bombed by the Americans, due to the "religious nature" of the buildings. USAID responded that the money had gone to repair facilities providing jobs, social services, food, and other basics, but that it had withheld payment of more than $45,000 for mosque repairs because "the contractor could not demonstrate that the work served a secular purpose."[75] As was also the case with RelHarmony, legal debates over the extraterritorial lives of the First Amendment come up short when faced with a situation in which the stability of the categories of law and religion has been so thoroughly eroded.[76] Developments on the ground are challenging the utility and the relevance of the establishment-disestablishment framework.[77] The repeated attempts at disestablishment that are associated with US domestic church-state history do not apply when it comes to foreign policy, and arguably never have.[78] Even in a domestic context, as Sullivan has argued, nondiscriminatory government support for religious institutions and activities is increasingly understood to not only be permitted by the First Amendment but also to be a necessary public good.[79] This suggests the need for a new approach to the intersection of religion and foreign policy.

BEYOND THE FIRST AMENDMENT

Historically, the Bill of Rights has been largely confined to domestic affairs. As American imperial reach has expanded over the past century, however, debates have arisen over constitutional limitations on the conduct of foreign policy.[80] The extraterritorial application of the First Amendment to the US Constitution, and the extent to which particular US overseas activities can be considered secular or religious,[81] have been subject to legal scrutiny, bureaucratic hand-wringing, and political debate in recent years.[82] It is unclear whether or to what extent the religion clauses of the First Amendment ("Congress shall make no law respecting an establishment of religion or prohibiting the free exercise thereof") apply to US actions abroad.[83] The Supreme Court has never ruled on whether the Establishment Clause applies to foreign policy, and the few lower court opinions on the subject are narrow and inconclusive.[84]

In a 1991 case, *Lamont v. Woods*, US taxpayers sued USAID for violating the Establishment Clause by funding Jewish and Catholic schools abroad.[85] The Second Circuit held that the Clause did apply, noting that its aim is to prevent governmental advancement of religion and that American taxpayers' grievances arose over the spending itself and not its location. But the court also observed that the standard of analysis for foreign affairs differs from that of domestic programs,[86] explaining that "domestic Establishment Clause jurisprudence has more than enough flexibility to accommodate any special circumstances created by the foreign situs of the expenditures, although the international dimension does, we believe, enter into the analysis." The court proposed a "balancing test" in which, even where American funds are going to a pervasively sectarian foreign organization, the government is allowed the opportunity to "demonstrate some compelling reason why the usually unacceptable risk attendant on such funding in such an institution should, in the particular case, be borne."[87]

Lamont was arguably superseded in 2007 by another decision, *Hein v. Freedom from Religion Foundation*, in which a group of US taxpayers brought an Establishment Clause challenge to the constitutionality of the White House Office of Faith-Based Community Initiatives, in particular the use of the office to convene conferences of religious groups, alleging that the meetings favored religion over nonreligion.[88] The Supreme Court ruled (five to four) that because no legislative body had directly authorized the funding, taxpayers did not have standing to bring suit in federal court to challenge the constitutionality of executive branch expenditures. Concerned about opening a floodgate of litigation, the Court held that as long as the government is not funding worship, and there is no coercive government proselytizing that harms an actual person, the government can essentially promote and fund religion as it chooses.[89]

As Austin Dacey points out in regard to this decision, "even if the State Department's new engagement activities resulted in direct funding to religious organizations, they might nevertheless be immune from constitutional challenge."[90] Practice on the ground reflects the legal uncertainty. During the occupation of Iraq, an American army colonel applied for funding from the Commander's Emergency Response Program to rebuild a mosque whose imam was wavering between working with the Americans and joining the insurgency. CERP rejected the colonel's request, so he changed the word "mosque" to "cultural site" and resubmitted the application. The funding was approved and the mosque was built.[91]

The debate over US religious engagement and religious reform is not about whether religion can be separate from government, ignored, or contained—as many separationists would have it. The notion of separation, as the editors of *After Secular Law* and others have suggested, has broken down as a useful description of the relationship between religion, law, and public policy.[92] There is no religion anywhere without government involvement in some form.[93] Religion never left public life. Instead, it has assumed different forms and occupied different spaces under modern regimes of governance, many of which are described as secular.[94] The debate over religious engagement and religious reform is also not about whether "persons of faith" should be included in public life to help achieve collective goals. Of course they should. The question is how these entanglements between governments and individuals and institutions abroad take shape: Who gets chosen, and why? How are they identified, and by whom? Which versions of which religion are supported? Which religious authorities are privileged, and who exactly are they understood to represent? Government-sponsored religious outreach inevitably enacts some version of what Lori Beaman and Winnifred Sullivan describe as "varieties of religious establishment."[95] It requires that governments decide which groups count as "religions" and that they choose among vying sects and denominations, privileging some at the expense of others. There is rarely, if ever, full agreement within any religious tradition on who speaks authoritatively for that tradition, which leader is in or out of favor, or which texts and practices represent the core of the tradition. The pretense that it is possible to identify and engage "religions" neutrally, on equal footing, masks the politics of government-sponsored religious engagement: it is always easier for the religion(s) of the majority, the religion of those who are in power, or the particular version of a religion supported for whatever reason by the United States, the United Nations, the

Chinese government, corporate interests, the European Union, or other power brokers to carry more weight politically than others. Groups that are disfavored are more likely to be classified as cults or extremists, while sympathetic allies are registered and protected as tolerant and orthodox. In the words of Suzan Johnson Cook, "there are certain areas where the U.S. government has muscle, and we can also promote religious leaders."[96]

Advocacy for spiritual health, tolerant religion, or interfaith cooperation, whether in 1950 or in 2020, involves singling out "religion" from a broader social field and identifying its representatives for strategic dialogue and other aims. There are no universal rules for distinguishing in any neutral or objective way between religion and nonreligion, moderate and extreme, tolerant and intolerant for the purposes of public policy or foreign policy. Lines have to be drawn. The religions of the majority, the politically powerful, or those sympathetic to US political and strategic interests will attract positive attention and material support. Groups that "look like a religion" to Americans are more likely to receive attention. Dissenters, doubters, and those on the edges fade into the margins. Nontraditional religions are met with skepticism and puzzlement or are ignored. In a faith-based world of religious engagement, the US government and other power brokers become the arbiters of "what and who counts in the construction of human activity as 'religious'"[97] and which versions of which religions count most. These selective dynamics are endemic to the process and project of engaging religion and cannot be ameliorated by increasing the number or diversity of religions engaged. As Martin Stringer observes in his description of an interfaith roundtable in England after 9/11, "it is, in fact, the so-called 'heterodox' groups . . . that have now been excluded at this higher level, partly because they are considered to be too small for representation and partly . . . because of an element of political exclusion on the part of the 'traditions from which they once seceded.'"[98]

The US commitment to religious engagement engenders support for religious leaders and groups that advance US political and economic interests. It gives an edge to those religions that conform to an American understanding of what it means for religion to be free. While some religions are "free of the need for regulation," others are not so free.[99] Intervention is required. During the occupation of Afghanistan, American soldiers built madrassas in Khost, a province on the border with Pakistan, with US funding and Afghan government approval. According to Frederick Barton, Shannon Hayden, and Karin von Hippel, the schools were built "with relatively little fanfare in the press, positive or negative. Nor did they engender any public discussion as to whether this violated the First Amendment. The soldiers just built the schools."[100] Commander David Adams, head of the US provincial reconstruction team, explained to the *Financial Times* that "we would like to see small religious schools in every district so that parents don't have to send their children over the border [to Pakistan]."[101] The attempt to situate this project in a First Amendment context hit a wall. As Barton and his co-authors concluded, "it is not clear what official overall legal guidance enabled these schools to be built—guidance that would also be applicable to other parts of the world—or if the 'national security concern' justification was invoked."[102] The soldiers built the schools to ensure that Afghan children would have the opportunity to be properly religious, pro-American, and free, which, in this case, and others discussed above, are understood to be indistinguishable. In this context the question of whether or not these activities are constitutional is, in some important sense, beside the point.

Of course selective dynamics apply to all civil society groups chosen for government engagement. Yet the instability of the category of religion makes it impossible for governments to engage in religious outreach without privileging particular authorities and communities over others. The claim to engage all religions evenhandedly obscures the political tensions and sharpened lines that emerge as a result of transforming diffuse and multiform fields of lived religious practice into bounded objects of legal and political regulation and reform, and beneficiaries of material support and political favoritism. Peter Mandaville has made a related point in reference to US government engagement with Muslims: "There is also a risk that, over time, singling Muslims out as being in need of special engagement becomes a hindrance to normalizing relations.... We will know that the Muslim engagement strategy has worked not when it becomes institutionalized, but rather when the activities that currently fly under this banner blend seamlessly into the broader panoply of U.S. global outreach ... we should yearn for the day when 'engaging global Muslim communities' sounds like an odd thing for the United States to be doing."[103] It is odd. When governments engage individuals and groups as religious groups they are forced to discriminate regarding who is chosen and which orthodoxies are enshrined as voices of authority. Engaging groups as religions requires choosing between them. It requires singling out particular authorities as representative of the whole. It requires deciding which groups and activities count as religious and which do not, as we shall see in Chapter 5. Religion or belief, as Sherwood reminds us, is "a limited membership club."[104]

CHAPTER 5

Minorities under Law

One cannot escape the fact that freedom of religion is limited in
Turkey, for Alevis and other religious minorities.
　—*Ali Yaman*

The whole notion of majority/minority in religious terms must be
categorically dismantled and overcome.
　—*Hamid Dabashi*

The fate of religious minorities in the Middle East and North Africa
(MENA) is in the spotlight.[1] Proponents of minority rights have
called for urgent measures to protect the Copts in Egypt, the Ahmadis in
Pakistan, and the Bahá'í in Iran, Egypt, and elsewhere. Legal protections
for religious minorities have become a "go-to" solution for supporting
religious diversity, shielding minority populations from discriminatory
practices and preventing religious violence. Enshrined in international
agreements and promoted by global experts and authorities, these protections are presented as the solution to the challenges of living with social
and religious diversity.[2]

Recent political transformations in the MENA region have shifted religious rights advocacy in Washington and Brussels into high gear. Calls for
the protection of Christians and other minorities became a cornerstone
of European and American policy as elites on both sides of the Atlantic
responded to developments through a framework that emphasizes the
rights of Christians and other minorities. In 2012 Roland Dubertrand, religious affairs advisor at the French Ministry of Foreign Affairs, observed
that his diplomatic apparatus had been "shocked" by the Arab Spring,
which brought Christian minorities to public attention in France and

forced Europeans to grapple with the question, "How could we find policy toward eastern Christians and mobilize more at the European and UN level?"[3] For Dubertrand, the "old approach to the protection of eastern Christians was no longer working" and a new focus on human rights was needed. The situation of the Eastern Christian, he observed, is the situation of a religious minority; France must recognize its historical links with these communities and defend their rights as a religious minority.

US decision makers also have interpreted developments in the region through the lens of Christian rights and freedoms. Howard Berman of the House Foreign Affairs Committee observed that the future of minorities is "on our agenda as we figure out how to help these countries" and their treatment of Christians and other minorities is a "'red line' that will affect future aid."[4] Senator Roy Blunt introduced legislation in March 2013 aimed at protecting the rights of religious minorities in the Middle East and South Asia, noting that "continued violence against Coptic Christians and other civilians in Egypt is incredibly disturbing and flies in the face of the religious freedoms and fundamental values that Americans hold dear."[5] The legislation, which passed in 2014 and was signed by President Obama that year, allocates one million dollars for a position at the rank of ambassador titled "Special Envoy to Promote Religious Freedom of Religious Minorities in the Near East and South Central Asia."[6] The Special Envoy, who will be housed in the Department of State, will "promote the right of religious freedom of religious minorities in the countries of the Near East and the countries of South Central Asia," "monitor and combat acts of religious intolerance and incitement targeted against religious minorities," and "work to ensure that the unique needs of religious minority communities in the countries of the Near East and the countries of South Central Asia are addressed."[7] According to the legislation, the Special Envoy "should be a person of recognized distinction in the field of human rights and religious freedom."[8]

This chapter explores the implications of adopting religion as a category to draw together individuals and communities as corporate bodies that are depicted as in need of legal protection to achieve their freedom. It draws on an extended case study of the Alevis in Turkey. Ongoing uncertainty about the legal and religious status of the Alevis opens a space in which to explore claims to the category of religious minority, constructs of religious freedom, and the implications of contemporary legal approaches to managing religious difference. The chapter begins with a short introduction to the Alevis, a social group that was formally constituted as a single community relatively recently as part of the Turkish nation-building project. It then evaluates two legal definitions of Alevism by the Turkish state and the European Court of Human Rights.[9] These distinct institutional contexts produce different constructions of Alevism with significant legal and political implications for arbitrating major social issues in Turkey, such as who is a Muslim, who is a minority, and what is religion. Both the Presidency of Religious Affairs and the European Court overstate the uniformity and obscure the deep multiplicity of Alevism as a lived tradition, while reinforcing the state's capacity to classify and govern its citizens as religious subjects. It is not simply that Alevi identity is indeterminate, then, but that legal constructions of Alevism as a religious tradition and Alevis as a religious minority shape both Alevism and the Turkish sociopolitical landscape in specific ways. This chapter explores the relations between the examples of "governed religion" represented by these two legal constructions of Alevism and the broader, multiform fields of lived practice, belief, and belonging that they shape and constrain.

The Presidency of Religious Affairs, or Diyanet Isleri Baskanligi (hereafter Diyanet) is the Turkish state agency charged with regulating acceptable Turkish religion at home and abroad. It is the primary government agency in which conflicting Alevi claims for recognition and religious agency are aired and contested. The Diyanet, as well as the Turkish Ministry of Education, which directly oversees religious education policy, both treat Alevism as a heterodox or "mystic" interpretation of Sunni Islam that departs from the mainstream.[10] This precludes Alevi claims for legal privileges granted by the state to Sunni institutions and practices, while also denying to Alevis the privileges granted to officially recognized religious minorities including Christians and Jews. Neither fish nor fowl, the Alevi exist in a kind of legal limbo.

This interpretation of Alevism has had adverse implications for Alevis due to a lack of official recognition for communal practices. It also has had an impact on other domains such as property rights, educational policy, and access to courts. A range of Alevi associations and foundations has challenged the state's official interpretation of Alevism and institutionalization of Turkish secularism (*laiklik*). While most Alevis regard Alevism as a non-Sunni variation of Islam, some claim that Alevism is not part of Islamic tradition, and others insist that it is not a religion at all. The Diyanet's move to incorporate and subsume the Alevis under Turkish religious (that is, Sunni) orthodoxy effaces this ambiguity and contestation.

The European Court of Human Rights, on the other hand, defines Alevis as a collective non-Sunni Muslim subject of minority rights guaranteed by the Turkish state and international law. The court's approach to Alevism in the *Zengin* opinion, discussed below, presumes that religious majorities and minorities are stable, well-defined groups that exist prior to law and politics. To refuse identity-based recognition for such already-existing groups, in this account, is to obstruct democratization and hinder the emergence of tolerant legal regimes for managing religious diversity. The court's inclination to support legal protection for Alevis and other "religious minorities" abroad is founded in a long and contested history of support for minority rights in the Middle East.[11] Attempts to defend an Alevi "religious minority" in Turkey are one element in a broader European- and American-sponsored set of international initiatives described in this book to institutionalize the right to legal personality for minority religions, create tolerant and democratic religious subjects, and promote a right to freedom of religion or belief globally. An example of such efforts to govern religion globally is the EU guidelines on the promotion and protection of freedom of religion or belief, adopted in June 2013 by the Council of Foreign Affairs of the European Union.[12]

Held up against the Diyanet's choice to fold Alevism into Sunni Hanefi interpretations of Islam, the European Court appears to offer an appealing compromise. Granting a degree of autonomy to the Alevis as a non-Sunni Muslim minority would seem to avoid trampling on Alevi collective agency and identity under the Diyanet's de facto Sunni majoritarian establishment. Rather than serving as a vector of religious liberalization, however, the court's attempt to fix a collective Alevi minority subject in law serves to distinguish Alevis officially from non-Alevi Turkish citizens in religious terms. This distinction has consequences not only for Alevis' official legal status in Turkey, but also for the lived practices associated with Alevism. Like all traditions, Alevism is shaped in particular ways when it is defined legally in religious terms. As Pamela Slotte explains, "When analyzing the case law of the Court, we are not just studying a legal vocabulary. We analyze a way to imagine human life that governs conduct. How does human rights law affect the way we think about religion, and how does it regulate the space in which people are given the opportunity to live out their faith?"[13] Efforts to secure legal recognition for Alevis as a static, collective object of minority (religious) rights, guaranteed by international authorities and recognized in state law, create specific kinds of spaces in which Alevis can "live out their faith."[14] These efforts prescribe a particular kind of social order that renders "specific notions of freedom and unfreedom possible and imaginable."[15] Legally designating groups of people as "Alevis," as "minorities," and as a "religion" has consequences for the people grouped together under these designations. Like all legal approximations of religion, the international religious rights "solution" formalizes and entrenches forms of social and religious difference that, while distinct from the forms and categories imposed by the Diyanet, also limit the spaces in which Alevis can individually and collectively articulate alternate forms of subjectivity, agency, and community. It stabilizes Alevi collective identity in religious terms, fixes its relationship to Sunni tradition, and reinforces a conventional Turkish statist approach to governing religion. Particular legalized religious distinctions become increasingly publically and politically salient. Naturally, many Alevis are also complicit in creating themselves as a minority in order to access these various legal goods.

FROM KIZILBAŞ TO ALEVIS: CONSTRUCTING AND CONTESTING ALEVISM

Defining Alevism is tricky. Though it is frequently described as a syncretic and heterodox cultural and religious tradition drawing on elements of pre-Islamic shamanism, Sufism, and Shi'a Islam, there are many views on the subject and little agreement. As Elise Massicard explains,

> Some define Aleviness as a religious phenomenon—as the true Islam, or a branch of Islam tinged with Shi'a elements and Turkishness, as a religion in its own right, or even as the essence of secularism. Others see it as a primarily political phenomenon—which can range from a philosophy of struggle and resistance against injustice, to a tolerant way of living or even as the epitome of democracy. Yet others emphasize its shamanistic (Turkish) or Zoroastrian (Kurdish) elements in order to define Aleviness in accordance to ethnic aspects.... Aleviness would seem to be an overarching way of life of groups who were rural for a long time: a religion, culture and affiliation to a group with its own rules, all at the same time.[16]

Media representations of the Alevis reflect this lack of agreement. Gareth Jenkins notes, "The Alevis are often described as a branch of the Shi'a Muslim tradition. This is misleading. Although they share with Shiites veneration for the Prophet Muhammad's nephew Ali, Alevism is not so much a form of Shi'a Islam as a syncretic, pluralistic tradition, including elements from Islam, shamanism, Christianity, and the pre-Christian religions of rural Anatolia."[17] The Turkish daily *Hurriyet* describes a diversity of understandings of Alevism, observing that "some Alevis perceive themselves as a sect of Islam, other Alevis see themselves as a different religion while others reject the notion that Alevism is a religion at all."[18]

The term Alevism (Turkish: *Alevilik*) is a relatively recent innovation. Though used sporadically in the last decades of the Ottoman Empire (in the late nineteenth century) among the Kızılbaş to indicate loyalty to or descent from Ali, the term became prevalent only in the early twentieth century to refer to "a new trans-regional identity linking previously only partially connected groups which shared similar narratives, beliefs, as well as social and ritual practices."[19] As Markus Dressler points out, the creation of Alevism as a category is inextricably bound up with the construction of Turkishness and the project of Turkish nation building: "Those groups that are today labeled Alevis in Turkey were historically referred to as *Kızılbaş*, 'Redhead.' What is important is that the name change came with a new signification. The heterogeneous Kızılbaş communities were, until the late Ottoman period, generally considered as heretics who were only, if at all, superficially Muslim, and not yet in any way associated with Turkishness. The concept Alevism homogenized these groups, connected them to Turkish culture, and integrated them into Islam, while at the same time asserting their 'heterodoxy.'"[20]

Definitions of Alevism as "heterodox" or "syncretistic" rely on an implicit normalization of legalist Sunni Islamic orthodoxy. This not only marginalizes Alevism in relation to Sunnism but also perpetuates a powerful myth purveyed by the Turkish state and others that Sunni Islam is a homogenous, stable, and fixed tradition with clearly defined boundaries. As Dressler explains, "the modern othering of the Alevis is dialectically related to the normalization of a Sunni-Muslim identity, just as in the 16th century the Kızılbaş question played an important role in the consolidation of Sunni Ottoman and Shiite Safavid doctrines, respectively."[21] In the early twentieth century the emergent Turkish state established a foundational connection between Sunni Muslim identity (*itthad-ı anasir İslamiye*, or "union of Muslim elements") and Turkish national identity in part through distinguishing both from something called "Alevism." Talal Asad's description of majority-minority relations in France makes the point in a different context: "the crucial difference between the 'majority' and the 'minorities' is, of course, that the majority effectively claims the

French state as its national state."[22] Alevis are eligible to be classified as a "minority" only to the extent that they cannot claim the Turkish state as their national state.

Today those groups distinguished as "Alevis" are estimated to constitute 15 to 20 percent of the Turkish population, of which approximately one-third speak Kurdish dialects (Kurmanji or Zazaki). Most do not attend mosques, but many hold rituals known as *cem*, which are held in *cemevi*, or meeting houses, presided over by *dedes*, or Alevi holy men. The cem ritual involves praying to Ali, recalling the names of the first twelve *imams*, and mourning the martyrdom of Hüseyin. Prayers, funerals, marriages, and other blessings not only draw on the Turkish prayers of the cem but may also involve a Sunni mosque *hoca*.[23] Turkish Alevis are sometimes confused with Arab Alawites, who live principally in Syria, with a significant number also in Turkey's Hatay province.[24]

In the 1980s a diverse set of social movements emerged that became known in Turkey and abroad as the "Alevi revival," a flowering of public activism and advocacy that attracted the attention of the EU and the international human rights community. A wide spectrum of Alevi organizations participated in the revival, ranging from the Pir Sultan Abdal Association, which approaches Alevism as a socialist resistance movement, to the Cem Foundation, which views Alevism as a Turkish interpretation of Islam, to the Ehl-i Beyt Foundation, which approaches it as a Shi'a interpretation of Islam.[25] Among other activities, some of these advocates began to lobby in favor of recognition of Alevism as a minority sect or religion understood as either a variation of Islam or, less frequently, as distinct from Islam altogether.[26] The diversity of interpretations of Alevism in relation to Islam among these groups is striking; as Talha Köse explains, those who believe that there can be "Alevilik" without Ali (*Alisiz Alevilik*) consider *Ehl-i Beyt*, or the family of the Prophet Mohammed and Islamic sources, as minor components of the syncretic tradition of Alevism, while others argue the Alevilik is the essence and/or Turkish interpretation of Islam.[27]

Alevi representatives are also divided over the advantages and drawbacks of being classified as a minority religion or ethnicity.[28] Some seek to entrench legally some form of communal identity through the Turkish legal system,[29] while others see minority status as a political liability to be rejected.[30] For historical reasons minority status in Turkey is connected at the most basic level to non-Muslim status—such that to be classified as a "minority" raises immediate questions about religion, and specifically one's relation to Islam and the Turkish nationalist project. As an Alevi from Yenibosna Cemhouse interviewed by Esra Özyürek explains, "I think being a minority is a bad thing in this country. We are not like Armenians or Jews. There is pressure on us but we also have some freedom. I am afraid that the term 'minority' in the European Union report can be used in a harmful manner. If they see us just like the way they see Armenians, it will be worse for us. You know, they may even see us in oppositional terms with nationalism."[31] This statement reflects the legacy of a suspicion of minority rights that emerged after the dissolution of the Ottoman Empire, when many Turkish statesmen attributed the empire's failure to the persistence of *millet* divisions and the inability of reform efforts (*ittihad-ı anasır*) to create an inclusive formula of Ottoman citizenship and nationality.[32] In this context claims to minority rights came to be seen with suspicion, "not as a matter of respect, freedom, liberty or equality within the borders of a shared polity, but more as the instrument of ethnic dismemberment and as a pretext for external interference."[33] The association between official minority status and being non-Muslim, and thus potentially subjected to social discrimination and marginalization, is a legacy of this era:[34] "In Turkey, minority status, defined by the 1923 Lausanne Treaty, acknowledges only non-Muslim groups such as Jews, Armenians, and Greeks. If people from Muslim ethno-linguistic groups such as Kurds, the Laz, and the Circessians make a claim about being minorities and start organizations to promote their rights, they are imprisoned 'for challenging the national unity and harming the country by being divisive.'"[35] European powers played a central role in negotiating the Lausanne Treaty, and contemporary European efforts to promote the rights of religious minorities in the Middle East—such as Dubertrand's, cited earlier—draw their legitimacy from a long history of European intervention on behalf of Christians in the region.[36] Given the complex history surrounding the term "minority" in Turkey and the region more broadly, it is not surprising that both the Pir Sultan Abdal Association and Cem Foundation prefer to describe the Alevis as *asli unsur*—a term used historically to refer to one of the founding constituents or "fundamental elements" of the Turkish Republic[37]—a classification that, in their view, emphasizes Alevis' status as long-standing and loyal citizens of the Republic.

Lobbying in favor of religious minority status, however, is an active Alevi diaspora, particularly in Germany where Alevism has attained legal recognition as a religion.[38] German Alevis tend to be more supportive of the recognition of Alevilik as a separate religion distinct from Islam.[39] In contrast with the Cem Foundation's support for an "Alevi Islam," the chairman of the Dede Commission of the Federation of Alevi Communities in Germany, Hasan Kılavuz, has rejected attempts to associate Alevism with Islamic tradition:

> Alevilik is a belief (*inanç*) in its own right. Alevis possess a belief that sees God everywhere in the universe. Alevis performed their worship and beliefs for a thousand years in a modest and extremely pure form; today, some dedes try to decorate this form of belief with fake pearls. These dedes, which are insecure about themselves, which are carried away by a minority complex towards the Sunni Muslim faith, distance the essence of Alevism from our traditions and customs. . . . We cannot connect the faith of the Anatolian Alevis with the basic principles of the Islamic religion.[40]

Özyürek attributes the emergence in Germany of a self-definition of Alevism as a publicly expressed independent religion to a 1986 decision by the European Parliament to subsidize associations promoting immigrant cultures and identities. This decision, alongside other factors such as the "minoritization" and "ethnicization" of Alevis through the German Foreigner's Law (Ausländergesetz),[41] illustrates the extent to which legal and administrative designations have shaped Alevism and Alevi self-understandings in particular ways. In this case, these designations incentivized Alevis living in Europe to organize *as* Alevis rather than along other lines of collective interest or affiliation, such as trade unions or neighborhood associations.[42] As Ayhan Kaya explains, "Turkish migrants have organized themselves along ethnic lines because the institutional context has made them do so."[43] German and European recognition of the Alevis as a religious minority separate from Sunnis, however, has been received with mixed feelings and considerable skepticism in Turkey, where many Alevis do not see minority status as a solution to their problems with the state. Under the Turkish regime of secularism, a minority designation marks them as non-Muslims, thereby excluding them from dominant renderings of Turkish citizenship and potentially subjecting them to increased social marginalization and discrimination.[44]

ALEVISM UNDER TURKISH SECULARISM

The Turkish state's definition of Alevism is an essential building block of Turkish secularism, known in Turkish as *laiklik*.[45] At the founding of the Republic, Nilüfer Göle explains, "secularism underpinned the ideal of a national community 'free of religion,' yet simultaneously it implicitly defined this community in terms of a Muslim and Sunnite majority, in counter distinction with non-Muslim minorities of the cosmopolitan empire as well as the Alevites and Kurds."[46] The arm of the state responsible for overseeing religious matters and ensuring their separation under law from other affairs of state is the Presidency of Religious Affairs, the Diyanet.[47] Established in 1924 by the same law that abolished the Caliphate and the Commissariat or Vekyalet for the Sheri'eh and Evqaf, the Diyanet is charged with "the dispatch of all cases and concerns of the Exalted Islamic Faith which relate to dogma and ritual, and for the administration of religious foundations."[48] The scope of the Diyanet's activities and its budget have changed over the years. In 2012 its budget was approximately two billion dollars, larger than that of the Ministry of Interior.[49] Reporting to the Prime Minister's Office, Diyanet is charged with doing research on Islamic-related matters, administering and maintaining mosques in Turkey,[50] and appointing and supervising Turkish imams, of which there are over eighty-five thousand. It has five departments: the Higher Committee for Religious Affairs (an advisory council), Education (including Koran courses for children and adults), Religious Services (services for families, discipleship, mosque services, and social and cultural services with a religious content), and Publications and Public Relations. While muftis and other religious personnel oversee domestic activities, the Diyanet also employs religious counselors, diplomatic attachés, and other personnel to conduct activities overseas.[51] As of 2011 there were approximately 1,350 Diyanet employees stationed in eighty-one countries, including a permanent representative in Washington, D.C.[52]

In contemporary Turkey the Diyanet promotes a version of Sunni Hanefi Islam that incorporates and defines Alevism as an interpretation of Islam. As Andrew Davison explains, "the state contains *established* relations of what are constituted as oversight, interpretation, service, and supervision for the teaching, training, and employment of all religious personnel and, through the offices of the mosques and publishing houses of the Directorate of Religious Affairs, the promotion and publication of a State Islam."[53] The Diyanet does not recognize Alevism as a complex of traditions whose identity is—like all religious traditions—fundamentally indeterminate and contested. Rather, it categorizes and stabilizes Alevism as an "interpretation of Islam" that is linked to the "common share of Islam." Former president of the Diyanet Ali Bardakoglu makes the state's approach to governed Alevism very clear: "Discussing whether Alevis are

Muslim or not is an insult against Islam. All Alevis are Muslim. Nobody should be deceived by the West and claim that Alevism is outside the fold of Islam."[54]

Alevis are ineligible for special treatment by the state as a religious minority while, at the same time, their non-Sunni practices are categorized by the state as "cultural" and not religious.[55] For instance most cemevi, or houses of worship, are treated as cultural centers. "Houses of worship are not recognized, nor are they provided the free water and property tax breaks that mosques, churches, and synagogues receive. Alevism is not taught in textbooks or in state divinity schools. Alevi prayer and community leaders are not trained or funded by state resources."[56] Since 2007 Alevism has appeared in textbooks under the section "Turkish Sunnite Islam," as discussed below;[57] nonetheless, the official co-optation and domestication of Alevism authorizes the state "to deny any support for or recognition of Alevi practices by branding them as particularist and thus in conflict with the supposedly impartial position of the state in its monopoly over religion in the public sphere."[58]

As is the case in all countries that privilege and regulate religion in law, the Diyanet's legal and religious definition and management of Alevism is a critical feature of Turkish nationalist discourse and the Turkish nation-building project. As İştar Gözaydın explains, "The Presidency of Religious Affairs claims that Alevis and Sunnites are not subject to discrimination because, except for certain local customs and beliefs, there are no differences between these two sects as to basic religious issues; and this actually indicates a denial of any separate 'Alevi' religious identity . . . The Presidency of Religious Affairs' pretending to be unaware of the religious belief of the Alevi population, and its building of mosques in Alevi villages, is obviously a pressure exerted by the state to implant the Sunnite belief in this section of society."[59]

Challenges to the state's official position on the status of Alevism are met with skepticism not only because they call into question official interpretations of Islam, but also and equally importantly because they destabilize a nationalist project that has subsumed the Alevis under the state's de facto Sunni establishment from the earliest days of the Republic. Today these challenges are proliferating, destabilizing the state's ambitious efforts to reproduce the Turkish nation through the centralized and hierarchical state regulation of its Muslim and non-Muslim citizen-subjects both at home and abroad. Since the 1980s, and particularly since the brief democratic opening in the second half of the 2000s, Alevis have responded to their predicament with a series of demands ranging from "restructuring the role of the *dedes'* spiritual leadership to employment of the *dedes* as religious personnel, from planning of *cemevis* as places of worship to the demand for an apology by the state for all the injustices done to them."[60] While some have sought official state recognition and a share of the religious affairs budget (Cumhuriyetçi Eğitim ve Kültür Merkezi Vakfı/Republican Education and Culture Center Foundation and the Ehli Beyt Foundation), others have demanded the outright closure of the State Directorate of Religious Affairs (Alevi Bektaşi Federation). Alevi-state tensions are palpable in disputes over the uncertain status of the Madımak Hotel—the site of the Sivas massacre where thirty-seven Alevi intellectuals were burned alive in July 1993[61]—the legal status of and state support for cemevis as places of worship, and the content of mandatory religious education courses in public schools.[62] In 2007 controversy over religious education reached the European Court of Human Rights, which settled on a different legal definition of Alevism.

ALEVISM UNDER EUROPEAN LAW

The European Court of Human Rights construes Alevism as a non-Sunni Muslim minority sect in need of legal protection. This treatment is evident in the court's October 2007 *Zengin v. Turkey* decision, which concluded that compulsory religious instruction in Turkish public schools violates the rights of religious minorities.[63] The opinion reflects an increasingly influential European expert consensus on the need to protect the rights of religious minorities globally. A central claim of this chapter is that rather than serving as a vector of religious liberalization and religious freedom, international pressure by the European Court and other outside actors and institutions to guarantee and govern the legal rights of a collective Alevi minority subject reinforces the distinction between Alevis and non-Alevi Turkish citizens in religious terms. It obscures a broader field of lived cultural and religious practices and traditions that are associated with Alevism, downplays the cross-cutting ties and affiliations between Alevi and non-Alevi communities, and reinforces the exclusionary connection forged by the Turkish state between governed Sunni Islam and Turkish nationalism.

The *Zengin* case involved the compatibility of compulsory public religious education in Turkey with the right to education in the European Convention on Human Rights. Some form of religious education in public schools is the norm in Europe, though there is significant variation within and among states.[64] Of the forty-six Council of Europe member states, forty-three provide religious instruction in state schools. In twenty-five of the forty-six, including Turkey, religious instruction is compulsory.[65] According to the Turkish Ministry of Education, "the aim of the course is to teach students how 'to put into practice the requirements of the belief individually, without any need of guidance from other authorities,' and to distinguish religious knowledge from superstitions and traditions."[66]

Although some Alevi groups have called for the state to abolish compulsory religious instruction altogether, others have sought curricular reform or the right to apply for an exemption to the requirement on a case-by-case basis. As legally recognized non-Muslim minorities,[67] Christians and Jews in Turkey have since 1990 been permitted to apply for an exemption from the "Religious Culture and Moral Knowledge" courses. However, as Türkmen explains, there has been confusion regarding this rule, and in 1992 the Ministry of Education circulated a memorandum denying the 1990 decision. The memo explained that the courses had been modified to reflect concerns for other religions and would henceforth be mandatory for all Turkish students, though non-Muslim students would not be responsible for the chapters on Islamic practices.[68] In any event, Alevis remained ineligible for an exemption: "in this decision, only non-Muslims can be exempt from some chapters of the course, whereas Muslims from other sects are not mentioned."[69]

In 2001 Hasan Zengin filed a complaint with the Istanbul Governor's Office, Istanbul Administrative Court, and the Council of State claiming that mandatory religious education classes forced his then seventh grade daughter, Eylem, to be inculcated with exclusively Sunni Islamic belief and practice, thereby infringing on her basic human rights. When the court ruled against him, Mr. Zengin appealed to the European Court of Human Rights, which heard the case in 2006. While the case ostensibly focused on whether Eylem's right to education had been violated by the compulsory religious education courses, in the background hovered a broader question of how Alevism should be construed by the court, legally and religiously.

The court's immediate task in *Zengin* was to assess the compatibility of the content of Turkish religious education courses with the right to education as outlined in the European Convention, not to weigh in on the relationship between Alevism and Sunni Islam as interpreted by the Turkish state. Judges were asked to determine "if the content-matter of

this subject is taught in an objective, critical and pluralist manner . . .
[and] whether appropriate provisions have been introduced in the Turkish educational system to ensure that parents' convictions are respected."[70]
The decision contains a lengthy discussion of the content of the religious education courses, noting that, although "the syllabus for teaching
in primary schools and the first cycle of secondary school, and all of the
textbooks drawn up in accordance with the Ministry of Education's decision no. 373 of 19 September 2000, give greater priority to knowledge of
Islam than they do to that of other religions and philosophies . . . this itself cannot be viewed as a departure from the principles of pluralism and
objectivity which would amount to indoctrination" because Islam is the
majority religion practiced in Turkey.[71] However, the court also observes
that the government's contention that adequate information about the
Alevis was taught in the ninth grade does not adequately compensate for
the "absence of instruction in the basic elements of this faith in primary
and secondary school" and that "the instruction provided in the school
subject 'religious culture and ethics' cannot be considered to meet the
criteria of objectivity and pluralism . . . and to respect the religious and
philosophical convictions of Ms Zengin's father, a follower of the Alevi
faith, on the subject of which the syllabus is clearly lacking."[72] It found
that the religious education classes, compulsory in Turkey since 1982,
violate Article 2 of the First Additional Protocol of the European Convention concerned with the "right to education,"[73] a violation it attributed
to "the inadequacy of the Turkish educational system, which, with regard
to religious instruction, does not meet the requirements of objectivity
and pluralism and provides no appropriate method for ensuring respect
for parents' convictions."[74] Turkey was enjoined to make adjustments to
the religious education curriculum or make the lessons optional.

A 2008 case brought by Alevi parents Ali Kenanoğlu and Hatice Köse
led to similar results, with the Turkish State Council agreeing with the
European Court that the religious education course could not be mandatory. In refusing to comply with these rulings, the Ministry of Education
explained that these decisions pertained to earlier course materials and
that the textbooks had since been revised in 2007–8 to include a new
chapter on Alevism. Opponents of the new version of the textbook coun-
tered that they disagreed with its representation of Alevism as a "mystic
interpretation of Sunnism."[75] Türkmen for instance describes the role of
the Alevis in the newer textbooks as little more than "the constitutive

other through which the domination of the Sunni interpretation of Islam imposes its legitimacy."[76] On November 6, 2010, one of Turkey's largest Alevi organizations, the Pir Sultan Abdal Cultural Association, staged a sit-down strike in Kadıköy Square in Istanbul to demand an end to mandatory religious education classes.[77] Activists cited the European Court's decision and the Turkish state's failure to act upon it as a factor in their mobilization.

In reaching a decision in *Zengin*, the court appears torn between two alternative approaches to Alevism, both of which are indebted to the criteria of assessment used by the Turkish state in matters of religion: either Alevis are a "religious minority" who deserve special dispensation with regard to compulsory religious education, or they are "Muslims" in the sense promoted by Bardakoglu and various arms of the Turkish state. "Muslims" in the latter sense would be individuals whose practices resemble those of the Sunni Muslim Turkish majority, with a particular version of Sunni Hanefi Islam serving as the de facto official religion of the secular Turkish state. So using the framework of this book, this would refer to those who practice some version of governed Turkish Sunni Islam. Departing from the Turkish government's position that subsumes Alevism under Turkish state Islam, the court concluded that the "Alevi faith" is "distinct from the Sunni understanding of Islam which is taught in schools" and allowed that the expression "'religious convictions' . . . is undoubtedly applicable to this faith."[78] Alevism, then, is a "religious" conviction within the meaning of Article 2, *and* it is distinct from Sunni Islam. Thus the question of whether Alevism should be understood legally as part of Islam as defined by the Turkish state, or as something else, was resolved—the court went with the latter. Note that the court joined the Turkish state's efforts to "pin down" a definition of Alevism in relation to Sunni Islamic tradition; it just reached a different conclusion about *how* to do so. It governs Alevism differently.

The Strasbourg court appears drawn to the emancipatory promise of legally enshrining the Alevis, and other "minorities" in other contexts, as a collective non-Sunni Muslim subject of minority rights guaranteed by state and international law. This tendency reflects the influence of a growing expert consensus in European and international public policy circles that majority and minority religions are natural groupings that exist prior to law and politics, and that it is the duty of the international community to guarantee their (religious) freedom.[79] As Austrian foreign minister and vice chancellor Michael Spindelegger stated in 2012 at the occasion of an "experts' seminar" on the freedom of religion in Brussels, "freedom of religion and the protection of religious minorities are central elements of Austria's human rights policy ... the events in the Arab World, in particular, remind us that freedom of religion of all citizens is also decisive for peace and security within a society. Religious minorities will therefore have to be involved in the redesign of the societies that is currently taking place in many Arab countries right from the beginning."[80] France and Italy have taken similar stands, promoting a narrative of religious freedom that, as Pasquale Ferrara explains, is "fundamentally based upon the concept of 'protecting' Christian minorities, although officially the rationale was advancement of religious freedom as a universal value."[81]

This position is voiced with increasing frequency in Europe, where protections for minority religions are seen by experts and governmental authorities alike as the key to unlocking democratic reform, ensuring the rule of law, and implementing tolerant legal regimes to manage what are depicted as unwieldy and recalcitrant sectarian differences in the Middle East and elsewhere. Support for a right to legal personality for minority religions is part of a European and North American commitment to international religious freedom, and denial thereof is categorized as a restriction on the right to religious freedom. According to the 2013 EU Guidelines on the Promotion and Protection of Religion or Belief, the right to freedom of religion or belief includes rights for communities that "include, but are not limited to, *legal personality* and non-interference in internal affairs, including the right to establish and maintain freely accessible places of worship or assembly, the freedom to select and train leaders or the right to carry out social, cultural, educational and charitable activities."[82]

In 2004, in part as a result of lobbying efforts by Alevi leaders in Europe, the EU officially categorized the Alevis as a "non-Sunni Muslim minority."[83] The Venice Commission has defined the Alevis as a disadvantaged minority in need of legal recognition and protection.[84] Since 1998 the annual reports of the European Commission have "insisted on the extension of official recognition of the three non-Muslim communities (Armenians, Greeks, and Jews) to the Kurdish, Alevi and Assyrian groups."[85] Turkey's accession process is also implicated: the commission's 2011 "Enlargement Strategy and Main Challenges" Turkey report cites freedom of religion and the protection of minorities (especially non-

Muslims and the Alevi community) as areas in which further efforts are required and calls for the establishment of a legal framework that aligns with the European Convention on Human Rights.[86] As noted previously, in 2013 the Council of Foreign Affairs Ministers of the EU adopted the EU Guidelines on the Promotion and Protection of Religion or Belief.[87] This instrument is said to provide staff in the European External Action Service, EU delegations, and embassies with an "operational set of tools to be used in dealings with third-countries, as well as with Churches and international and civil society organizations, in order to *protect all individual believers and religious minorities* within its external action."[88]

Initiatives that single out religion and religious affiliation as the basis for formulating European foreign policy are reminiscent of the colonial and postcolonial history of European intervention on behalf of Christians in the Middle East and North Africa, many of which had violent consequences for the people of the region.[89] As Ussama Makdisi has shown, European colonial powers played a significant role in introducing sectarian distinctions by intervening in the region on an explicitly sectarian basis, with the French backing the Maronites and British protecting the Druze. Under the Ottomans, for example, Makdisi explains, "the operative social and political distinction in rural Mount Lebanon was between knowledgeable elites and ignorant commoners regardless of religious affiliation. Both Christian and Druze religious authorities legitimized the traditional secular political and social order. It was the Europeans, who insisted on saving the 'subjugated' Christians of the Orient, that singled out religion in Mount Lebanon as the basis for, and sign of, modern reform."[90] Benjamin White has shown similarly that the construct of "minority" is itself a recent invention accompanying the creation of the modern nation-state.[91]

As the prioritizing of religious rights occupies an increasingly central position in the European external relations portfolio, the impact of the religion agenda will be felt in Turkey and elsewhere. In the Turkish case, the religious rights model has its appeal when contrasted with the Diyanet's move to subsume Alevism under Sunni Hanefi interpretations of Islam—thereby marginalizing Alevi voices, practices, and traditions that locate themselves outside the Sunni Hanefi umbrella. Ensuring a degree of autonomy to the Alevis as a non-Sunni Muslim minority appears as a reasonable alternative to trampling Alevi collective identity by ignoring demands for communal autonomy and recognition. Rather than serving as an instrument of religious liberalization, however, the European attempt to fix a collective Alevi non-Sunni Muslim minority subject in law serves to distinguish Alevis from non-Alevi Turkish citizens in religious terms. This has important consequences for the politics of religious difference in Turkey.

CREATING APOSTATES AND INSURGENTS: THE LEGAL CONSTITUTION OF RELIGIOUS DIFFERENCE

Turkish citizens of different backgrounds have voiced concerns about state persecution and discrimination against Alevis. Many have petitioned for public recognition of Alevi identity, collective practices, and historical grievances. For these critics, the Kemalist project—named after the first president of Turkey, and the primary framework in which Turkish national identity has been negotiated and legitimated since the founding of the Republic in 1923—is distinguished by a concerted nationalistic attempt to force Alevis, Kurds, Armenians, and others to "abandon their traditional attachments."[92] Activists and spokespersons challenging the exclusionary dimensions of Turkish nationalism often counter the assimilationist narrative by calling for a public revalorization of Alevism, alongside other non-Sunni identities and histories, through the promotion of Alevi rights and freedoms. Fueled by external pressure from the EU and encouraged by recent attempts to prioritize religious freedom and the rights of religious minorities as a European external relations objective, the revalorization of Alevism is presented as the antidote to the Kemalist effacement of cultural and religious difference. In 2007 the ruling party, Adalet ve Kalkınma Partisi (AKP), initiated an "Alevi opening," consisting of a series of workshops, in an attempt to address these concerns.[93] As part of the "opening" the Ministry of Education modified textbooks for the Religious Culture and Ethics courses to include more information on the Alevis, as discussed above; some municipalities recognized cemevis as "houses of worship"; and the state nationalized the Madımak Hotel in Sivas.[94] These limited concessions were received by Alevis as "falling far short of the general recognition to which Alevis aspire" and as "showing no intention to restructure the current system of state organization and control of religion."[95]

Despite the important differences between the Turkish state's treatment of Alevism as part of the "common share of Islam" and the European Court's approach to Alevism as a "religious conviction distinct from

Sunni Islam," both constructions of Alevism efface the profound heterogeneity (and even inconsistency) of practices associated with lived Alevism while reinforcing the Turkish state's capacity to classify and govern its
citizens as *religious* subjects. To classify the Alevis—despite their substantial internal diversity and the unsettled nature of their identity claims—
as a collective subject of religious rights and religious freedom that is
guaranteed by the state and backed up by international legal instruments
reinforces a long-standing statist tradition of Turkish secularism in which
an implicit Sunni-majority state serves as the official arbiter of religious
identity and practice. This is a political and social order characterized
by centralized, and at times authoritarian, forms of governance, as Gözaydın explains: "From the very first days of the Republic, secularism in
Turkey has meant safeguarding the state against social forces, as the 1982
Constitution has once again strongly proven. The official conception of
secularism in Turkey complements this statist tradition. This tradition is
characterized by a denial of the existence of autonomous political and
cultural realms within society, regarding these as threats against the existence of the state and advocating that legitimate social practices are limited to practices supervised by the state. The official ideology inevitably
approaches religion in line with this statist tradition."[96] The social forces
behind the Gezi protests in Turkey united in opposition to this statist tradition.[97] When external actors classify and govern Alevism as a religious
conviction that is distinct from Sunni Islam—as some form of a religious
"minority" in the Turkish context—this stabilizes Alevism, an otherwise
more indeterminate collective identity, in religious terms, cements a fixed
relationship to Sunni tradition, and reinforces a conventional Turkish
statist approach to governing religion. In the name of protecting social
and religious diversity, it occludes the undecidability and indeterminacy
of Alevism as a heterogeneous and contested set of lived practices and
traditions that may fade away at the margins, shift depending on time
and locale, and even be indifferent to the relationship between Alevism
and Turkish or other official "state Islams."

To depict the Alevis as a religious minority in law and international
public policy is therefore to endow an otherwise more open and unstable
religious, ethnic, social, and cultural identity with more pointed religious
and legal salience in the eyes of individual citizens, including many Alevis
who are shaped by these legal constructions, the state, and the international community. This "fixing" of Alevi identity produces a perception
of stable and nonnegotiable differences among Alevis, other minorities,

and (unmarked) Sunni Turkish citizens. This overcoding of the boundaries between groups, as discussed in Chapter 3, formalizes identity in religious terms and contributes to a confessionalization of social order. Michael Wahid Hanna makes a related point in reference to the effects of US-based Coptic diaspora lobbying on behalf of Egyptian Copts. Hanna suggests that pro-Coptic interventions by external actors risk inflaming, rather than calming, Coptic-Muslim tensions in Egypt. Citing the internal diversity of the Coptic community, and Copts' diverse life experiences, disparate socioeconomic positions, and different geographic locations, Hanna argues that while there may be a place for outside lobbying "it would be perverse if the efforts of Coptic diaspora activists were a further cause of strife and a rallying cry for Islamists who seek to implement a vision of religious supremacy."[98] Nukhet Sandal discusses a contrasting case in which experts, authorities and external lobbies have not (as yet) contributed to the consolidation of a politicized "Christian community" in Turkey that stands apart from other communal groups. Juxtaposing the Egyptian Copts discussed by Hanna and Turkish Christians, Sandal concludes that "there is no 'Christian' discourse or a unified Christian public theology in the Turkish public sphere that is equivalent to the Coptic public theology in Egypt. The Christian communities have defined themselves either by the word 'non-Muslim' or by their ethnicity, and focused on their own communities' problems rather than on the problems of the Christian community in general."[99] The situation in Turkey is likely to change as an active European and global Christian rights lobby, including but not limited to spokespersons for various churches, contributes to the social production of a public and politicized "Christian community" in Turkey and elsewhere. This emergent faith-based global political landscape exhibits the complex interplay among expert religion, lived religion, and governed religion described in this book.

To enshrine Alevism legally as a protected, governed minority religion contributes to a perception of social space as structured around an Alevi-Sunni opposition.[100] Political identity and subjectivity defined in religious terms comes to "occupy the full terrain of the thinkable."[101] This conceals the ways in which collective needs cut across these contrived divides. It obscures the ways forward that emerge when the focus is not on communities of believers but on shared goods, goals, and crosscutting affiliations and allegiances. These observations apply equally to other groups perched on the threshold of official recognition and naturalization as "religious" minorities, both past and present.[102] To officially "religionize"

Alevism risks contributing to the perception that natural sectarian lines divide Turkish Alevis, Arab Alevis residing in Turkey, the Sunni majority in Turkey, and the (mainly Sunni) Syrian refugees fleeing the violence to take refuge in southeastern Turkey.[103] It heightens the risk that social tensions emerging from the Syrian and Iraqi wars will be cast as intractable religious or sectarian problems rather than acknowledging their political and economic dimensions.

And yet, importantly, this is not only a question of misconstruing or oversimplifying a complex situation. Enshrining Alevism as an official minority religion also catalyzes a series of internal dynamics within Alevi communities. The process of being "religionized" empowers particular authorities to represent and speak on behalf of *the* Alevi religious community, a dynamic discussed in the two preceding chapters. The socio-legal transformation of Alevis into official collective religious subjects under state law, and Alevism into an official religion (whether understood as a variation of Islam or not) sanctifies particular understandings of Alevism as orthodox while marginalizing others. Necdet Subaşı, ministerial advisor and general coordinator of the Alevi Initiative, lists the steps to be taken on the road to Alevi state recognition as including "improvement of the conditions of the *cemevis*, elimination of the obstacles before the status of *cemevis* as houses of worship, *public acknowledgement and appreciation of the leading Alevi men of faith by the state, and strengthening the role and status of these leaders.*"[104] Dissenters and those making claims on behalf of Alevism deemed unorthodox or threatening by "leading Alevi men of faith" are disenfranchised. Those who claim that Alevism is not a religion at all, that it is not a heterodox sect of Islam, or are indifferent to such claims, fall below the threshold of public discourse and political and juridical recognition, both nationally and internationally.[105] Some Alevis naturally become complicit in creating themselves as a minority in order to access these various legal goods. Others do not. To raise Alevis above the official threshold of legal recognition as a minority enshrines *particular* authorities as the arbiters of religious orthodoxy: Who is a religion? Who decides? Who speaks for a religious community?

Paul Sedra identifies similar dynamics in the intracommunal politics of Egyptian sectarianism. Sedra is interested in the consequences for the Coptic laity of Article 3 of the Egyptian constitution, adopted under former president Morsi but retained in the 2014 version under the new regime. Article 3 formally vests power over personal status in the Coptic Church, stating that "the canon principles of Egyptian Christians and Jews are the main source of legislation for their personal status laws, religious affairs, and the selection of their religious leaders."[106] As Sedra points out, Article 3 disempowers and marginalizes Coptic laypeople whose views do not necessarily align with those of the Coptic hierarchy:

> Now that Egypt's new constitution has vested power over personal status in the church on a formal basis, in a sense codifying this mil-let partnership and, by extension, the triumph of clerical forces over their rivals in the Coptic laity for control of the church and community, one cannot help but wonder what roles Coptic laypeople will find for themselves in communal and national politics. In the face of determined church efforts to marginalize them, as well as the state's support for these efforts, are Coptic laypeople who want a meaningful say in their community's and nation's future, destined to become apostates and insurgents?[107]

Are Alevis whose views do not necessarily align with those of the "leading Alevi men of faith" but who want a meaningful say in their community's and nation's future destined to become apostates and insurgents? Is there an alternative?

RELIGION AND POLITICS BEYOND RELIGIOUS RIGHTS

In *Emergency Politics*, Bonnie Honig observes that new rights inaugurate new relations and realities by presupposing the world they seek to bring into being.[108] Adopting religion as a category to distinguish groups that are seen as in need of legal protection inaugurates new relations and realities. It impacts the lives of those who live under these designations. It creates a world in which citizens are governed as religious subjects, contributing to the consolidation of a social order in which groups are distinguished by perceived religious differences, creating apostates and insurgents on the margins of legal religion. It effaces forms of agency and subjectivity that fall outside or cut across the boundaries of political constituencies defined by religious community.[109] Legal classifications of Alevism by the Turkish state and the European Court work to define the Alevis and to determine how Alevism relates to purportedly stable and unchanging dominant renderings of Sunni Islamic tradition.[110] Both of these classifications impact Alevis directly by transforming the experiences, ambiguities, and inconsistencies that attend their affiliations and practices into something more fast and fixed—nudging and funneling individuals into discrete "faith communities" through which they are legally and collectively defined, overseen, and spoken for.[111] These designations marginalize multiform and dissenting forms of religiosity, occluding a broader field of human activity, investments, and practices that may or may not be captured in the set of human goings-on identified as religion for the purposes of Turkish and transnational law. They embolden those empowered to speak in the name of orthodoxy. They obscure the fuzziness and diversity within and between communities, submerging their histories and traditions "in the mill of modernist discourses and the homogenizing machinery of the nation state."[112] To fix Alevism in law through guarantees for religious rights—whether domestic or international—effaces the indeterminacy and heterogeneity of Alevism as a set of lived traditions while shoring up efforts to regulate acceptable Turkish religiosities in the service of the state.

Returning to Hamid Dabashi's admonition in the epigraph to this chapter, what would it look like to take seriously the need to dismantle the notion of majority/minority in religious terms? If the logic of religious rights diminishes the range of lived possibilities of Alevism while occluding alternative political goals, alliances, and allegiances, is there an alternative? Such an alternative would necessarily be based on a different set of assumptions about Alevism, Sunnism, rights, and freedom. Alevism would be understood as an evolving and contesting set of lived traditions with ambiguous and unsettled relations to various orthodoxies, including Sunnism. Scholars and experts who produce knowledge about contemporary Turkish religious governance would pay closer attention to the distinctions among governed Alevism, expert Alevism, and lived Alevism— and their complex interactions and mutual imbrications. Modes of social order, practices of citizenship and rights, and public and political goods and goals that rely on a rigid Alevi-Sunni distinction would no longer be privileged, or even make sense. Rights would also be understood differently. Rather than attaching to the self as a (religious) subject, a different conception of rights would attach to what William Connolly, drawing on Foucault's work, describes as "that which is defined by the normalized subject as otherness, as deviating from or falling below or failing to live up to the standards of subjectivity."[113] Rather than as a solution to the question of social difference that expands autonomy and choice without constraint, rights would be approached as contingent political constructs that, as Wendy Brown has argued, carry normative and subject-producing dimensions, embody particular cultural assumptions and aims, prescribe and proscribe, and configure the political in particular ways, always competing with other possibilities and discourses.[114] Freedom too would appear differently. Invoking William James's anarchist vision, as described by Alexander Livingston, freedom would be located in the arc of critically negotiating norms imposed by the authorities.[115] In a Jamesian political ethos, Livingston suggests, drawing also on Gilles Deleuze's philosophy of becoming, multiple sites in different jurisdictions are linked in a continuing network of political actions and struggles. Local energies do not coalesce into a coherent, unitary package. There is no single politics or prescriptive program. There is no larger unity that gathers up all lived experience into a whole, no consensus or solution to be determined. As Talal Asad concludes, "the modern *idea* of religious belief (protected as a right in the individual and regulated institutionally) is a critical function of the liberal-democratic nation-state but not of democratic sensibility."[116]

CHAPTER 6

Beyond Religious Freedom

E stablished in 2005, the Trans-Sahara Counterterrorism Partnership
(TSCTP) is an interagency public diplomacy program among the US
Department of State, Department of Defense, and USAID designed to
combat violent extremism in the Sahel and Maghreb. Partnering with Tunisia, Algeria, Morocco, Niger, Mauritania, Burkina Faso, Chad, Senegal,
Nigeria, and Mali, it is intended, among other aims, to address humanitarian needs, quash violent extremism, and promote the development
of civil society in partner states. One of its more popular programs is a
radio broadcast featuring news in local languages and educational programs promoting peace, religious tolerance, and healthy gender relations.
A State Department report explains that one of the program's main objectives is "preserving traditional tolerance and moderation displayed in
most African Muslim communities and countering the development of
extremism, particularly in youth and rural populations."[1] TSCTP funds
governance programs that support democracy building and economic
development in the Sahel, strengthening those states' "ability to with-
stand internal threats" in part by "discrediting terrorist ideology."[2] It also
has a military component known as Operation Enduring Freedom Trans-
Sahara, which relies on "hard" power to enhance stability and deter terrorist activity on the continent. Enduring Freedom is a project of the US
Africa Command, or Africom.

TSCTP is among a proliferating number of North American and
European-sponsored initiatives designed to cultivate religiously free polities, harness interfaith cooperation, teach religious subjects to be tolerant, and guarantee the freedom of religious minorities under secular law.
Like other programs of its kind, TSCTP approaches religion as an aspect
of social difference that is a potential problem, a cause of violence and

discrimination, and its own solution, insofar as interfaith cooperation and toleration can be institutionalized, extremists marginalized, and religion's benevolent tendencies harnessed for the greater good. Religions appear as coherent entities with licensed representatives, as actors on a global political stage. Religion needs to be put to work, partnering with governments and other international authorities to foster its benevolent aspects while subduing its potential to incite violence.

In North America and European public discourse, older conceptions of religion as "private" and largely irrelevant to global governance have been partially displaced in favor of this understanding of religion as a public good and, simultaneously, a potential source of violence. Universities, think tanks, and foundations fund policy-relevant research on religious freedom, persecution, and rights. Scholars weigh the best techniques to "manage" religion by measuring the impact of religion in public life, applying the insights of religious traditions to international public policy, and building a field of interfaith studies that bridges across academic, advocacy, and policy-making communities.[3] Religion is accepted in many circles as a plausible explanation of political behavior, rendering natural and necessary political interventions to engage, temper, and shape it. The government's job is to identify and nurture religion's transformative and benevolent powers while softening or disciplining its exclusionary edges. This demands particular forms of religious stewardship, partnership, and interventionism, including efforts to reform religion, create religiously tolerant subjects, and guarantee religiously free societies and minorities in law. The new global politics of religion has created new categories of actors in world politics. It has spawned new mandates and commissions. It has disseminated and naturalized new modes of social, legal, and religious organization. It has created a flourishing international political economy of good religion. Bureaucracies and foundations have been established, careers made, and professional reputations secured. Online resources, workshops, training programs, and interfaith dialogues proliferate. Discussions of religion and politics in political science, policy studies, and adjacent fields debate to what extent religion and religious actors should be overseen by, and be incorporated into, projects of government and governance. Legal and constitutional models for the treatment of religion are considered and compared.

This book has raised concerns about the value of the category of religion used to organize a set of social facts collected together for international legal and political purposes. Underscoring the instability and even incoherence of the category of religion as the basis of legal protection, it has questioned the sociological coherence and the political consequences of singling out religion as a basis from which to conduct foreign policy, write laws and constitutions, and pursue rights advocacy. While religious practices are an important dimension of human life, the category of religion is too complex and unstable to serve as a platform from which to pursue these political ends. The adoption of religion as a legal and policy category helps to create the world that it purports to oversee. It naturalizes religious-religious and religious-secular distinctions as the natural building blocks of social order. In presupposing discrete religious identities as the foundation of social order, it produces a legal and political landscape defined and populated by "faith communities" and "religious actors." These become larger than life. Winnifred Sullivan and Lori Beaman describe this "overemphasis on religion as a key identity marker and as a basis of rights claims" as the "cornering" of religious identity.[4] As Beaman argues, "rather than normalizing religion as one identity point among many, or as a complex category that often defies easy characterization, it becomes fetishized such that the identification of religion becomes the beginning point from which social relations are enacted and from which institutional policy is developed."[5]

Religion is being cornered in international relations, particularly in European and North American academic and policy circles, but elsewhere as well.[6] States and international authorities identify individuals and groups as religious citizens and subjects, and position them on a legal landscape of majority and minority religions. Such groups are presumed to be not only distinct from each other but to exist ontologically prior to the state, transnational law, and other forms of collective governance. Privileging religion as an object of law and policy reduces complex and multidimensional affiliations, desires, and actions to a question of religious identity and community. It lends special significance to that which is identified as "religion" and politicizes the process through which this designation is made. Cornering religion fortifies particular lines of division between communities as social divisions are defined in religious terms. Some groups are protected and privileged and others are not. Discrete and bounded religious communities and identities are taken for granted. Politics take shape around secular-religious and religious-religious distinctions. Governments and courts become arbiters of religious authenticity and orthodoxy. Politically and legally authorized forms of religious being and belonging are privileged. Individuals and groups are funneled into discrete faith communities with identifiable leaders and recognizable orthodoxies. Citizens appear on the world stage as religiously motivated actors waiting to be engaged by the United States, the European Union, or the United Nations, rather than as human beings living in history with complex and shifting needs, desires, and affiliations.[7]

Singling out religion for legal and political purposes also shapes religious possibilities for the individuals and communities these projects seek to redeem or protect. It privileges certain forms of religion at the expense of the rest of the world's religious and spiritual practices, enacting a series of "mini-establishments" in the process. It distils an amorphous, messy field of practice into bounded entities with neatly trimmed orthodoxies and discernible hierarchies that are legible to modern legal and administrative bodies. It transforms states, courts, and other authorities into arbiters of orthodoxy, weighing in and enforcing, often in law, distinctions between insider and outsider, believer and nonbeliever, orthodox and unorthodox, religious and secular. Governments, judges, and international authorities become entangled in the adjudication of religious and religious-secular identity, difference, belonging, and orthodoxy. This raises the local political stakes of these distinctions by forcing to the surface tensions between official, sanctioned religion and a broader field of practices that mix and mingle across traditions, occupy the borderlands at the edges of the religious-secular divide, or fall outside of the religion that is selected for engagement or dialogue. To rely on the category of religion as an object of foreign policy and human rights advocacy privileges certain forms of expression and ways of life while marginalizing others. It puts pressure on nonestablished, unorthodox, nonconforming ways of being religious, and of being human. Doubters, dissidents, and those who identify with nonorthodox versions of protected traditions struggle for air on a landscape politically defined and divided by religious-religious and religious-secular distinctions. Those who would like to speak but prefer not to do so in their capacity *as* believers, nonbelievers, Muslims, Buddhists, Jews, or Christians are rendered inaudible. Slipping below the threshold of political and juridical recognition, these voiceless constituencies raise important questions about the compatibility of the legalization of religious freedom with processes of deep and multidimensional democratization and pluralization.[8]

The new global politics of religion further shapes the landscapes in which it intervenes by inviting individuals and groups to self-identify as religions. It transforms local self-definitions and self-understandings. To make religion the point from which social relations are enacted and institutional policy is developed contributes to the production of new forms of politicized religious difference. As global ecologies of affiliation based on religious-religious and religious-secular distinctions are disseminated and normalized, individuals and groups in search of international backing are prompted to articulate claims for resources, justice, and dignity in terms that reflect and reinforce those distinctions. It is a self-fulfilling prophecy—groups confronted with political and material incentives to frame identities, make political claims, and specify collective needs as religious actors, religious minorities, and religious communities in search of their freedom have every reason to do so. Faced with these powerful incentives, particular groups are distilled and distinguished from broader and more amorphous fields of identity, practice, and ways of being and belonging. Drawn to the sociopolitical and material rewards that follow from identifying themselves, each other, and their interests in a recognizably "religious" register, the Rohingya, Ahmadi, Christian, Alevi, and other faith communities emerge to take their place on the international public stage as religious minorities, reaping the benefits of being classified by the state or other power brokers as religions, faith communities, or (persecuted) religionists. As Sudanese refugees in Egypt explained to Melani McAlister, "being a 'persecuted Christian' was a good idea if you wanted to get asylum status or help from UN programs."[9] Groups that are positioned to tap into the new global politics of religion are showered with material and institutional benefits from state and international donors. Trade deals flourish. Security cooperation improves. Development assistance coffers open. Asylum is granted. Sanctions are lifted. In a world of religionists, those marked as nonreligious, as dissenters, or as doubters, and those who simply choose not to speak *as* religionists are silenced. As McAlister says, the State Department has found religion, but whose?[10]

The political risks of privileging religion as the basis of designing foreign policy have not gone unrecognized. In April 2013, the US Commission on International Religious Freedom (USCIRF) issued a report on religious freedom in Syria calling for "projects that promote multireligious and multi-ethnic efforts to encourage religious tolerance and understanding . . . [and help] religious minorities to organize themselves."[11] Curiously, three of the eight USCIRF commissioners dissented from the report's conclusions because, in their words, "the facts about and the relation between issues of religious freedom and the political dynamics of the armed struggle there are not sufficiently clear to enable us to draw conclusions or make recommendations."[12] In other words, the report had "cornered" religion. Citing the complexity and uncertainty surrounding the role of religion in the Syrian conflict, the dissenters puzzled over the notion that religious hostilities were causing the war and suggested instead that privileging religious freedom and the rights of religious minorities as political objectives would fail to do justice to the complex causes of the uprising.

The dissenting commissioners were right to question the report's attempt to corner religion. The goal of the Syrian opposition in spring 2011 was to put an end to the state's brutal treatment and exploitation of the Syrian people. As is also the case in Egypt, Bahrain, Libya, and Tunisia, the Syrian war has complex roots in economic deprivation, social injustice, and everyday oppression. To reduce the multiplex grievances of the Syrian people to a problem of religious difference, and their solution to religious freedom, is to play into the hands of the Assad regime, which has benefited for decades from the politicization of sectarian difference to justify autocratic rule. Privileging religion in these circumstances lends undue weight to a sectarian reading of the conflict that excludes the possibility of antiregime Syrian Alawites, reinforcing the regime's dangerous propaganda that to be an Alawite is to stand with Assad.[13] The result, as Mohja Kahf has suggested, is to "make any person of Alawite background open target for hatred by anyone rightly outraged at the regime's atrocities."[14]

Given these concerns about the distortions and losses that result from cornering religion, what would it mean to dethrone religion as a stable interpretive and policy category as suggested in this book? What would it entail to disaggregate religion and consider the interrelations between expert, lived, and governed religion? What if we were to accept both that secularization theory was misguided and that religion is also deeply problematic as a political category? That the category of religion loosely organizes a domain of academic inquiry, religious studies, which is itself the product of a particular modern concept of religion does not mean that it can be used innocently to motivate political projects. There are other ways to respond to the critique of secularization theory and its descriptive and normative pretensions. Religion cannot simply be "brought back in" to international relations as an agentive force by inviting whatever is identified as "religious"—religious leaders, texts, or perspectives—into social science analysis, policy debate, and government. To attempt to do so is to miss the point of recent efforts to historicize and politicize secularism. It is to take for granted the very processes of privatization and differentiation that have been, and continue to be, interrogated, problematized, and renarrated across disciplines and historical contexts as part of a sweeping reconsideration of secularism and secularity.[15] There is no unmarked religion to be recovered by incorporating leaders, beliefs, doctrine, or behavior into social scientific theories, models, or modes of collective governance. There is no stable core of any religion that can be mobilized for such purposes. As Justin McDaniel describes his approach to the study of Thai Buddhism, "instead of trying to find what is 'Buddhist' about what a particular person holds, chants, and values, I look first to how they do something, how they say they do something, and the material and social contexts they do it in."[16] How might such a postseparationist—and postreligionist—ethos be reflected in the study of global politics? The next section explores a preliminary response to this question in reference to what is often named as "religious" violence and persecution, revisiting the puzzle with which this book began.

"RELIGIOUS" VIOLENCE RECONSIDERED

In late 2013 a group of armed men on a motorbike attacked a Christian wedding at the Coptic Orthodox Church of the Virgin Mary in Cairo's Warraq district. Four people were killed and several wounded. The Egyptian government blamed the Muslim Brotherhood for the attack.[17] The Muslim Brotherhood denied involvement and accused the army of using the allegation to justify a crackdown. Investigating the attack for the Egyptian newspaper *Aswat Masriya*, journalist Yasmine Saleh interviewed local residents of the lower-class neighborhood of Cairo in which the Virgin Church is located. Church officials told Saleh that they had informed the police about threats received before the shooting but to no avail. According to a guard at the church compound, "the Interior Ministry is not equipped to station a police car outside each church." Eyewitnesses said that despite numerous distress calls, police and ambulances did not arrive on the scene until two hours after the shooting began. Security personnel sent by the Ministry of the Interior to protect the building were seen fleeing up a side street during the attack, leaving the church unguarded. Addressing the possibility that the authorities had a role in this and other attacks, Ishaq Ibrahim of the Cairo-based Egyptian Initiative for Personal Rights told another journalist that "churches were torched, Christians kidnapped and now gunned down, and there is no security guarding the churches. I believe there is collaboration."[18] Importantly, Yasmine Saleh also reported that there had been "no signs of Muslim-Christian tension" in the neighborhood prior to the attack. To the contrary, as one resident explained, "Muslims would protect Christians whenever pro-Mursi supporters held protests in the dusty area, where piles of garbage lie in narrow dirt lanes beside crudely built brick homes. Some fear that such cross-sectarian solidarity was the real target of the perpetrators of the wedding shooting." The supervisor of the church library, Essam Iskander, also concluded that "those who carried out the attack were not only tackling Christians, but both Christians and Muslims, to spread terrorism and make the new state fail. Some of the injured people were Muslims. And many Muslims who sit in a nearby cafe protect the church."[19]

The Egyptian government, international media, and other observers described the attack on the Virgin Church as religious or sectarian in nature.[20] Christians are being persecuted in Egypt, it is said, in the same way that Muslims are being persecuted in Myanmar. While sectarian explanations of violence and discrimination saturate popular, governmental, and scholarly accounts of developments in the Middle East and North Africa, particularly in the wake of the Arab Spring and surging violence in Syria and Iraq, these explanations should sound a warning bell to readers of this book. Dethroning religion as a singular and stable interpretive category requires revisiting the legitimacy of claims to "religion" or "sect" as comprehensive explanations of violence, discrimination, or persecution—or for that matter, freedom, peace, or toleration. The discourse of sectarianism relies on a fixed and totalizing representation of the shifting and complex roles of religion and religious difference in politics and society. This discourse transforms the complexities and contingencies of human affiliation, behavior, and motivation into a singular explanation of political outcomes: "religion made them do it." This book has questioned such an approach. Many aspects of human being and belonging fail to conform to such all-encompassing narratives of sectarian difference. These divergences become all the more apparent when we delve more deeply into the circumstances surrounding a particular episode named as "sectarian violence." They are evident in Saleh's reporting on the lack of Muslim-Christian tension in the local neighborhood before the attack and her description of Muslims in a nearly café who protected the church. They are evident in the response of local citizens of Tripoli, Lebanon to the arson of the Saeh library discussed in the introduction. These episodes are suggestive of the tensions between sectarian discourses of entrenched religious difference authorized by those in positions of power, and religious difference as lived and experienced by other individuals and groups.

The idea is not only to stress the instability of the category of religion in these circumstances but also to underscore the sociological implausibility of narratives that rely on the modifier "religious" as an explanation of acts of violence or persecution. The complex and at times conflicting amalgamation of interests, fears, motivations, and forms of agency that come together to result in tragic events such as those in Warraq and Tripoli, and many others named as sectarian violence, undercut the stable presuppositions about "religious" motivation and causation that form the bedrock in which sectarian accounts comfortably rest. This book has chipped away at this bedrock, insisting on the instability of the category of religion, citing the complex interplay and fluid distinctions between religion and religious difference as authorized by those in positions of power and as lived and experienced by those without it.

Ussama Makdisi has shown that the advent of modern sectarian discourse and practice became possible only due to a "rupture, a birth of a new culture that singled out religious affiliation as the defining public and political characteristic of a modern subject and citizen."[21] Makdisi's study of the outbreak of violence in the Shuf, in Lebanon in 1841, illuminates this distinction in a set of historical circumstances in which, as he explains, religion became "detached from its social environment" and treated by those in positions of power as "a cohesive, exclusivist, and organic force."[22] As Makdisi, Benjamin Kaplan, Evan Haefeli, and others have shown, and as I have emphasized in this book, the drive to isolate and privilege religion as a cohesive social force detached from its local environment is a political gesture, a distinctive form of politics.[23] It is not inevitable. Sectarian accounts of violence marginalize its spontaneity and minimize the agency of its perpetrators.[24] Persecution narratives simplify messy and heterogeneous social and religious landscapes. Alternative modes of construing and living with social and religious diversity compete with, subvert, ignore, and at times overturn grand narratives of religious being and belonging, such as sectarianism and persecution narratives, while never escaping their influence entirely.

This is not to say that religious or sectarian difference is irrelevant to politics. It is to suggest rather that an uncritical reliance on sectarian explanations of events, processes, and political outcomes effaces the broader context and eclipses other modes of sociality and relationality—religious, secular, both, neither—that compete with, downplay, ignore, or subvert the rigid lines of sectarian difference defended by those most invested in them. These alternate forms of sociality and religiosity easily escape the field of vision of scholars and practitioners who have been socialized to hone in on the realization of religious freedom, religious peace making, religious tolerance, interfaith understanding, and so on. Opening the field onto a broader social and interpretive landscape requires not simply deconstructing sectarian explanations of all kinds—which are likely to remain powerful for some time—but pulling back, looking elsewhere, and allowing these narratives to destabilize themselves by drawing attention to the alternatives.[25] In this context, religious and communal practices that downplay or may be indifferent to the rigidity of confessional boundaries, doctrinal purity, and identity markers take on heightened significance. While leaders privilege interfaith dialogue, religious freedom, religious rights, and the taming of sectarian difference, many individuals and groups may have only a passing familiarity with these constructs and their legal and political entailments. Some may engage in practices that are illegible or invisible when viewed through the interpretive rubrics of secularism, separationism, sectarianism, or church-state politics. Yet despite—or because of—their illegibility, these alternate forms of sociality and religiosity offer a different vantage point on the analytical frames and political sensibilities associated with "big religion" and "big politics." To see them requires resisting the easy appeal of concepts such as sectarian violence, Christian persecution, religious freedom, or other formulations of religion-in-power, and seeking out the ambiguities, multiplicities, and paradoxes of multiple religions in politics more broadly construed.

Disaggregating political sectarianism also yields more immediate analytical benefits. In the context of the contemporary transformations of the Middle East, it calls attention to the distinction between the Bahraini Al-Khalifa regime's mobilization of sectarian politics and the nonsectarian agenda of much of the Bahraini democratic opposition. Opponents of the regime not only denounced a state-sponsored sectarian agenda but also worked to promote cross-sectarian solidarity and to articulate political demands that reflected these crosscutting allegiances. As Toby Jones observes, "the opposition's demands include judicial reform, electoral reform, release of opposition political prisoners, and an elected government with full legislative powers." The detention of the opposition, he concludes, amounts to "little more than a brazen effort to silence a set of critics, but also those who have most effectively laid bare the distortions peddled by the government."[26] Disaggregating sectarianism also illuminates the distance between the Israeli government's political mobilization of sectarian difference through the recruitment of Christian

Palestinians to serve in the Israeli military, and the multiform politics of dissent among much of the Israeli Palestinian Christian community, and select other parts of Israeli society.[27] As Jonathan Cook explains, the overwhelming majority of Palestinian Christians opposes military service. Church authorities in Israel and abroad are caught between the demands of the laity and the Israeli government, fearful of antagonizing the latter but attentive to the dissenting politics of the former, which accuses the state of attempting to achieve "the disintegration of the Palestinian national minority into warring sects."[28] Disaggregating sectarianism also draws attention to the contrast between the defensive mobilization of sectarian politics by the Assad regime in Syria and the practices of the nonviolent, now largely marginalized, revolutionary opposition. Contra the regime's narrative, political allegiances among the multiple nodes of the Syrian opposition took shape not only in relation to sectarian difference but as a result of a complex set of factors including personal history, employment background, geographical location, family situations, and past experience with the regime.[29] To describe the Syrian war, or any war, as "sectarian" is to single out a particular, politicized construal of religious difference as the most salient and significant among the many aspects of human identity, history, political allegiance, sociality, and experience— including alternative religiosities—that are relevant to the conflict. It is to privilege epistemologically this particular rendering of religious difference above others. This not only obscures other dimensions of conflict, as seen in the case of the Rohingya, but it also makes life more difficult for those who refuse to assent to the terms of a particular, politicized rendering of sectarian difference.[30] An example is the punk rock band Rebel Riot, from Yangon, whose lead singer Kyaw Kyaw has spoken out against Buddhist monks and others instigating violence against the Rohingya. "If they were real monks," Kyaw Kyaw said, "I'd be quiet, but they aren't, they are nationalists, fascists. No one wants to hear it, but it's true."[31]

The histories and motivations behind acts of violence, persecution, and discrimination are complex. Forcing them into the "religion box" does not bring clarity and, in some cases, reinforces the very lines of division that make the violence seem possible, and in the worst cases, unavoidable. There is no unitary and universal conception of religion or sect that can be conjured to stabilize the shaky foundations of sectarian accounts of action, decision, desire, persecution, violence, and affiliation, in the Middle East or elsewhere. In the United States, as Robert Orsi observes, there is "no such thing as a 'Methodist' or a 'Southern Baptist' who can be neatly summarized by an account of the denomination's history or theology."[32] There are Methodists and Southern Baptists in particular times and places immersed in their worlds and struggling with local realities of work, life, gender, politics, illness, sexuality, race, class, violence, and other constraints and possibilities that are part of the contemporary human condition. The same observation holds for Sunnis, Druze, Jews, Alevis, atheists, Zoroastrians, and Buddhists.[33]

THINKING OTHERWISE ABOUT RELIGION

Of crucial importance is the question of how scholars of religion and politics might serve not as producers of information, the epistemological premises of which are already set by the policy world, but rather as carriers of critical insights that can be brought to bear on how policy is developed and implemented. This book has questioned the notion that religion is a self-evident category that motivates a host of actions, whether good or bad. It has pursued an approach to the study of religion and global politics that goes beyond celebrating good religion as a source of morality and reassurance while surveying and disciplining bad religion as a danger to be contained or suppressed.[34] Religion is never simply one or the other. In Orsi's words, "Religion does not make the world better to live in (although some forms of religious practice might); religion does not necessarily conform to the creedal formulations and doctrinal limits developed by cultured and circumspect theologians, church leaders, or ethicists; religion does not unambiguously orient people toward social justice. . . . Religion is often enough cruel and dangerous, and the same impulses that result in a special kind of compassion also lead to destruction, often among the same people at the same time."[35]

Religion cannot be divided into good and bad. Rather, as Salomon and Walton explain, it is "the product of a creative symbiosis of insiders and outsiders, populated by individuals who cannot simply be placed into the rigid categories of believer and unbeliever. . . . Religion is neither an object to be redeemed by theory nor an authentic truth to be protected from theory's detrimental incursions."[36] In this view, which I share, believing and belonging is a complex and messy business. It is not always easy to determine what makes someone a believer or a member of a "faith community" and what makes someone not so. It is often difficult to settle on what life experiences, confessional commitments, or ritual practices qualify one as an insider, and which prohibit an individual from inclusion. It is not always clear when an individual's degree of group affiliation tips the balance, thereby qualifying him or her as a member of a group. "Insider" and "outsider" are not permanent categories—and individuals often move creatively between them.[37] There are no universal criteria that can be invoked to enable judicial or political authorities—whether domestic or international—to identify and mark out a sphere of "religion" in a manner that is neutral to all religions.[38] It is impossible to determine, once and for all, what counts as religion with such a strong degree of certainty as to permit the enactment of laws and regulations that discriminate among individuals and groups on those grounds.[39] There are no religions with clean boundaries and neat orthodoxies that are waiting on the sidelines to be engaged or reformed, condemned or celebrated. One can study the ways in which religion is delimited and deployed in specific legal, institutional, historical, and political contexts, by whom, and for what purposes, as this book has done in the context of contemporary international relations. But religion is too unstable as a category to be treated otherwise.[40] To the extent that scholars of religion and global politics fail to acknowledge this instability they risk reproducing the very normative distinctions and discourses that are in need of interrogation and politicization.

It is worth considering in this context whether the complexities inherent to the category of religion resemble other objects of modern legal and political regulation such as race, class, ethnicity, custom, or gender. On the one hand, certain dilemmas produced by governing social difference through religious rights and freedoms also trouble other categories of modern governance. All rights constructions are weighty, institutionalized cultural practices that, as Michael McCann observes, are "harnessed to constellations of group power, institutional arrangements, and state force" and are "difficult or costly for most people, and especially subaltern or disadvantaged groups, to challenge and change."[41] This applies not only to religious rights but also to other markers of group identity such as gender, ethnicity, culture, and race. And yet each of these categories invokes very different histories and catalyzes different forms of politics depending on the specific historical context.[42] While there is insight to be gained from comparison across cases, as suggested in the discussion of the "Gay International" in Chapter 3, the politics of singling out religion as a stable, reliable object of law and policy generates social and political consequences that are not easily generalizable. Religion is not just any category. It has a history. To invoke religious rights or religious freedom is also to invoke the history of the category of religion, including its long and complex genealogy as discussed in the introduction.

This book has cautioned against attempts to posit religion as a stable basis from which to formulate foreign policy, pursue rights advocacy, and govern internationally. It has emphasized the need to better understand the complex interplay between expert religion, lived religion, and governed religion. To rely uncritically on "religion" as an object of law and policy, whether domestically or internationally, exacerbates the very problems that many modern attempts to govern deliberatively and democratically have sought to manage or resolve. It does so by authorizing specific forms of law, politics, and administration that heighten the public and political salience of *that which the authorities identify as* religious-religious and religious-secular difference. It generates particular questions and problems that, though always distinctive from one context to the next, share family resemblances, enabling leaders in Myanmar to tap into particular construals of religious difference to support new forms of exclusionary nationalism and fueling efforts by the Egyptian government to repress political opponents demonized for their alleged associations with Islamism.

To move beyond both the reproduction and the critique of the new global politics of religion requires thinking differently about religion, politics, law, history, and culture. Religious discourses are part of complex and evolving fields of practice that cannot be singled out from other aspects of human activity and yet also cannot simply be identified with these either. This approach to religion, as historian Sarah Shortall explains,

> demands an appreciation of the way in which religious discourses interact with, but are not exhausted by, the political, social, and cultural contexts of their production. In some cases, these utterances may reinforce existing power relations, but in other cases they may resist or transform them, and indeed they can do both at the same time. This transformative power arises from the fact that religious discourses emerge in conversation both with the particular historical context of their production, and with the manifold internal resources of a much longer religious tradition. It is the conjunction of these two contextual forces that lends religious phenomena their irreducible ambivalence and renders them excessive to the particular historical moment in which they are uttered.[43]

Rather than approach religion and politics as discreet entities that "influence" one another or are even mutually constitutive, this book has questioned the basis of their conceptual and disciplinary separation. In questioning the concept of policy-relevant knowledge about religion, it has emphasized the need to make connections as Orsi, Shortall, Sullivan, and others have done between religious discourses and their broader social, intellectual, political, and institutional contexts. A number of other scholars doing historical, comparative, and contextualized work also have sought to refashion the study of religion, law, and governance along these lines. Critical histories of attempts to subsume complex histories of contentious politics under claims to religious freedom, such as C. S. Adcock's rereading of the history of Tolerance, discussed in Chapter 3, show not only that other modes of coexistence and forms of political struggle across intersecting lines of difference (class, caste, religion) have existed historically but also that other possibilities are available in the present. In his work on ruling religion in Sri Lanka, Benjamin Schonthal moves back and forth between past and present, inside and outside the boundaries of official law and administration, to demonstrate how constitutional law shapes, and limits, local religious self-understandings and possibilities for coexistence.[44] Anver Emon's *Religious Pluralism and Islamic Law* questions the coherence of "tolerance" as a concept for understanding the significance of the *dhimmī* rules that governed non-Muslim permanent residents in Islamic lands, suggesting instead that these rules are "symptomatic of the messy business of ordering and regulating a diverse society."[45] Moving to colonial India but maintaining a focus on the sociolegal constitution and governance of religious diversity, Nandini Chatterjee's *The Making of Indian Secularism* analyzes "the complex, contradictory and often unintended trajectory of a bundle of laws, political ethics and institutional cultures of dealing with religion that are distinctly modern and distinctly Indian."[46] In his study of the making of Sudanese Islam, Noah Salomon explores the unexpected historical continuities, and the ruptures, between British colonial state-building efforts that intervened to create appropriate and civilized Sudanese Islamic religiosities and repress what the British saw as "unorthodox fanaticism," and current efforts by the Sudanese government to position the "Islamic state" as the potential solution to Sudan's woes after the departure of the majority non-Muslim south. Both the colonial and current authoritarian states, he shows, placed the making of Islam at the center of government strategy.[47] Finally, illustrating the potential of a phenomenological turn in the study of law, Benjamin Berger explores the Canadian constitutional rule of law's construal of religion, the limits of liberal legal subjectivity, and the complications of dominant conceptions of multiculturalism, pluralism, and tolerance. In drawing attention to what he describes as the "liberally-unruly dimensions of religion-as-lived," Berger's book explores what it means to be subjected to, and shaped by, the culture of law's rule in a particular set of circumstances.[48]

In interrogating the presumption of the inevitability and neutrality of secular governance, establishing the impossibility of disestablishment, exploring the limits of tolerance, examining the creation of minorities as rights holders, and exploring aspects of religion that are left "on the cutting-room floor" by constitutional culture, these scholars carve out new spaces for the study of religion, law, and governance. They document the distance to be traveled between grand constructs of religious governance and the actual experiences of those they govern. They approach religion as always already entangled with specific modes of governance, particular histories, and forms of sociality without being reducible to them.[49] Importantly, they also evince an awareness of the "limits of law's ability to speak to the full range of the meaningful contours of personal and collective life."[50] Excessive privileging of law and legal speech, Berger cautions, and I agree, can "efface the affective and relational dimensions of our social worlds." Wary of chipping away at the richness of experience through the "march of juridification," he calls for "modesty about the reliance on legal tools."[51] Winnifred Sullivan's *A Ministry of Presence: Chaplaincy, Spiritual Care, and the Law* is exemplary in this regard, describing the practices associated with contemporary spiritual care in the United States, understanding the needs served by these forms of ministry under modern secular governance, and situating these developments as part of a broader naturalization and deconstitutionalization of religion and spirituality.

Normalizing religion in academic scholarship would perhaps find policy expression in programming that avoids singling out religion and faith communities as the basis for developing policy, protecting human rights, and responding to global crises. An example is a State Department program called the US Ambassadors Fund for Cultural Preservation (AFCP).[52] Between 2001 and 2007 AFCP disbursed approximately eleven million dollars for 437 grants in 119 countries, supporting "a wide range of projects to preserve cultural heritage, such as the restoration of historic buildings, assessment and conservation of museum collections, archaeological site preservation, documentation of vanishing traditional craft techniques, improved storage conditions for archives and manuscripts, and documentation of indigenous languages."[53] While many sites restored by the fund are places of worship, the program's guiding rationale does not privilege religious actors or institutions. This does not mean that the fund shuns those who identify as religious; in fact, critics have attacked AFCP and the Obama administration for "funding mosque development around the world," citing the fund's support for heritage preservation projects that involve restoring mosques in Muslim-majority countries.[54] It also does not mean that the fund's activities are apolitical. As is the case with all essentially contested categories, that of culture is not innocent. The politics of designating particular activities, places, or practices as cultural and not religious carries its own risks and liabilities.[55] In the case of the AFCP, grants are awarded based on a number of considerations, among them the "anticipated benefit to the advancement of U.S. diplomatic goals as a result of the selection."[56] While always privileging particular cultural sites and understandings of culture, this program's rationale and selection process stand at a distance from, and may in some circumstances be indifferent to, the historical problem space of secularism. It is worth considering other social movements, modes of governance, and forms of political sociality that are characterized by the indifference that Hussein Agrama has described as *asecularity*, referring to "a situation not where norms are no longer secular, but where the questions against which such norms are adduced and contested as answers are no longer seen as necessary. It is a situation where we can be genuinely *indifferent* to those questions, the ways that particular stakes are attached to them, and their seeming indispensability to our ways of life."[57]

The possibility of thinking otherwise about religion in global politics will require not only policy reform or new scholarly frameworks—though neither should be underestimated—but also self-reflection on the part of scholars and practitioners. In many North American and European diplomatic, academic, and advocacy circles, the religious practices of others—though rarely those of social scientists and policy makers themselves—appear to have been reduced to little more than bounded objects of secular law and governance. It is as if the religious practices of scholars, analysts, and advocates stand apart and at a distance from those of their subjects, immune from scrutiny. This can be attributed to a number of historical factors, including a politics of religious containment going back to the wars of religion and the European Enlightenment(s). It is frequently remarked that religion—or at least the all-encompassing, embodied "presecularized" religion that seems to command the attention of government leaders and other elites—is something that "they" and not "we" are assumed to possess. As Elizabeth Pritchard observes, "religion as an identity is applied to various 'others' with whom the scholar or liberal secularist critically engages."[58] The tendency among many scholars and practitioners of global politics to distance themselves from the objects of intervention may also be due to a lack of interest in, or ability to focus on, the subject. Many appear to be torn between an anxious desire to locate actionable solutions to the problems that are said to be generated by (other people's) religions, while simultaneously being drawn to the political benefits of tapping into the (allegedly) domesticating tendencies of certain forms of religion, in particular those with distantly familiar institutionalized hierarchies.

Resisting both of these options, this book has destabilized and disaggregated the category of religion that made the "return of religion" to international relations legible and, for many, reassuring. It has distinguished between religion as construed by those in power for purposes of law and governance and religion as lived by those without it, stressing the complex interplay and porous boundaries between the fields of practice, tradition, belonging, and governance indexed by these distinctions while strenuously resisting any strict dichotomy between them. There is no unmarked religion, anywhere. This book has drawn attention to religion beyond that which is sanctioned by either political or religious authorities, to "religious messiness, to multiplicities, to seeing religious spaces as always, inevitably, and profoundly intersected by things brought into them from outside, things that bear their own histories, complexities, meanings different from those offered within the religious space."[59] It has historicized and politicized the agendas of reassurance and surveillance in their academic and policy guises. And it has generated discussion of the terms and conditions under which research is conducted, and knowledge produced, about the diverse and shifting field that is named as religion and its deep imbrication with specific global historical, legal, and political processes. To take this inquiry to the next level will require that scholars of international relations engage substantively with scholars of contemporary religion working across academic disciplines.[60] It will require asking new kinds of questions about religion and governance. Which activities in the vast sea of human affiliations and actions are designated as religious and primed for engagement, partnership, and dialogue, and which are not? Whose version of which religion is under scrutiny? Which authorities speak in its name, and on whose behalf? What is the relationship between these authorities and the individuals and communities in whose name they allegedly speak? How do researchers account for the practices of individuals that may have tense or nonexistent ties to such institutions or authorities? Conversely, how do researchers consider those who have ties to many simultaneously?

The religion that is chosen for protection under modern law, the religion that is subjected to state and international legal administration, does not, and cannot, exhaust this vast and diverse field of human goings-on. Many practices are eclipsed, and all are transformed, through the selective processes of modern religious governance. At the same time, modern subjects are neither fully determined by their legal and discursive environments nor fully captured by orthodoxy of any kind.[61] Individuals and groups are adaptive and acculturating, mixing and borrowing not only from other traditions but also with practices from the cultural repertoires that surround them, including business practices, politics, art, literature, media, and popular culture.[62] Religious practices are often public, improvised, and embedded in everyday life, and take place outside of churches, synagogues, and mosques.[63] Such "DIY religion" is often relatively free from the regulation of religious authorities.[64] It generally fails to make the headlines. It is often ignored or shuffled off to the wings. It does not have a seat at the interfaith table. It is rarely studied or spoken of by scholars of religion and global politics. It is neither free nor unfree. The imperatives of religion under law, the inventories of religious freedom, tolerance, and rights, and the subjectivities and social fields they reflect and create are always part of a much larger story.

Notes

NOTES TO PREFACE

1. Mohamed Elshinnawi, "Conflicts Engulf Christians in Mideast," *Voice of America*, August 30, 2014, http://www.voanews.com/content/conflicts-engulf-christians-in-middle-east/2432773.html.

2. Quoted in Ruth Alexander, "Are There Really 100,000 New Christian Martyrs Every Year?," *BBC News Magazine*, November 12, 2013, http://www.bbc.com/news/magazine-24864587. On the history of the "persecuted Church," see Melani McAlister, "US Evangelicals and the Politics of Slave Redemption as Religious Freedom in Sudan," *South Atlantic Quarterly* 113, no. 1 (2014): 87–108; Elizabeth A. Castelli, "Praying for the Persecuted Church: US Christian Activism in the Global Arena," *Journal of Human Rights* 4, no. 3 (2005): 321–51; and Castelli, "Persecution Complexes: Identity Politics and the 'War on Christians,'" *Differences: A Journal of Feminist Cultural Studies* 18, no. 3 (2007): 152–80.

3. Pew Forum on Religion and Public Life, "Religious Hostilities Reach Six-Year High" (Washington, DC: Pew Research Center, January 14, 2014), http://www.pewforum.org/2014/01/14/religious-hostilities-reach-six-year-high/.

4. Similar reports are issued on a regular basis by the US State Department, the US Commission on International Religious Freedom, the UN Special Rapporteur on Freedom of Religion or Belief, the Council of the European Union, the UK Foreign and Commonwealth Office, Human Rights Watch, the International Crisis Group, Freedom House, Amnesty International, and others.

5. All quotations in the following paragraphs are from Alexander, "Are There Really 100,000 New Christian Martyrs Every Year?"

6. John L. Allen, Jr., *The Global War on Christians: Dispatches from the Front Lines of Anti-Christian Persecution* (New York: Image, 2013).

CHAPTER I: INTRODUCTION

1. The *New Yorker* described Sarrouj as a longtime resident of Tripoli's Serail neighborhood who had "amassed a large collection of books—rare first editions of scholarly texts, novels in different languages, dictionaries, encyclopedias, out-of-print magazines—in the

forty-plus years since he opened for business." Elias Muhanna, "Letter from Lebanon: A Bookshop Burns," *New Yorker*, January 16, 2014, http://www.newyorker.com/online /blogs/books/2014/01/letter-from-lebanon-a-bookshop-burns.html.

2. "Some sources suggested that there may be a link between what happened and a real estate dispute between Sarrouj and the building's owners, who had made several failed attempts through the judiciary to evict Sarrouj." Ghassan Rifi, "Tripoli Residents Condemn Burning of Saeh Library," trans. Rani Geha, *Al-Monitor*, January 8, 2014, http:// www.al-monitor.com/pulse/security/2014/01/tripoli-library-burned-islamists-condemned .html#ixzz2tzynmuzU. Muhanna asks, "Were the arsonists somehow connected with the building's owners, who had been trying to muscle the recalcitrant priest out for years?" Muhanna, "Letter from Lebanon."

3. "The unprecedented political, religious, civil, and popular solidarity seen in Tripoli, the support shown to the Orthodox Church and Father Sarrouj, and the rush to contain what happened mitigated the crime's consequences and asserted that Tripoli will remain committed to its knowledge, intellectuals, customs, traditions, diversity and its Muslim-Christian coexistence." Rifi, "Tripoli Residents Condemn Burning of Saeh Library."

4. Antoine Amrieh, "Tripoli Mobilizes after Historic Library Torched," *Daily Star*, January 4, 2014, http://www.dailystar.com.lb/News/Lebanon-News/2014/Jan-04/243098-historic -library-torched-in-n-lebanon.ashx#axzz2pisNlpFu. Thanks to Jeremy Menchik for drawing my attention to this incident.

5. Both statements are cited in Tyler O'Neil, "Over 50,000 Books Burned in Christian Library in Lebanon over Blasphemy Claim; US Leader Says 'Violent Hysteria' Spreading in Muslim World," *Christian Post*, January 7, 2014, http://www.christianpost.com/news /over-50000-books-burned-in-christian-library-in-lebanon-over-blasphemy-claim-us -leader-says-violent-hysteria-spreading-in-muslim-world-112133/cpt.

6. Chris Hann and Mathijs Pelkmans, "Realigning Religion and Power in Central Asia: Religion, the Nation-State and (Post)socialism," *Europe-Asia Studies* 61, no. 9 (2009): 1520.

7. Winnifred Fallers Sullivan, *The Impossibility of Religious Freedom* (Princeton: Princeton University Press, 2005), 111.

8. Pamela Slotte, "The Religious and the Secular in European Human Rights Discourse," *Finnish Yearbook of International Law* 21 (2010): 54.

9. Liora Danan, "Mixed Blessings: U.S. Government Engagement with Religion in Conflict-Prone Settings" (Washington, DC: Center for Strategic and International Studies, August 2007): 2.

10. Ibid., 26n114, emphasis added.

11. For example, José Casanova explains that rather than privatizing religion, Westphalia inaugurated a new mode of managing it by territorializing religion in separate confessional states. José Casanova, "Religion, the New Millennium, and Globalization," *Sociology of Religion* 62, no. 4 (2001): 424, 428. See also Peter Beyer, "Deprivileging Religion in a Post-Westphalian State," in *Varieties of Religious Establishment*, ed. Lori G. Beaman and Winnifred Fallers Sullivan (London: Ashgate, 2013), 78–79.

12. Noah Salomon, *"The People of Sudan Love You, Oh Messenger of God": An Ethnography of the Islamic State* (Princeton: Princeton University Press, 2016), chap. 1.

13. Nandini Chatterjee, "English Law, Brahmo Marriage, and the Problem of Religious Difference: Civil Marriage Laws in Britain and India," *Comparative Studies in Society and History* 52, no. 3 (July 2010): 539, 528.

14. Michael Goldfarb, "Napoleon, the Jews and French Muslims," *New York Times*, March 18, 2007, http://www.nytimes.com/2007/03/18/opinion/18iht-edgoldfarb.4943373.html. On the adjudication of Jewish identity through secular law in the contemporary United Kingdom in the *Jews Free School* case, see Heather Miller Rubens, " . . . 'Something Has Gone Wrong:' The JFS Case and Defining Jewish Identity in the Courtroom," and Peter G. Danchin and Louis Blond, "Unlawful Religion? Modern Secular Power and the Legal Reasoning in the *JFS* Case," in "Politics of Religious Freedom: Case Studies," ed. Peter G. Danchin, Winnifred Fallers Sullivan, Saba Mahmood, and Elizabeth Shakman Hurd, special issue of *Maryland Journal of International Law* 29 (2015): 361–413 and 414–75.

15. President's Advisory Council on Faith-Based and Neighborhood Partnerships, "A New Era of Partnerships: Report of Recommendations to the President" (Washington, DC: White House Office of Faith-Based and Neighborhood Partnerships, March 2010), 85.

16. Cited in Toby Helm, "Extremist Religion Is at Root of 21st-Century Wars, Says Tony Blair," *Guardian*, January 25, 2014, http://www.theguardian.com/politics/2014/jan/25/extremist-religion-wars-tony-blair.

17. Peter Baker, "Religious Freedom Is a Tenet of Foreign Policy, Obama Says," *New York Times*, February 6, 2014, http://www.nytimes.com/2014/02/07/us/politics/obama-denounces-religious-repression.html?emc=eta1&_r=0.

18. Religious institutions are also turning to secular law to seek out "juridical personalities" for faith communities. Archbishop Silvano Tomasi, head of the Holy See's permanent observer mission in Geneva, explained in a 2012 speech to the Human Rights Council that "the task of the government is not to define religion or recognize its value, but to confer upon faith communities a juridical personality so that they can function peacefully within a legal framework." Kevin J. Jones, "Vatican Urges UN to Help Protect Religious Freedom," *EWTN News*, March 3, 2012, http://www.ewtnnews.com/catholic-news/World.php?id=5006#ixzz20XM0PhXR.

19. In 2005 the UK Department for International Development (DFID)—the British equivalent of USAID—launched a five-year, £3.5 million research program on "faiths in development," and in 2003 the British government launched a cross-Whitehall dialogue on faith issues to coordinate interdepartmental engagement with UK faith communities. Gerard Clarke, "Agents of Transformation? Donors, Faith-Based Organisations and International Development," *Third World Quarterly* 28, no. 1 (2007): 85. Under James Wolfensohn, the World Bank and World Health Organization also became interested in religion, as seen in the "Development Dialogue on Values and Ethics" program described by Katherine Marshall in "Journey towards Faith Development Partnerships: The Challenge and the Potential," in *The World Market and Interreligious Dialogue*, ed. Catherine Cornille and Glenn Willis (Eugene, OR: Cascade Books, 2011), 190–210.

20. Gerd Bauman, *Contesting Culture, Discourses of Identity in Multi-ethnic London* (Cambridge: Cambridge University Press, 1996), 30.

21. Manuel Vásquez observes that "the shifting boundaries of what we call religion will continue to defy our most astute efforts to fix them once and for all. . . . Such an indeterminacy does not mean that anything goes in the study of religion or that all approaches are equally fruitful (or ineffectual)." Manuel A. Vasquez, *More Than Belief: A Materialist Theory of Religion* (Oxford: Oxford University Press, 2010), 10.

22. See also the publications from the Politics of Religious Freedom: Contested Norms and

Local Practices collaborative research project, funded by the Henry Luce Foundation, including Winnifred Fallers Sullivan, Elizabeth Shakman Hurd, Peter Danchin, and Saba Mahmood, eds., *Politics of Religious Freedom* (Chicago: University of Chicago Press, 2015); "Politics of Religious Freedom: Contested Genealogies," ed. Saba Mahmood and Peter G. Danchin, special issue of *South Atlantic Quarterly* 113, no. 1 (2014); "Symposium: Re-thinking Religious Freedom," ed. Elizabeth Shakman Hurd and Winnifred Fallers Sullivan, *Journal of Law and Religion* 29, no. 3 (2014); the collection of essays at the Social Science Research Council's website the *Immanent Frame*, edited by Hurd and Sullivan, "Politics of Religious Freedom," http://blogs.ssrc.org/tif/the-politics-of -religious-freedom; and "Politics of Religious Freedom: Case Studies," ed. Peter G. Danchin, Winnifred Fallers Sullivan, Saba Mahmood, and Elizabeth Shakman Hurd, special issue of *Maryland Journal of International Law* 29 (2015): 288–542.

23. Markus Dressler and Arvind-Pal S. Mandair, "Introduction: Modernity, Religion-Making, and the Postsecular," in *Secularism and Religion-Making*, ed. Markus Dressler and Arvind-Pal S. Mandair (Oxford: Oxford University Press, 2011), 21–22.

24. As Courtney Bender asks, "what would a sociology of modern religious life look like if it did not begin with the expectation or the view that social differentiation frees religion, politics, and economics from each other in the way that we have so frequently claimed?" Courtney Bender, "The Power of Pluralist Thinking," in Sullivan et al., *Politics of Religious Freedom*, 74. For a related argument developed in the context of a sociological and philosophical critique of the laïcité-religion framework and the paradox of assimilation in France, see Yolande Jansen, *Secularism, Assimilation and the Crisis of Multiculturalism: French Modernist Legacies* (Amsterdam: Amsterdam University Press, 2013), 286–87.

25. Robert A. Orsi, *Between Heaven and Earth: The Religious Worlds People Make and the Scholars Who Study Them* (Princeton: Princeton University Press, 2005), 166.

26. Dressler and Mandair, "Introduction," 18.

27. Linda Woodhead, "Diversity in Religious Practice: Examples from the UK" (lecture, India International Centre, New Delhi, February 18, 2013).

28. Linda Woodhead, "Tactical and Strategic Religion," in *Everyday Lived Islam in Europe*, ed. Nathal Dessing, Nadia Jeldtoft, Jørgen Nielsen, and Linda Woodhead (London: Ashgate, 2013).

29. Akeel Bilgrami, "Slouching toward Bethlehem: Secularism in the MENA Region" (lecture, Conference on Crepuscular Secularism, Ann Arbor, MI, March 18, 2013). See further Akeel Bilgrami, *Secularism, Identity, and Enchantment* (Cambridge, MA: Harvard University Press, 2014).

30. Wilton Park, "Conference Report: Promoting Religious Freedom around the World" (July 2012), https://www.wiltonpark.org.uk/wp-content/uploads/wp1108-report.pdf.

31. For an example, see Ed Husain, "A Global Venture to Counter Violent Extremism" (Council on Foreign Relations Policy Innovation Memorandum 37, September 2013), http://www.cfr.org/radicalization-and-extremism/global-venture-counter-violent -extremism/p30494.

32. For an early harbinger of this logic, see R. Scott Appleby, *The Ambivalence of the Sacred: Religion, Violence, and Reconciliation* (Oxford: Rowman & Littlefield, 2000).

33. C. S. Adcock, *The Limits of Tolerance: Indian Secularism and the Politics of Religious Freedom* (Oxford: Oxford University Press, 2013), 7.

34. "Modern government has unfolded . . . through the development of new forms of expertise, which among other things define problems and issues upon which government

can operate. . . . Again and again government itself operates—as Foucault has taught us—simultaneously as fields of knowledge and fields of power. And the objects brought into being in this way—defined in important ways through the development of expert knowledge—become in themselves modes through which political power operates." Timothy Mitchell "Timothy Mitchell on Infra-Theory, the State Effect, and the Technopolitics of Oil" (Theory Talk no. 59, October 25, 2013), http://www.theory-talks .org/2013/10/theory-talk-59.html.

35. See the pathbreaking work of Talal Asad. See also Hussein Ali Agrama, *Questioning Secularism: Islam, Sovereignty, and the Rule of Law in Modern Egypt* (Chicago: University of Chicago Press, 2012) and Saba Mahmood, "Secularism, Hermeneutics, and Empire: The Politics of Islamic Reformation," *Public Culture* 18, no. 2 (Spring 2006): 323–47. Dressler and Mandair describe the Asadian approach as one of three strands in the critique of secularity including "(i) the socio-political philosophy of liberal secularism exemplified by Charles Taylor (and to some extent shared by thinkers such as John Rawls and Jürgen Habermas); (ii) the 'postmodernist' critiques of ontotheological metaphysics by radical theologians and continental philosophers that have helped to revive the discourse of 'political theology'; (iii) following the work of Michel Foucault and Edward Said, the various forms of discourse analysis focusing on genealogies of power most closely identified with the work of Talal Asad." Dressler and Mandair, "Introduction," 4.

36. Martin D. Stringer, *Discourses on Religious Diversity: Explorations in an Urban Ecology* (Farnham: Ashgate, 2013), 1–2.

37. Pamela E. Klassen and Courtney Bender, "Introduction: Habits of Pluralism," in *After Pluralism: Reimagining Religious Engagement*, ed. Pamela Klassen and Courtney Bender (New York: Columbia University Press, 2010), 22.

38. Robert A. Orsi, "Afterword: Everyday Religion and the Contemporary World: The Unmodern, or What Was Supposed to Have Disappeared but Did Not," in *Ordinary Lives and Grand Schemes: An Anthropology of Everyday Religion*, ed. Samuli Schielke and Liza Debevec (New York: Berghahn Books, 2012), 149.

39. This is also true of US federal law enforcement officials as discussed by Nancy Ammerman in the context of expert responses to the standoff with David Koresh and the Branch Davidians in Waco in 1993. Nancy T. Ammerman, "Waco, Federal Law Enforcement, and Scholars of Religion," in *Armageddon in Waco: Critical Perspectives on the Branch Davidian Conflict*, ed. Stuart A. Wright (Chicago: University of Chicago Press, 1995), 282–96.

40. Samuli Schielke, "Second Thoughts about the Anthropology of Islam," *ZMO Working Papers* 2 (2010): 4–5.

41. I agree with Laborde that "it would be a mistake to think that conceptual imprecision is in itself an obstacle to scholarly inquiry." Cécile Laborde, "Three Approaches to the Study of Religion," *Immanent Frame*, February 5, 2014, http://blogs.ssrc.org/tif/2014 /02/05/three-approaches-to-the-study-of-religion/.

42. Orsi, "Afterword," 150–53. Nancy T. Ammerman, ed., *Everyday Religion: Observing Modern Religious Lives* (Oxford: Oxford University Press, 2006) and David D. Hall, ed., *Lived Religion in America: Toward a History of Practice* (Princeton: Princeton University Press, 1997).

43. Sullivan, *Impossibility of Religious Freedom*.

44. Winnifred Fallers Sullivan, "We Are All Religious Now. Again." *Social Research* 76, no. 4 (2009): 1197.

45. "Following 9/11 and 7/7 the need, in some way or another, to 'manage' religious diversity, or at least certain aspects of religious extremism within the UK and elsewhere, became imperative." Stringer, *Discourses on Religious Diversity*, 134.

46. Winnifred Sullivan discusses the new spiritual governance in her study of chaplains in the United States. *A Ministry of Presence: Chaplaincy, Spiritual Care, and the Law* (Chicago: University of Chicago Press, 2014).

47. Ibid., 11.

48. Adcock, *Limits of Tolerance*, 50.

49. For the impact of colonial interactions on the formation of the modern category of religion, see Peter Van der Veer, *Imperial Encounters: Religion and Modernity in India and Britain* (Princeton: Princeton University Press, 2001), Van der Veer, *The Modern Spirit of Asia: The Spiritual and the Secular in China and India* (Princeton: Princeton University Press, 2013), Jason Ānanda Josephson, *The Invention of Religion in Japan* (Chicago: University of Chicago Press, 2012), David Chidester, *Savage Systems: Colonialism and Comparative Religion in Southern Africa* (Charlottesville: University of Virginia Press, 1996), and Jean and John Comaroff, *Of Revelation and Revolution: Christianity, Colonialism, and Consciousness in South Africa*, vol. 1 (Chicago: University of Chicago Press, 1991). See also Brent Nongbri, *Before Religion: A History of a Modern Concept* (New Haven: Yale University Press, 2013).

50. Helge Årsheim, "Legal Secularism? Differing Notions of Religion in International and Norwegian Law," in *Secular and Sacred? The Scandinavian Case of Religion in Human Rights, Law and Public Space*, ed. Rosemary Van Den Breemer, José Casanova, and Trygve Wyller (Göttingen: Vandenhoeck & Ruprecht, 2013), 124.

51. Thanks to Courtney Bender for helping me to see this point.

52. A point Talal Asad makes cogently: "Legal definitions of religion are not mere academic exercises: they have profound implications for the organization of social life and the possibilities of personal experience." "Response to Gil Anidjar," *Interventions: International Journal of Postcolonial Studies* 11, no. 3 (2009): 398.

53. Robert A. Orsi, *The Madonna of 115th Street: Faith and Community in Italian Harlem, 1880–1950*, 3rd ed. (New Haven: Yale University Press, 2010), 226.

54. Ibid., 220.

55. A point made differently by Bruno Latour: "There is no right way to speak religiously. Who would dare claim he has the right, the precise, the definitive, the orthodox metalanguage to talk about these things?" Bruno Latour, *Rejoicing: Or the Torments of Religious Speech* (Cambridge: Polity, 2013), 117.

56. Lila Abu-Lughod, comments at a workshop on "Policy-Relevant Knowledge about Religion: Promises and Perils" (New York: Luce Foundation, September 2013).

CHAPTER 2: TWO FACES OF FAITH

1. For the epigraphs, see Yvonne Sherwood, "On the Freedom of the Concepts of Religion and Belief," in Sullivan et al., *Politics of Religious Freedom*, 33; and Tony Blair, "Taking Faith Seriously," *New Europe Online*, January 2, 2012, http://www.neurope.eu/blog/taking-faith-seriously.

2. Similar assumptions underlay US and British counterradicalization programs, as Samuel Rascoff has shown. "The theory underlying counterradicalization—and especially underlying efforts aimed at transforming entire communities—treats Muslims as *simultaneously posing a unique threat to security and possessing the distinctive capacity to address that threat.*" Samuel J. Rascoff, "Establishing Official Islam: The Law and Strategy of Counter-Radicalization," *Stanford Law Review* 64 (2012): 173, emphasis added.

3. Quoted in Dressler and Mandair, "Introduction," 26. See Brian Goldstone, "Secularism, 'Religious Violence,' and the Liberal Imaginary," in Dressler and Mandair, *Secularism and Religion-Making*, 104–24. This narrative has a long history. See John Locke, *A Letter Concerning Toleration*, ed. James H. Tully (Indianapolis: Hackett, 1983) and the discussion in chapter 3 of Locke's religious psychology. For a rereading of Locke's political theology that challenges the widespread assumption that his theory of toleration privatized religion, see Elizabeth A. Pritchard, *Religion in Public: Locke's Political Theology* (Stanford: Stanford University Press, 2013).

4. A 2010 report from the US President's Advisory Council on Faith-Based and Neighborhood Partnerships captures this excitement about the rediscovery of religion, recommending that the president "request the appointment of senior staff for multi-religious engagement in each of the major agencies tasked with international affairs, including the Department of State, the U.S. Agency for International Development (USAID), the National Security Council (NSC), and the Department of Defense." President's Advisory Council on Faith-Based and Neighborhood Partnerships, "New Era of Partnerships," 71.

5. "The armed services are still determining how such knowledge should be used in practice. Much of the *strategic implementation of religious knowledge* today is occurring at the Joint Intelligence Operations Centers and the regionally focused Combatant Commands." Danan, "Mixed Blessings," 26n114, emphasis added.

6. The US government refers to these efforts to bring the "religion factor" back in as "operationalizing religion." Danan, "Mixed Blessings," 25.

7. Blair, "Taking Faith Seriously."

8. See Monica Duffy Toft, Daniel Philpott, and Timothy Samuel Shah, *God's Century: Resurgent Religion and Global Politics* (New York: Norton, 2011).

9. Noah Toly, "Reports Analyzing Issues around the World Oddly Silent on Religion," *Sightings*, March 6, 2014, http://divinity.uchicago.edu/sightings/reports-analyzing-issues -around-world-oddly-silent-religion——noah-toly.

10. Olivia Ward, "Meet Canada's Defender of the Faiths," *Toronto Star*, February 14, 2014, http://www.thestar.com/news/world/2014/02/14/meet_canadas_defender_of_the _faiths.html. In 2013 Canadian Prime Minister Stephen Harper launched an Office of Religious Freedom at the Department of Foreign Affairs, Trade, and Development (DFATD) modeled on the US Department of State Office.

11. Robert Joustra, "Century for Sale," Review of *God's Century: Resurgent Religion and Global Politics* by Monica Duffy Toft, Daniel Philpott, and Timothy Samuel Shah, *Books & Culture: A Christian Review*, September/October 2011, http://www.booksandculture .com/articles/2011/sepoct/centurysale.html?paging=off.

12. Similar objectives animated the Save Darfur Coalition that, according to Rosemary Hicks, "reinvigorated diverse, longstanding narratives that establish American moral authority

with military endeavors to save women from Islam." Rosemary R. Hicks, "Saving Darfur: Enacting Pluralism in Terms of Gender, Genocide, and Militarized Human Rights," in Klassen and Bender, *After Pluralism*, 255. On the salvation narratives of Americans engaged in efforts to save Darfur, see also Jodi Eichler-Levine and Rosemary Hicks, "As Americans Against Genocide: The Crisis in Darfur and Interreligious Political Activism," *American Quarterly* 59, no. 3 (September 2007): 711–35.

13. On gender and the politics of secularism, see Elizabeth Shakman Hurd, "Rescued by Law? Gender and the Global Politics of Secularism," in *Religion, the Secular, and the Politics of Sexual Difference*, ed. Linell E. Cady and Tracy Fessenden (New York: Columbia University Press, 2014), 211–28. Joan Scott compares Laura Bush's campaign to liberate the women of Afghanistan to the "racist benevolence" of French feminists who abandoned their critique of the status quo to support a 2004 law that offered *laïcité* as the singular ground for gender equality and French national identity. Joan Wallach Scott, *The Politics of the Veil* (Princeton: Princeton University Press, 2007), 172.

14. Dana Cloud makes a related point about the *Time* magazine photo essay "Kabul Unveiled," in which "liberation" is defined as "the exposure of women to the consumer market and to the mass media." Cloud points out that images of the oppression of Afghan women in the American media "operate within a rhetorical discourse that becomes more forceful when images of oppression are contrasted with images of women granted entry—by the arrival of US forces—into modern, Western-style, market-driven 'civilization.'" Dana L. Cloud, "To Veil the Threat of Terror: Afghan Women and the 'Clash of Civilizations' in the Imagery of the U.S. War on Terrorism," *Quarterly Journal of Speech* 90, no. 3 (2004): 294. The connections between free market ideology and the religious economies model are discussed further in the next chapter.

15. Eric Fassin, "National Identities and Transnational Intimacies: Sexual Democracy and the Politics of Immigration in Europe," *Public Culture* 22, no. 3 (2010): 510.

16. Agrama, *Questioning Secularism*. Årsheim has a nice description of the intersection of law and religion: "law constantly creates and patrols the borders of social practices, and whenever these regulations designate certain spaces for religion, legal rules run the errands of secularism." Årsheim, "Legal Secularism?," 125–26.

17. This brings to mind Charles Hirschkind's observation that "the incorporation of what had been modernity's other—religion—into its very fabric does not decenter the conceptual edifice of European modernity in any way that might allow a reconsideration of Europe's religious minorities, but on the contrary redoubles it, deepening the fundamental otherness of those who cannot inhabit its Christian genealogy." Charles Hirschkind, "Religious Difference and Democratic Pluralism: Some Recent Debates and Frameworks," *Temenos* 44, no. 1 (2008): 72.

18. See Kathleen Sands's forthcoming book on this subject for an innovative and historically rich discussion of the American case that goes beyond the tired polarities of the culture wars.

19. André Laliberté, "The Communist Party and the Future of Religion in China," *Immanent Frame*, October 4, 2013, http://blogs.ssrc.org/tif/2013/10/04/the-communist-party -and-the-future-of-religion-in-china/.

20. Peter W. Edge, "Hard Law and Soft Power: Counter-Terrorism, the Power of Sacred Places, and the Establishment of an Anglican Islam," *Rutgers Journal of Law & Religion* 12, pt. 2 (Spring 2010): 375, citing a publication of the Foreign and Commonwealth Office,

"Preventing Violent Extremism," (Sixth Report of Session 2009–10, March 16, 2010), http://www.publications.parliament.uk/pa/cm200910/cmselect/cmcomloc/65/65.pdf.

21. According to Maïla the office has four objectives: "Alert and anticipation through observation and analysis of tendencies and movements that affect religions throughout the world; following the positions and orientations of religions on major international questions such as human rights, racial discrimination, bioethics ... or religious freedom; assisting in diplomatic efforts and advising regional ministerial offices on difficult ('hot') topics; and sensitizing diplomats to religious questions and concerns." Anne-Bénédicte Hoffner and Frédéric Mounier, "Quand l'Etat Est Amené à Traiter des Questions Religieuses," *La-Croix*, December 16, 2011, http://www.la-croix.com/Religion/Approfondir /Spiritualite/Quand-l-Etat-est-amene-a-traiter-des-questions-religieuses-_NP_-2011-12 -16-747748 (author's translation).

22. See, for example, Jeffrey Haynes, *Religion, Politics and International Relations: Selected Essays* (London: Routledge, 2011).

23. See, for example, the Berkley Center at Georgetown University's project on "Christianity and Freedom," which describes itself as an attempt to "explore Christianity's contribution to the construction and diffusion of freedom." http://berkleycenter.georgetown .edu/rfp/themes/christianity-freedom-historical-and-contemporary-perspectives.

24. Ron E. Hassner, *War on Sacred Grounds* (Ithaca, NY: Cornell University Press, 2009).

25. Monica Duffy Toft, "Religion, Rationality and Violence," in *Religion and International Relations Theory*, ed. Jack Snyder (New York: Columbia University Press, 2011), 115–40.

26. There are dissenters. See, for example, Erin K. Wilson's *After Secularism: Rethinking Religion in Global Politics* (New York: Palgrave Macmillan, 2012).

27. On immanent causality as an alternative to efficient causality in the study of international relations, see Lars Tønder, "Ideational Analysis, Political Change and Immanent Causality," in *The Role of Ideas in Political Analysis: A Portrait of Contemporary Debates*, ed. Andreas Gofas and Colin Hay (New York: Routledge, 2009), 56–77.

28. Two exemplary collections are Craig Calhoun, Mark Juergensmeyer, and Jonathan VanAntwerpen, eds., *Rethinking Secularism* (Oxford: Oxford University Press, 2011) and Michael Warner, Jonathan VanAntwerpen, and Craig Calhoun, eds., *Varieties of Secularism in a Secular Age* (Cambridge, MA: Harvard University Press, 2010). My first book, *The Politics of Secularism in International Relations* (Princeton: Princeton University Press, 2008), also contributed to this effort.

29. José Casanova, *Public Religions in the Modern World* (Chicago: University of Chicago Press, 1994); Bruno Latour, *We Have Never Been Modern* (Cambridge, MA: Harvard University Press, 1993); Bruno Latour, *An Inquiry into Modes of Existence: An Anthropology of the Moderns*, trans. Catherine Porter (Cambridge, MA: Harvard University Press, 2013).

30. On its website, KAICIID is described, rather improbably, as "an independent, autonomous, international organisation, free of political or economic influence." http://www .kaiciid.org/en/the-centre/.

31. Casanova's *Public Religions in the Modern World* may be seen as having opened the floodgates for public consumption and eventual widespread acceptance of this narrative.

32. See Daniel Philpott, "What Religion Brings to the Politics of Transitional Justice," *Journal of International Affairs* 61, no. 1 (2007): 93–110.

33. See Séverine Deneulin and Masooda Bano, *Religion in Development: Rewriting the Secular Script* (London: Zed Books, 2009), and Gerard Clarke and Michael Jennings, eds., *Development, Civil Society and Faith-Based Organizations* (New York: Palgrave Macmillan, 2008).

34. Thomas Banchoff and Robert Wuthnow, "Introduction," in *Religion and the Global Politics of Human Rights*, ed. Thomas Banchoff and Robert Wuthnow (Oxford: Oxford University Press, 2011), 5.

35. "Those many people in the West today who decry the singular intolerance of Islam are mistaken not because Islam is really 'tolerant' (whatever that might mean), but because it makes no sense to talk about the 'essence of Islam'—or of any other 'religion' for that matter—if one is not already in some sense committed to it. Talk about the essence of a religious or non-religious tradition is part of a political discourse of persuasion or dissuasion; it is not a neutral exercise of Reason." Talal Asad, "Muhammad Asad between Religion and Politics," *Islam Interactive*, n.d., http://www.islaminteractive.info/content/muhammad-asad-between-religion-and-politics#.T7omUh6JUTM.

36. Årsheim, "Legal Secularism?," 123.

37. Elena Fiddian-Qasmiyeh, "The Pragmatics of Performance: Putting 'Faith' in Aid in the Sahrawi Refugee Camps," *Journal of Refugee Studies* 24, no. 3 (2011): 533–47. See also Fiddian-Qasmiyeh, *The Ideal Refugees: Gender, Islam, and the Sahrawi Politics of Survival* (Syracuse, NY: Syracuse University Press, 2013).

38. Fiddian-Qasmiyeh, "Pragmatics of Performance," 537.

39. Stephen Zunes, "The Last Colony: Beyond Dominant Narratives on the Western Sahara Roundtable," *Jadaliyya*, June 3, 2013, http://www.jadaliyya.com/pages/index/11992/the-last-colony_beyond-dominant-narratives-on-the-.

40. Christ the Rock has been working in the camps since 1999. The organization provides summer host families in the United States for Sahrawi children, teaches English in the Smara camp, and develops programs to "build bridges between people in the United States and Saharawis forced to live in the arid Saharan Desert." Timothy Kustusch, "Muslim Leaders and Christian Volunteers Host Religious Dialogues in Saharawi Camps" (Union de Periodistas y Escritores Saharauis [UPES], April 2, 2009), http://www.upes.org/bodyindex_eng.asp?field=sosio_eng&id=1501.

41. Fiddian-Qasmiyeh, "Pragmatics of Performance," 539.

42. Ibid., 539.

43. Ibid., 537.

44. Ibid., 542.

45. Kustusch, "Muslim Leaders and Christian Volunteers," cited in Fiddian-Qasmiyeh, "Pragmatics of Performance," 542.

46. Fiddian-Qasmiyeh, "Pragmatics of Performance," 544.

47. Ibid., 544, citing Barbara Harrell-Bond, "The Experience of Refugees as Recipients of Aid," in *Refugees: Perspectives on the Experience of Forced Migration*, ed. Alastair Ager (London: Pinter, 1999), 136–68.

48. Wendy Brown, *Regulating Aversion: Tolerance in the Age of Identity and Empire* (Princeton: Princeton University Press, 2008).

49. As Blair insists, "those who feel that their faith compels them to act in a way destructive of mutual respect must be persuaded that this is a wrong reading of their faith." Blair, "Taking Faith Seriously."

50. Orsi, "Afterword," 148.

51. Samuel Moyn, "Soft Sells: On Liberal Internationalism," *Nation*, October 3, 2011, 41.

52. Robert M. Bosco, "Persistent Orientalisms: The Concept of Religion in International Relations," *Journal of International Relations and Development* 12, no. 1 (2009): 108. See also Robert M. Bosco, *Securing the Sacred: Religion, National Security, and the Western State* (Ann Arbor: University of Michigan Press, 2014).

53. "Modernity, an inconsistent and paradoxical combination of claims about nature and culture, passes itself off as the clean, enlightened alternative to a messy, primitivistic cosmology that confuses the natural with the cultural, mixes the animal with the human, mistakes the inanimate for the animate, and contaminates the moral with the prudential." Jane Bennett, *The Enchantment of Modern Life: Attachments, Crossings, and Ethics* (Princeton: Princeton University Press, 2001), 97–98.

54. Describing the rationale for the UK counterextremism program PREVENT, former director of the Office for Security and Counter-Terrorism at the Home Office Charles Farr observed that "there is a much larger group of people who feel a degree of negativity, if not hostility, towards the state, the country, the community, and who are, as it were, the pool in which terrorists will swim.... [U]nless we reach that group they may themselves *move into the very sharp end*, but even if they do not they will create an environment in which terrorists can operate with a degree of impunity that we do not want." Quoted in Rascoff, "Establishing Official Islam," 143.

55. Blair's statement to this effect was quoted in the introduction: "The purpose should be ... to start to treat this issue of religious extremism as an issue that is about religion as well as politics, to go to the roots of where a *false view of religion* is being promulgated and to make it a major item on the agenda of world leaders to combine effectively to combat it." Blair quoted in Helm, "Extremist Religion."

CHAPTER 3: INTERNATIONAL RELIGIOUS FREEDOM

1. Louis de Bernières, *Birds Without Wings* (New York: Vintage, 2004), 265. This novel is set in a village in rural southwestern Anatolia during the transition from Ottoman to Turkish governance amid the upheaval of World War I and the Greek-Turkish population exchange. It depicts the costs paid by local inhabitants as various aspects of their collective identities were assigned from above and then relied upon to determine their futures as citizens and subjects during the unstable and violent transition to modern Turkish statehood. This exchange between two childhood friends, one Muslim and the other Christian, took place on the eve of the former's departure to fight with Atatürk's forces.

2. For a list of possible presidential actions ranging from a private démarche to the suspension of US development or military assistance and to directing the US executive directors of international financial institutions to oppose loans benefiting the foreign government, agency, instrumentality, or official found by the president to be responsible for violations, see sec. 405 of the act. The president may also waive the application of the act if "the important national interest of the United States requires the exercise of such waiver authority." International Religious Freedom Act of 1998, HR 2431, 105th Cong., 2nd Sess. (1998), sec. 407.

3. The UN Office of the Special Rapporteur for Freedom of Religion or Belief has promoted religious freedom for three decades, focusing on state compliance with international and regional human rights conventions including the 1948 Universal Declaration of Human Rights (Article 18), the European and American human rights conventions of 1950 and 1978, the two human rights conventions of 1976, the 1981 UN Declaration on the Elimination of All Forms of Intolerance and of Discrimination Based on Religion or Belief, and regional human rights instruments such as the 1986 African Charter on Human and Peoples Rights and the 1990 Cairo Declaration on Human Rights in Islam. For a compelling argument that "Article 18 was not the result of some abstract overlapping consensus but rather a triumph for a few actors to whom its details mattered" and a "product of persistence, not consensus" see Linde Lindkvist, "The Politics of Article 18: Religious Liberty in the Universal Declaration of Human Rights," *Humanity: An International Journal of Human Rights, Humanitarianism, and Development* 4, no. 3 (2013): 430, 444. On this history, see also Årsheim, "Legal Secularism?."

4. Since 2009 the FCO has distributed a "toolkit" on "Freedom of Religion or Belief" to foreign service officers. The toolkit observes that "many conflicts find their roots in, or are exacerbated by, religious differences." UK Foreign and Commonwealth Office, "Freedom of Religion or Belief—How the FCO Can Help Promote Respect for This Human Right" (June 2010), https://www.gov.uk/government/uploads/system/uploads/attachment_data/file/35443/freedom-toolkit.pdf.

5. In 2012 the Italian foreign ministry signed a protocol of understanding with the city of Rome to create an Italian Oversight Committee for Religious Freedom to monitor religious freedoms both in Rome and globally. The chairman of the US Bishops' Ad Hoc committee for liberty, Archbishop William E. Lori, addressed the newly established observatory with a speech titled "Religious Liberty: God's Gift to all Nations is our Responsibility to Defend," quoted in Ann Schneible, "Global Zenit News," June 28, 2012, http://www.catholic.net/index.php?option=zenit&id=35107.

6. Launched in 2012, L'observatoire du Pluralisme des Cultures et des Religions (Pharos) issues "Pluralism Status Reports" and "Pharos Watch" reports on a country-by-country basis beginning in 2012 with Syria, India, Cuba, and Greece. http://www.pharos observatory.com.

7. The National Association of Evangelicals, which led the campaign for IRFA's passage in the 1990s, describes religious freedom as a God-given human right that occupies a privileged position above other rights claims. Elizabeth A. Castelli, "Theologizing Human Rights: Christian Activism and the Limits of Religious Freedom," in *Non-governmental Politics*, ed. Michel Feher, Gaëlle Krikorian, and Yates McKee (New York: Zone Books, 2007), 675.

8. See, for example, H. Knox Thames, Chris Seiple, and Amy Rowe, *International Religious Freedom Advocacy: A Guide to Organizations, Law, and NGOs* (Waco, TX: Baylor University Press, 2009).

9. Thomas F. Farr, "Religious Freedom Abroad," *First Things*, March 2012, 21–23.

10. The IRFA legislation attributes the failure to achieve religious freedom to a lack of social and cultural maturity: "In many nations where severe violations of religious freedom occur ... there is not sufficient cultural and social understanding of international norms of religious freedom." International Religious Freedom Act, sec. 501.

11. The Georgetown Berkley Center's Christianity & Freedom: Historical and Contemporary Perspectives project builds on a history of attempts to cement and to celebrate the alleged connection among Christianity, human rights, democratic pluralism, and political freedom. The project continues in the Christian triumphalist tradition of Lebanese philosopher, diplomat, and contributing author of the UDHR, Charles Malik, who in 1968 observed, "There is nothing that has been proclaimed about human rights in our age, nothing, for instance, in our Universal Declaration of Human Rights, which cannot be traced to the great Christian religious matrix. . . . Even those in our own day who carry on a non-religious or even on an anti-religious basis the burden of human rights with such evident passion and sincerity . . . owe their impulse, knowingly or unknowingly, to the original inspiration of this tradition." Quoted in Samuel Moyn, *The Last Utopia: Human Rights in History* (Cambridge, MA: Belknap, 2010), 127. On Malik, see further Lindkvist, "Politics of Article 18," 436–38.

12. Slotte, "Religious and the Secular in European Human Rights Discourse," 54. See also Paul Kahn, *The Cultural Study of Law: Reconstructing Legal Scholarship* (Chicago: University of Chicago Press, 1999).

13. Sarah Shields, "Mosul, the Ottoman Legacy, and the League of Nations," *International Journal of Contemporary Iraqi Studies* 3, no. 2 (2009): 218.

14. Hann and Pelkmans make a related point in an article on post-Soviet Central Asia in transition: "The promotion of religious human rights and the concomitant ideal of a 'religious marketplace' prioritise individual freedom of expression, but the unbridled religious market may lead in practice to social friction and new pathologies." Hann and Pelkmans, "Realigning Religion and Power in Central Asia," 1538.

15. Castelli, "Theologizing Human Rights," 684.

16. David Campbell, *National Deconstruction: Violence, Identity, and Justice in Bosnia* (Minneapolis: University of Minnesota Press, 1998).

17. Castelli, "Theologizing Human Rights," 684.

18. For the Comaroffs the commodification of ethnicity "has the curious capacity to conjure a collective imagining and to confer upon it social, political, and material currency—not to mention 'authenticity,' the spectre that haunts the commodification of culture everywhere." John L. Comaroff and Jean Comaroff, *Ethnicity, Inc.* (Chicago: University of Chicago Press, 2009), 10; Schielke, "Second Thoughts about the Anthropology of Islam," 4–5.

19. Michael Peletz, "Malaysia's Syariah Judiciary as Global Assemblage: Islamization, Corporatization, and Other Transformations in Context," *Comparative Studies in Society and History* 55, no. 3 (2013): 626.

20. Sophia Akram, "Cutting Borders: Ethnic Tensions and Burmese Refugees," *Fair Observer*, September 18, 2013, http://www.fairobserver.com/article/cutting-borders-ethnic-tensions-and-burmese-refugees.

21. "A document on Burmese languages dating to 1799 refers to Rooinga as "natives of Arakan [Rakhine]," but it is widely believed that most Rohingya came over from Bangladesh around 1821, when Britain annexed Myanmar as a province of British India and brought over migrant Muslim laborers." Kate Hodal, "Trapped Inside Burma's Refugee Camps, the Rohingya People Call for Recognition," *Guardian*, December 20, 2012, http://www.guardian.co.uk/world/2012/dec/20/burma-rohingya-muslim-refugee-camps.

22. Ibid.

23. Jonathan Head, "The Unending Plight of Burma's Unwanted Rohingyas," *BBC News*, July 1, 2013, http://www.bbc.co.uk/news/world-asia-23077537.

24. Elliott Prasse-Freeman, "Scapegoating in Burma," *Anthropology Today* 29, no. 4 (2013): 2. Thanks to Nicole Loring for helping me navigate academic accounts of developments in Burma.

25. "As Myanmar has liberalized, outsiders who had called for the US to overthrow the military dictatorship and install Aung San Suu Kyi have turned their attention to the plight of the Muslims, especially the Rohingya. They castigate Myanmar's current government and insist on making protection of Muslims a condition for better relations with the West." David I. Steinberg, "Myanmar: Buddhist-Muslim Tensions," *Sightings*, July 24, 2014, https://divinity.uchicago.edu/sightings/myanmar-buddhist-muslim-tensions-%E2%80%94-david-i-steinberg.

26. Head, "Unending Plight."

27. In an interview Wirathu explained that in his organization's name, 969, "the first 9 stands for the nine special attributes of the Lord Buddha and the 6 for the six special attributes of his Dhamma, or Buddhist Teachings, and the last 9 represents the nine special attributes of Buddhist Sanga [monks]. Those special attributes are the three Gems of the Buddha. In the past, the Buddha, Sangha, Dhamma and the wheel of Dhamma were Buddhists' sign. And the same goes for 969; it is another Buddhist sign." "Interview: Nationalist Monk U Wirathu Denies Role in Anti-Muslim Unrest," *Irrawaddy*, April 2, 2013, http://www.irrawaddy.org/interview/nationalist-monk-u-wirathu-denies-role-in-anti-muslim-unrest.html.

28. According to one account, "the 969 movement is controlled by disgruntled hardliners from the previous junta, who are fomenting unrest to derail the reforms and foil an election landslide by Suu Kyi's NLD." Andrew R. C. Marshall, "Myanmar Gives Official Blessing to Anti-Muslim Monks," Reuters, June 27, 2013, http://www.reuters.com/article/2013/06/27/us-myanmar-969-specialreport-idUSBRE95Q04720130627.

29. Cited in ibid.

30. Benjamin Schonthal, "The 'Muslim Other' in Myanmar and Sri Lanka," in *Islam and the State in Myanmar: Muslim-Buddhist Relations and the Politics of Belonging*, ed. Melissa Crouch (in progress).

31. "Eventually, even traditional Buddhists were marginalized, as dictators employed a grotesque parody of their religion to manipulate the masses. The leaders portrayed themselves as devout, but showed no compassion in brutally repressing minorities and dissidents." Aung Zaw, "Are Myanmar's Hopes Fading?," *New York Times*, April 24, 2013, http://www.nytimes.com/2013/04/25/opinion/will-hatred-kill-the-dream-of-a-peaceful-democratic-myanmar.html?_r=0.

32. Ibid.

33. Martin Smith, "Ethnic Politics in Myanmar: A Year of Tension and Anticipation," *Journal of Southeast Asian Affairs* 2010 (2010): 214–15.

34. Ibid., 224.

35. Prasse-Freeman, "Scapegoating in Burma," 2; Jared Ferrie, "Why Myanmar's Rohingya Are Forced to Say They Are Bengali," *Christian Science Monitor*, June 2, 2013, http://www.csmonitor.com/World/Asia-Pacific/2013/0602/Why-Myanmar-s-Rohingya-are-forced-to-say-they-are-Bengali.

36. Ibid.
37. Smith, "Ethnic Politics in Myanmar," 223. SPDC is the State Peace and Development Council, known formerly as the SLORC, State Law and Order Restoration Council.
38. Ferrie, "Why Myanmar's Rohingya Are Forced."
39. Prasse-Freeman, "Scapegoating in Burma," 3.
40. John Campbell, "Africa Update" (panel presentation, Seventh Annual Religion and Foreign Policy Summer Workshop, New York, June 25, 2013).
41. William E. Connolly, *The Ethos of Pluralization* (Minneapolis: University of Minnesota Press, 1995), 167.
42. Stringer, *Discourses on Religious Diversity*, 137.
43. US Agency for International Development, "Religion, Conflict and Peacebuilding: An Introductory Program Guide" (Washington, DC: Office of Conflict Management and Mitigation, Bureau for Democracy, Conflict, and Humanitarian Assistance, 2009), 11, emphasis added.
44. David S. Cloud and Jeff Gerth, "Muslim Scholars Were Paid to Aid U.S. Propaganda," *New York Times*, January 2, 2006, http://www.nytimes.com/2006/01/02/politics/02 propaganda.html?_r=0.
45. Jessica Powley Hayden, "Mullahs on a Bus: The Establishment Clause and U.S. Foreign Aid," *Georgetown Law Journal* 95 (2006): 171–206. There is however a significant gap between official First Amendment jurisprudence as represented by Hayden and others and what is actually occurring on the ground in the United States, which has involved various forms of cooperation and collaboration between law enforcement and religious authorities, suggesting less divergence between US domestic and international activities than is often assumed. Thanks to Winni Sullivan for this clarification.
46. UK Foreign and Commonwealth Office, "Freedom of Religion or Belief," 17.
47. Néstor Quiroa, "The Popol Vuh and the Dominican Religious Extirpation in Highland Guatemala: Prologues and Annotations of Fr. Francisco Ximénez," *Americas* 67, no. 4 (2011): 468. The story is more complicated because the Popol Vuh as we know it is itself, according to Quiroa, "the product of a colonial encounter between Maya and European civilization." Fr. Francisco Ximénez's treatise is "an expression of the Dominican evangelization campaign at the beginning of the eighteenth century—a tool intended to destroy native religion in order to replace it with European Christianity." Ibid., 472, 479.
48. Dianne Post, "Land, Life, and Honor: Guatemala's Women in Resistance," *Fair Observer*, October 4, 2013, http://www.fairobserver.com/article/land-life-honor-guatemala -women-resistance.
49. Greg Johnson, *Sacred Claims: Repatriation and Living Tradition* (Charlottesville: University of Virginia Press, 2007); Huston Smith, *A Seat at the Table: Huston Smith in Conversation with Native Americans on Religious Freedom*, ed. Phil Cousineau (Berkeley: University of California Press, 2005).
50. Tisa Wenger, *We Have a Religion: The 1920s Pueblo Indian Dance Controversy and American Religious Freedom* (Chapel Hill: University of North Carolina Press, 2009).
51. Noah Salomon and Jeremy F. Walton, "Religious Criticism, Secular Criticism, and the 'Critical Study of Religion': Lessons from the Study of Islam," in *The Cambridge Companion to Religious Studies*, ed. Robert A. Orsi (Cambridge: Cambridge University Press, 2012), 406.

52. Ambassador Campbell observed that although adherents to African traditional religions had previously been in the majority in Nigeria, today many have "both faiths" such as Yoruba/Christian. Campbell, "Africa Update."

53. Noah Salomon, "Freeing Religion at the Birth of South Sudan," *Immanent Frame*, April 12, 2012, http://blogs.ssrc.org/tif/2012/04/12/freeing-religion-at-the-birth-of-south -sudan/.

54. Rosalind I. J. Hackett, "Traditional, African, Religious, Freedom?" in Sullivan et al., *Politics of Religious Freedom*, 90–91, 96. See further David Chidester, *Wild Religion: Tracking the Sacred in South Africa* (Berkeley: University of California Press, 2012) and Makau Mutua, *Human Rights: A Political and Cultural Critique* (Philadelphia: University of Pennsylvania Press, 2008). Mutua argued that "liberal generic protection of religious freedoms" favors mission-related religions and is inimical to indigenous African religions and lifestyles. Quoted in Hackett, 91.

55. Adcock, *Limits of Tolerance*, 14, 20, 121, 145, 163. As Adcock concludes, "Tolerance supported a 'secular majoritarianism' that served to disempower and minoritize non-caste-Hindus by a combined strategy of encompassment and exclusion." Ibid., 168. Makdisi argues along related lines that the discourse of sectarianism under the Ottomans in late nineteenth-century Mount Lebanon "masked a final restoration of an elitist social order in Mount Lebanon and marked the end of a genuinely popular, if always ambivalent, participation in politics." Ussama Makdisi, *The Culture of Sectarianism: Community, History, and Violence in Nineteenth-Century Ottoman Lebanon* (Berkeley: University of California Press, 2000), 147.

56. For an analysis of the role of Japanese political theorists, constitutional scholars, and scholars of religion in the construction of new theories of religious freedom as a human right in US-occupied Japan, see Jolyon Thomas, "Japan's Preoccupation with Religious Freedom" (Ph.D. thesis, Department of Religion, Princeton University, 2014). On the role of Japanese intellectuals, policymakers, and diplomats in producing a category of religion in Japan during the Meiji epoch "that carved out a private space for belief in a set of officially recognized religions, but also embedded Shinto in the very structure of the state and exiled various 'superstitions' beyond the sphere of tolerance," see Josephson, *Invention of Religion in Japan*, 257.

57. The ReligioWest research project, directed by Olivier Roy and based at the European University Institute, is studying the processes associated with the "formatting" of religion in Europe. http://www.eui.eu/Projects/ReligioWest/Home.aspx.

58. An example is the tense relationship between the Catholic Church and the southern Italian popular religion of Italian Harlem's Catholic community as described by Robert Orsi, who observes that the Church's "cultural distaste for the immigrants amounted to an existential rejection of their whole value system." Orsi, *Madonna of 115th Street*, 189.

59. "The people knew, of course, that the leaders of the American church downtown frowned upon their devotion, upon this public display of a Catholicism that was viewed as pagan and primitive." Ibid., 220–21.

60. Amahl Bishara, "Covering the Christians of the Holy Land," *Middle East Report* 267 (Summer 2013): 14.

61. On recognition as a political good, see the classic statement by Charles Taylor, *Multiculturalism and "The Politics of Recognition": An Essay with Commentary*, ed. Amy Gutmann (Princeton: Princeton University Press, 1992).

62. Patchen Markell, *Bound by Recognition* (Princeton: Princeton University Press, 2003).
63. Elizabeth Povinelli, *The Cunning of Recognition: Indigenous Alterities and the Making of Australian Multiculturalism* (Durham, NC: Duke University Press, 2002).
64. Maria Birnbaum, "Becoming Recognizable: Postcolonial Independence and the Reification of Religion in International Relations" (Ph.D. thesis, European University Institute, Florence, 2015).
65. "It is these missionary tasks, the discourse that produces them, and the organizations that represent them that constitute what I call the *Gay International*." Joseph A. Massad, "Re-orienting Desire: The Gay International and the Arab World," *Public Culture* 14, no. 2 (2002): 362. Thanks to Evren Savci and Noah Salomon for bringing this comparison to my attention.
66. "In contradistinction to the liberatory claims made by the Gay International in relation to what it posits as an always already homosexualized population, I argue that it is the discourse of the Gay International that both produces homosexuals, as well as gays and lesbians, where they do not exist, and represses same-sex desires and practices that refuse to be assimilated into its sexual epistemology." Ibid., 363.
67. A longer version of this section appears as "Believing in Religious Freedom," in Sullivan et al., *Politics of Religious Freedom*, and a shorter one on the *Immanent Frame*, March 1, 2012, http://blogs.ssrc.org/tif/2012/03/01/believing-in-religious-freedom/.
68. "Freedom in this sense—and this market-based sense of freedom becomes dominant in modernity—is not the repression of activity, but it is the regulated enactment of activity along particular lines." Janet R. Jakobsen, "Sex + Freedom = Regulation. Why?," *Social Text* 23, nos. 3/4 (2005): 285.
69. "Freedom of religion becomes important when you profess a certain religion. This kind of consciousness does not exist in the vast majority of Japanese. Most die without professing a certain religion. In other words, we have to start by learning the very basics, what is meant by believing in religion." Hiroi Takase, "Religious Freedom and the New Millennium" (address, International Coalition for Religious Freedom Conference, Takushoku University, Tokyo, May 23–25, 1998), http://religiousfreedom.com/index.php?option=com_content&view=article&id=375&Itemid=18. On the history of the process through which Japanese officials invented religion in Japan, see Josephson, *Invention of Religion in Japan*, showing that "defining religion in Japan was a politically charged, boundary-drawing exercise that extensively reclassified the inherited materials of Buddhism, Confucianism, and Shinto." Josephson further argues that "looking at the formation of religion in Japan not only reveals its global diplomatic contours but also shows how the discourse of religion is woven into the fabric of modernity and how guarantees of religious toleration function to increase state power and to reconfigure entire cultural systems." Ibid., 2, 4.
70. UK Foreign and Commonwealth Office, "Freedom of Religion or Belief," 4. The FCO guidelines continue, "The following are examples of beliefs considered to fall within the protection of this freedom: druidism, veganism, pacifism, the divine light mission, scientology, Krishna Consciousness Movement, humanism, atheism and agnosticism." Ibid., 4.
71. Constance M. Furey, "Body, Society, and Subjectivity in Religious Studies," *Journal of the American Academy of Religion* 80, no. 1 (March 2012): 8–9.
72. Sherwood, "On the Freedom of the Concepts," 34. She continues, "How ironic that even

as the contemporary field of religious studies has striven for a law court model of religion based on witnessing and experience, law—oblivious to this—has reinstated and reinvigorated the old category of belief." Ibid., 35.

73. Jon Butler, "Disquieted History in A Secular Age," in Warner, VanAntwerpen, and Calhoun, *Varieties of Secularism in a Secular Age*, 206–7. Butler goes on to say, "The presence in modern times of choice to believe, as well as choice about what to believe, is the modern representation of long difficulties and complexities of belief itself, certainly in the West." Ibid., 215.

74. Ibid., 211.

75. T. M. Luhrmann, "Belief Is the Least Part of Faith," *New York Times*, May 29, 2013, http://www.nytimes.com/2013/05/30/opinion/luhrmann-belief-is-the-least-part-of-faith.html?emc=eta1&_r=0.

76. Orsi, *Between Heaven and Earth*, 18.

77. At least some of this normative force can be attributed to the specific historical and political context in which Article 18 of the UDHR emerged, including, as Linde Lindkvist has shown, the influence of Christian missionaries whose interests lay in advancing a version of religious freedom that stressed the freedom to change one's religion. As Lindkvist concludes, "The stress on the freedom of religious choice and the freedom to change was not derived from an abstract notion of what religious liberty is but rather stemmed from tangible concerns voiced by missionary organizations. By having this component of religious liberty recognized as a universal human right, they sought international legitimacy for those forces that worked to transform the political and religious landscapes of 'Mohammedan societies.'" Lindkvist, "Politics of Article 18," 441–42.

78. Talal Asad, "Thinking about Religion, Belief, and Politics," in Orsi, *Cambridge Companion to Religious Studies*, 40.

79. Ibid., 43.

80. Donald S. Lopez, Jr., "Belief," in *Critical Terms for Religious Studies*, ed. Mark C. Taylor (Chicago: University of Chicago Press, 1998), 31.

81. Asad, "Thinking about Religion, Belief, and Politics," 44, citing Dorothea Weltecke, "Beyond Religion: On the Lack of Belief during the Central and Late Middle Ages," in *Religion and Its Other: Secular and Sacral Concepts in Interaction*, ed. Heike Bock, Jörg Feuchter, and Michi Knecht (Frankfurt: Campus Verlag, 2008).

82. Ibid., 46–47.

83. Sherwood, "On the Freedom of the Concepts," 41.

84. William Cavanaugh, *The Myth of Religious Violence: Secular Ideology and the Roots of Modern Conflict* (New York: Oxford University Press, 2009), 17.

85. Malcolm Evans, "Advancing Freedom of Religion or Belief: Agendas for Change" (Lambeth Inter Faith Lecture, London, June 8, 2011). See further Malcolm Evans, *Religious Liberty and International Law in Europe* (Cambridge: Cambridge University Press, 1997).

86. Evans, "Advancing Freedom of Religion or Belief."

87. Orsi, *Between Heaven and Earth*, 18.

88. Thanks to Noah Salomon for helping me think through these issues.

89. "The question is this: What are to count as *religious* beliefs? Should beliefs denounced by the Medieval Latin Church as *superstitio* (wrongheadedness) therefore be regarded as secular beliefs? Or should they be pronounced religious on the criteria provided by late-

Enlightenment critics for whom all religion was superstition? Is the intention to carry out a particular act always crucial to its religiosity? If so, how and by whom is that to be judged?" Asad, "Thinking about Religion, Belief, and Politics," 46.

90. Slotte, "Religious and the Secular," 56.

91. Thanks to Yvonne Sherwood for her contributions to this section.

92. Lila Abu-Lughod, "Against Universals: The Dialects of (Women's) Human Rights and Human Capabilities," in *Rethinking the Human*, ed. J. Michelle Molina and Donald K. Swearer (Cambridge, MA: Harvard University Press, 2010), 85.

93. Suzan Johnson Cook, "Religious Tolerance at Home and Abroad" (panel presentation, Seventh Annual Religion and Foreign Policy Summer Workshop, New York, June 25, 2013).

94. Sherwood, "On the Freedom of the Concepts," 39.

95. Talal Asad, *Genealogies of Religion: Discipline and Reasons of Power in Christianity and Islam* (Baltimore: Johns Hopkins University Press, 1993), 41.

96. Webb Keane, *Christian Moderns: Freedom and Fetish in the Mission Encounter* (Berkeley: University of California Press, 2007), 67.

97. Thomas F. Farr, *World of Faith and Freedom: Why International Religious Liberty Is Vital to American National Security* (Oxford: Oxford University Press, 2008).

98. William Inboden, "Religious Freedom and National Security," *Hoover Institution Policy Review*, no. 175 (2012), http://www.hoover.org/research/religious-freedom-and-national -security.

99. For a history of the improvised arrangements through which ordinary early modern Europeans sometimes coexisted peacefully across lines of social and religious difference without religious freedom, see Benjamin J. Kaplan, *Divided by Faith: Religious Conflict and the Practice of Toleration in Early Modern Europe* (Cambridge, MA: Belknap, 2007).

100. Lars Tønder, *Tolerance: A Sensorial Orientation to Politics* (Oxford: Oxford University Press, 2013), 55.

101. Asad's observation is about the Universal Declaration of Human Rights (UDHR). He goes on to point out that, in privileging the state's (or associations thereof) norm-defining function, the UDHR encourages the thought that "the authority of norms corresponds to the political force that supports them as law." Talal Asad, *Formations of the Secular: Christianity, Islam, Modernity* (Stanford: Stanford University Press, 2003), 138.

CHAPTER 4: RELIGIOUS ENGAGEMENT

1. For the epigraphs, see US Information and Education Exchange, quoted in Jonathan P. Herzog, *The Spiritual-Industrial Complex: America's Religious Battle Against Communism in the Early Cold War* (Oxford: Oxford University Press, 2011), 128; and World Learning, "Fostering Religious Harmony in Albania: Final Report" (June 30, 2007), http://pdf .usaid.gov/pdf_docs/PDACK058.pdf. For background on the creation of the Office of Faith-Based Community Initiatives, see Austin Dacey, "Why Is the State Department Opening an Office of 'Religious Engagement?,'" *Religion Dispatches*, August 8, 2013, http://religiondispatches.org/why-is-the-state-department-opening-an-office-of -religious-engagement/.

2. Melissa Rogers, director of the White House Office of Faith-Based and Neighborhood Partnerships, "Comments at the Launch of the Office of Faith-Based Community Initiatives" (August 7, 2013), http://www.state.gov/secretary/remarks/2013/08/212781.htm. According to former executive director of the White House Office of Faith-based and Neighborhood Partnerships Josh DuBois, "faith leaders are among the most trusted members of their society around the world ... and religious networks often reach places where we are not, especially in remote, difficult to access locations, and faith leaders often wield credibility that government actors lack." Quoted in Robert T. Lalka, "Engaging Faith-Based Communities on Foreign Policy Objectives," *DipNote*, April 1, 2011, http://blogs.state.gov/stories/2011/04/01/engaging-faith-based-communities-foreign -policy-objectives#sthash.Kind5R8c.dpuf.

3. "As a result of this work, we've seen new courses in religious engagement at the Foreign Service Institute, new efforts on religion and global affairs at the State Department, and a renewed focus on the intersection of religion and foreign policy across the United States Government." Joshua DuBois, "The White House, Religion, and Global Affairs" (Washington, DC: Office of Faith-based and Neighborhood Partnerships, July 11, 2011), http://www.whitehouse.gov/blog/2011/07/11/white-house-religion-and-global-affairs.

4. US Department of State, "US Strategy on Religious Leader and Faith Community Engagement" (n.d.), http://www.state.gov/s/rga/strategy/.

5. US Department of Homeland Security, "Faith-Based Security and Communications Advisory Committee" (Washington, DC: Homeland Security Advisory Council, 2012), http://www.dhs.gov/xlibrary/assets/hsac/hsac-faith-based-security-and-communications -advisory-committee-final-report-may-2012.pdf.

6. The 2010 report of the US President's Advisory Council on Faith-Based and Neighborhood Partnerships notes that "the U.S. Government currently partners with a wide range of secular entities to achieve its domestic and international objectives. The Federal Government also recognizes that religiously affiliated persons, communities, specialized agencies, and multireligious bodies can be vital partners in both domestic and international affairs." President's Advisory Council on Faith-Based and Neighborhood Partnerships, "New Era of Partnerships," 71, http://www.whitehouse.gov/sites/default/files /microsites/ofbnp-council-final-report.pdf.

7. Douglas Johnston and Cynthia Sampson, eds., *Religion, the Missing Dimension of Statecraft* (Oxford: Oxford University Press, 1995).

8. US Agency for International Development Bosnia-Herzegovina, World Conference of Religions for Peace, Inter-Religious Action for Tolerance and Co-Existence in the Balkans, "Final Narrative Report, March 1, 2004–March 31, 2005" (New York: World Conference of Religions for Peace, June 2005), http://pdf.usaid.gov/pdf_docs/pdacd982.pdf.

9. Courtney Bender, "Power of Pluralist Thinking," 75.

10. Herzog discusses the understanding of the United States as the leader of the free world and the world's greatest champion of free religion in *Spiritual-Industrial Complex*, 127. For a critique of this account, see David Sehat, *The Myth of American Religious Freedom* (Oxford: Oxford University Press, 2011). For a defense of special treatment for religion in American constitutional law under the rubric of religious neutrality, see chap. 4 of Andrew Koppelman, *Defending American Religious Neutrality* (Cambridge, MA: Harvard University Press, 2013); for an opposing viewpoint, see Brian Leiter, *Why Tolerate Religion?* (Princeton: Princeton University Press, 2012).

11. The US Army Human Terrain System (HTS) was a response to combat brigade commanders' demand for "operationally relevant cultural knowledge." The HTS program sent teams of three anthropologists and three military members (known as "human terrain teams") into the field to help soldiers counter insurgents. Bill Stamets, "Anthropologists at War," *In These Times*, June 19, 2008, http://inthesetimes.com/article /3749/anthropologists_at_war/.

12. As this book demonstrates, building on my earlier work and that of others, the secularization thesis is mistaken, while at the same time an overreliance on religion as a transhistorical and transcultural category is also deeply problematic.

13. For a cultural history of American empire during a period in which the United States colonized Hawaii, Samoa, the Philippines, and Guam (1876–1917), see Matthew Frye Jacobson, *Barbarian Virtues: The United States Encounters Foreign Peoples at Home and Abroad* (New York: Hill & Wang, 2000).

14. Elizabeth Shakman Hurd, "Religious Freedom, American-Style," *Quaderni di Diritto e Politica Ecclesiastica*, no. 1 (April 2014): 231–42.

15. Sarah E. Ruble, *The Gospel of Freedom and Power: Protestant Missionaries in American Culture after World War II* (Chapel Hill: University of North Carolina Press, 2014); Ussama Makdisi, *Artillery of Heaven: American Missionaries and the Failed Conversion of the Middle East* (Ithaca, NY: Cornell University Press, 2009); Tracy Fessenden, *Culture and Redemption: Religion, the Secular, and American Literature* (Princeton: Princeton University Press, 2007); and Stuart Creighton Miller, *"Benevolent Assimilation": The American Conquest of the Philippines, 1899–1903* (New Haven: Yale University Press, 1984).

16. State-sponsored religious reform is also not unique to the United States. An example are the religious reforms undertaken in Thailand in the mid-nineteenth century, when successive royal regimes introduced comprehensive schemes to "purify" Buddhism, which, among other objectives, underscored the importance of texts and sought to remove astrology, spirits, exorcism, and cosmology from Thai practices. See Donald K. Swearer, "Center and Periphery: Buddhism and Politics in Modern Thailand," in *Buddhism and Politics in Twentieth Century Asia*, ed. Ian Harris (London: Continuum, 2001), 194–228.

17. "One of the most important developments in Cold War historiography of late is to show, even as the US Supreme Court turned to impose a 'wall of separation' between church and state, how the country's self-avowed Christian statesmen viewed their task as a holy crusade against secularism." Samuel Moyn, "From Communist to Muslim: European Human Rights, the Cold War, and Religious Liberty," *South Atlantic Quarterly* 113, no. 1 (2014): 69. For a defense of what Thomas Farr refers to as "the spiritual side of containment," see William Inboden, *Religion and American Foreign Policy, 1945–1960: The Soul of Containment* (Cambridge: Cambridge University Press, 2008). Thomas F. Farr, "Cold War Religion," *First Things*, June 2009, http://www.firstthings.com/article/2009/06 /cold-war-religion.

18. Herzog, *Spiritual-Industrial Complex*, 127. As Moyn explains, "From its origins until a few decades ago, the norm [religious freedom]—including in its form as an international human right codified in the middle of the twentieth century—frequently served as a Christian principle of discrimination. Its purpose was to secure a social and global tilt not against Islam but against secularism." Moyn, "From Communist to Muslim," 67.

19. Herzog, *Spiritual-Industrial Complex*, 126.

20. According to Farr, Myron Taylor, Truman's unofficial envoy to the Holy See, "shared

Truman's vision of a pan-Christian and pan-religious front against communism, and he spent years working covertly with the Vatican and lobbying powerful Protestant organizations, such as the World Council of Churches, to cooperate with Catholics in the Cold War." Farr, "Cold War Religion."

21. Herzog, *Spiritual-Industrial Complex*, 127. Serving on the committee were Monsignor Thomas J. McCarthy of the National Catholic Welfare Council, Reverend E. N. Pruden of the American Baptist Convention, and Isaac Franck of the Washington Jewish Council. Cardinal Spellman was also involved. Ibid., 245n51.

22. Quoted in Herzog, *Spiritual-Industrial Complex*, 127. Returning to the epigraph to this chapter, the report concluded that "if the threat of Communism is to be met effectively, a moral and spiritual offensive is necessary" (128).

23. Ibid., 128. Reinhold Niebuhr also contributed to Voice of America programming at the time.

24. Herzog, *Spiritual-Industrial Complex*, 151. "The CPL strived to convince Americans that God was the guarantor of true freedom." The committee's efforts in this area are similar to the Fortnight for Freedom campaign of the US Conference of Catholic Bishops, described on the USCCB website as follows: "Culminating on Independence Day, this special period of prayer, study, catechesis, and public action will emphasize both our Christian and American heritage of liberty. Dioceses and parishes around the country have scheduled special events that support a great national campaign of teaching and witness for religious liberty." USCCB, "Fortnight for Freedom" (2014), http://www .usccb.org/issues-and-action/religious-liberty/fortnight-for-freedom/.

25. Herzog, *Spiritual-Industrial Complex*, 163. Herzog emphasizes that during the Cold War, attempts to link US national identity and Christianity/moral order not only were right-wing talking points but also came from moderates like Truman and liberals like Niebuhr. Ibid., 197.

26. Mark Hulsether, "Review of *Religion and American Foreign Policy, 1945–1960: The Soul of Containment,* by William Inboden." *American Studies*, Vol. 51, nos. 1–2 (2010): 127.

27. Quoted in Farr, "Cold War Religion."

28. Herzog, *Spiritual-Industrial Complex*, 134.

29. Seth Jacobs, *America's Miracle Man in Vietnam: Ngo Dinh Diem, Religion, Race, and U.S. Intervention in Southeast Asia* (Durham, NC: Duke University Press, 2005), 51.

30. See Ian Harris, *Cambodian Buddhism: History and Practice* (Honolulu: University of Hawaii Press, 2005), chap. 7 and Martin Stuart-Fox and Rod Bucknell, "Politicization of the Buddhist Sangha in Laos," *Journal of Southeast Asian Studies* 13, no. 1 (1982): 60–80. Thanks to Ben Schonthal for the references.

31. David E. Kaplan, "Hearts, Minds, and Dollars," *U.S. News & World Report*, April 17, 2005, http://www.globalissues.org/article/584/hearts-minds-and-dollars.

32. There was no conflict at the time that RelHarmony began its work. Presumably to justify its existence in a place where there is no such conflict, the Project's final report cites the Albanian writer Ismail Kadare, who observes that "the history of religious harmony in Albania is not an idyllic history. In its essence it has always been and remains dramatic. Nowadays, in democratic Albania, all the dangers that have been overcome are still potential. Religious harmony is as majestic an establishment as it is a fragile one. The first serious radicalism of one of the faiths is sufficient for the establishment to come down." World Learning, "Fostering Religious Harmony in Albania," 2.

33. Ibid., i.

34. Ibid., 19.

35. USAID worked with other donors in a complex network of interconnected projects. For a discussion of the Bosnian Women's Working Group (a subgroup of the Inter-Religious Councils of Bosnia and Kosovo also engaged by RelHarmony) that adopts many of the same presuppositions about the irenic qualities of religion on which the program itself is based, see Pauline C. H. Kollantai, "Finding a Path to a Common Future: Religion and Cosmopolitanism in the Context of Bosnia-Herzegovina," in *Cosmopolitanism, Religion and the Public Sphere*, ed. Maria Rovisco and Sebastian Kim (New York: Routledge, 2014), 48–67.

36. "In Albania, no laws regulate the relationship between religious communities and the state. Instead, the constitution calls for the establishment of agreements to define state-religious relations. The State Committee on Cults (a government established group) received a grant to form an Inter-Ministerial Working Group to draft three separate agreements that faith communities signed as well as a template agreement that the state can sign with interested religious communities. The agreements will regulate the relationship between religious communities and the state in the fields of culture, education, property, taxes, customs, religious matters, and other key issues. Agreements have been approved by the Government of Albania and are awaiting formal approval through Parliament." USAID, "Religion, Conflict and Peacebuilding," 21.

37. World Learning, "Fostering Religious Harmony in Albania," 20–21. According to the final report, the film titled *Living Together* "shows that Albanian national identity is based on interfaith harmony and the common values of all faiths merge together in shaping the spiritual dimension of the Albanian nation." Ibid., 20.

38. Ibid., 17.

39. Ibid., 27.

40. Courtney Bender, "Secularism and Pluralism" (unpublished manuscript, June 2012), 20.

41. As Dacey points out, "when the U.S. government bestows high-level diplomatic attention instead on select (typically male, adult, and non-democratically appointed) spokespersons, it aids them in consolidating their own power and authority within their communities." Dacey, "Why Is the State Department Opening an Office of 'Religious Engagement?'"

42. Bender, "Power of Pluralist Thinking," 71.

43. World Learning, "Fostering Religious Harmony in Albania," 21.

44. USAID, "Religion, Conflict and Peacebuilding," 10; see also 27–30 on the KEDEM project.

45. "Street Law courses are being taught to male and female students in Islamic institutes and madrasas, most of whom are between the ages of 15–18, although there are adult and some younger students as well. Full-time madrasa instruction is open to any student who has completed the compulsory nine years of basic education. Islamic Institutes in Kyrgyzstan serve students who have completed their secondary, as well as basic education. To date, the program has trained 126 students (90 male and 36 female). The program continues to grow and in February 2007 was given permission from religious leaders to begin teaching in additional madrasas. The program also began working in an Islamic NGO that provides Qur'anic instruction for adults." Ibid., 17.

46. Robert W. Hefner and Krishna Kumar, "Summary Assessment of the Islam and Civil

Society Program in Indonesia: Promoting Democracy and Pluralism in the Muslim World," PPC Evaluation Brief 13 (Washington, DC: USAID, Bureau for Policy and Program Coordination, February 2006).

47. US Agency for International Development Bosnia-Herzegovina, World Conference of Religions for Peace, "Inter-Religious Action for Tolerance," 3.

48. The project's final report notes that several groups, including the Catholic Church and the Orthodox community, refused to participate in the council at various times for political reasons. The Orthodox community withdrew in protest against a NATO raid on an Orthodox parish in an attempt to apprehend Radovan Karadic that severely injured a priest and his son and destroyed their home. The Catholic Church froze its status within the council to protest a refusal by other religious leaders to support an agreement between the state and Vatican City that would have given the Catholic community additional rights and privileges. Ibid.

49. In describing the ubiquity of this model, Bender observes that "even the staunchest sociological critics of the religious economies models share its basic premise—namely that a plurality of religious groups is needed to indicate a thriving religious freedom, and that the American example presents a clear case of actually free religion." Bender, "Power of Pluralist Thinking," 71. See also Rick Moore, "The Genres of Religious Freedom: Creating Discourses on Religion at the State Department," in *History, Time, Meaning and Memory: Ideas for the Sociology of Religion*, ed. Barbara Jones Denison (Leiden: Brill, 2011), 223–53.

50. "The U.S. does not have a church, in the church-state sense, because American Christianity, as well as the other US-based religious communities that have adopted its institutional forms, have been dominated historically by the free-church model of the antinomian branch of the Reformation, through an explicit rejection of the Church of England—and later in a negative response to Catholic immigration." Lori G. Beaman and Winnifred Fallers Sullivan, "Neighbo(u)rly Misreadings and Misconstruals: A Cross-Border Conversation," in Beaman and Sullivan, *Varieties of Religious Establishment*, 3.

51. World Learning, "Fostering Religious Harmony in Albania," 31–32.

52. USAID, "Religion, Conflict and Peacebuilding," 22.

53. Ibid., 12.

54. Ibid., 13, emphasis added.

55. Hurd, "Religious Freedom, American-Style."

56. The US Army Chaplain Corps was founded July 29, 1775, with a general order from George Washington. Rev. William Emerson, the grandfather of Ralph Waldo Emerson, became the first recognized chaplain of the American Army as he ministered to soldiers on the battlefield of Lexington and Concord, Massachusetts, in April 1775. Gary Sheftick, "Chaplain Corps Turns 236 with New Strength" (July 28, 2011), http://www.army.mil/article/62568/Chaplain_Corps_turns_236_with_new_strength/.

57. Army chaplains are commissioned officers that are formally endorsed as chaplains by their faith group. The Department of Defense Chaplain's Board approves endorsees, and applications are made individually to the service the chaplain candidate wishes to join.

58. U.S. Navy, Religious Ministry in the U.S. Navy, Navy Warfare Publication (NWP) 1–05 (Newport, RI: Department of the Navy, August 2003), para. 5.2.7, quoted in George

Adams, "Chaplains as Liaisons with Religious Leaders," *Peaceworks*, no. 56 (2006): 15, http://www.usip.org/publications/chaplains-liaisons-religious-leaders-lessons-iraq-and-afghanistan.

59. Chaplains provide "religious services to persons who would not otherwise be able to access the preferred free market in religious options," including "soldiers, prisoners, and other government personnel who are away from their home communities on government business." Winnifred Fallers Sullivan, "After Secularism: Governing through Spiritual Care" (paper, Center for Law and Public Affairs, Princeton University, March 7, 2011), 19.

60. *Baz v. Walters*, 782 F.2d 701 (1986).

61. *Larsen v. United States Navy*, 486 F. Supp. 2d 11, 18 (D.D.C. 2007).

62. Pauletta Otis, "An Overview of the U.S. Military Chaplaincy: A Ministry of Presence and Practice," *Review of Faith and International Affairs* 7, no. 4 (2009): 3–15.

63. Adams, "Chaplains as Liaisons," 13.

64. Stacey Gutkowski and George Wilkes, "Changing Chaplaincy: A Contribution to Debate over the Roles of US and British Military Chaplains in Afghanistan," *Religion, State, and Society* 30, no. 1 (2011): 111, quoting US Joint Chiefs of Staff, Religious Affairs in Joint Operations (Washington, DC: Office of the US Chief of Chaplains, Joint Publication 1–05, November 13, 2009): chap. 3, 5.

65. Adams, "Chaplains as Liaisons," 6.

66. Ibid., 43.

67. The Commander's Emergency Response Program "enables local commanders in Afghanistan and Iraq to respond with a nonlethal weapon to urgent, small-scale, humanitarian relief, and reconstruction projects and services that immediately assist the indigenous population and that the local population or government can sustain." http://www.globalsecurity.org/military/library/report/call/call_09-27-ch04.htm.

68. Adams, "Chaplains as Liaisons," 16–17. "Unquestionably, a chaplain's primary responsibility is to provide for the free exercise of religion for soldiers, sailors, airmen, and marines, their families, and other authorized personnel. Nevertheless, communicating with local religious leaders in a commander's area of responsibility (AOR) for the purpose of establishing mutual trust and understanding also is within the scope of a chaplain's function." Ibid., 12–13.

69. Brian Mockenhaupt, "Enlisting Allah," *Atlantic*, July 24, 2011, http://www.theatlantic.com/magazine/archive/2011/09/enlisting-allah/308597/.

70. Rich Bartell, "U.S. Army Africa Chaplains Teach Resiliency in Africa," March 6, 2012, http://www.army.mil/article/75110/U_S__Army_Africa_chaplains_teach_resiliency_in_Africa/.

71. Danan, "Mixed Blessings," 25, emphasis added, quoting Major Laura Geldhof et al., "Intelligent Design: COIN Operations and Intelligence Collection and Analysis," *Military Review*, September/October 2006, reprinted from the original publication in *Special Warfare*, May/June 2006.

72. In the words of former DIA director Lt. Gen. Clapper, "In the threat environment we're in now, understanding village dynamics is critical." Quoted in Danan, "Mixed Blessings," 24.

73. "Since 1998 the Department of Defense's share of U.S. Official Development Assistance

increased from 3.5 percent to 22 percent. The Department of Defense has dramatically expanded its relief, development, and reconstruction assistance through programs such as Section 1207, the Commanders' Emergency Response Program (CERP), and the Combatant Commanders' Initiative Fund, as well as through the activities of the regional combatant commands, particularly AFRICOM and SOUTHCOM, and the Provincial Reconstruction Teams (PRTs)." President's Advisory Council on Faith-Based and Neighborhood Partnerships, "New Era of Partnerships," 110. DOD funds humanitarian operations such as digging wells and providing food security in northern Nigeria, with similar operations in the region expected to increase in coming years. Danan, "Mixed Blessings," 38.

74. "One of the most significant challenges for USAID in engaging religious communities is the Establishment Clause of the First Amendment to the U.S. Constitution. In a 1991 decision, the United States Court of Appeals for the Second Circuit concluded that the Establishment Clause (separation of church and state) was applicable to USAID grants under the American Schools and Hospitals Abroad (ASHA) program. As a result, USAID implements all of its programs overseas as if the Establishment Clause were applicable. This means that *USAID will finance only activities and programs that have a secular purpose and which do not have the primary effect of advancing or inhibiting religion.* Accordingly, USAID-financed activities and programs may not (i) result in government indoctrination of religion, (ii) define its recipients by reference to religion, or (iii) create an excessive entanglement with religion. *USAID grantees and other recipients of funds must allocate assistance on the basis of neutral, secular criteria* that neither favor nor disfavor religion, and such assistance must be made available to both religious and secular beneficiaries on a nondiscriminatory basis. USAID funds may not be used to finance inherently religious activities, such as worship, religious instruction, or proselytization. Thus, before development professionals 'plunge into the thicket of Establishment Clause jurisprudence,' as the Court of Appeals for the Second Circuit stated in a non-USAID case, development planners in USAID should consult with their Regional Legal Advisor or with the Office of General Counsel in Washington to ensure that planning is consistent with applicable law." USAID, "Religion, Conflict and Peacebuilding," 7.

75. Colum Lynch, "In Fighting Radical Islam, Tricky Course for U.S. Aid," *Washington Post*, July 30, 2009, http://www.washingtonpost.com/wp-dyn/content/article/2009/07/29/AR2009072903515.html. The relevant passage from 22 C.F.R. Section 205.1(b) (2010) reads, "USAID funds may not be used for the acquisition, construction, or rehabilitation of structures to the extent that those structures are used for inherently religious activities. USAID funds may be used for the acquisition, construction, or rehabilitation of structures only to the extent that those structures are used for conducting eligible activities under this part. Where a structure is used for both eligible and inherently religious activities, USAID funds may not exceed the cost of those portions of the acquisition, construction, or rehabilitation that are attributable to eligible activities in accordance with the cost accounting requirements applicable to USAID funds in this part."

76. Winnifred Fallers Sullivan, Robert Yelle, and Mateo Taussig-Rubbo, "Introduction," in *After Secular Law*, ed. Winnifred Fallers Sullivan, Robert Yelle, and Mateo Taussig-Rubbo (Stanford: Stanford University Press, 2011), 9.

77. Beaman and Sullivan, "Neighbo(u)rly Misreadings and Misconstruals," 6. See also Rich-

ard C. Schragger, "The Relative Irrelevance of the Establishment Clause," *Texas Law Review* 89 (2011): 583–649.

78. For a history of attempts at disestablishment in the United States and their origins in colonial America and the American Revolution, see Evan Haefeli, "Toleration and Empire: The Origins of American Religious Pluralism," in *British North America in the Seventeenth and Eighteenth Centuries: Oxford History of the British Empire Companion*, ed. Stephen Foster (Oxford: Oxford University Press, 2014), 103–35.

79. Winnifred Fallers Sullivan, *Prison Religion: Faith-Based Reform and the Constitution* (Princeton: Princeton University Press, 2009), 221. "Universalist spiritual care is a constitutionally appropriate role of government. In a case of curiously circular reasoning, all that is necessary to constitutionalize religion is to say that it serves a secular purpose." Sullivan, *Ministry of Presence*, 268; Sullivan, "We Are All Religious Now," 1192.

80. On this history, see Kal Raustiala, *Does the Constitution Follow the Flag? The Evolution of Territoriality in American Law* (Oxford: Oxford University Press, 2009).

81. USAID contractors are required to show that their activities are not inherently religious and that they promote a "secular purpose." An administrative regulation known as the "Rule" stipulates that organizations receiving direct financial assistance from USAID "may not engage in inherently religious activities, such as worship, religious instruction, or proselytization." 22 C.F.R. sec. 205.1(b) (2010). Government restrictions on faith-based activities published by the GAO stipulate that "FBOs are not permitted to use direct federal funds for inherently religious activities such as prayer, religious instruction, worship, or proselytization. If an FBO conducts such activities, the activities must be separated by time or location from federally funded services or programs and must be voluntary for the beneficiary. However, they are allowed to retain religious art, icons, or symbols in the facilities where they provide services. In addition, for the programs in our review, FBOs generally are not prohibited under federal law from making employment decisions based on religious grounds, even after receiving federal funds." US Government Accountability Office, "Faith-Based and Community Initiative: Improvements in Monitoring Grantees and Measuring Performance Could Enhance Accountability" (Washington, D.C.: BiblioGov, 2011).

82. See for instance the report of the Chicago Council's Task Force on Religion and the Making of U.S. Foreign Policy, which suggests that legal confusion is undermining the effectiveness of US foreign policy by hindering the government's ability to engage effectively religious communities abroad. The report criticizes the Justice Department's Office of Legal Counsel (which has authority over these matters for the executive branch) for failing to provide legal clarity and calls on the government to resolve "legal uncertainty about the extent to which the Establishment Clause applies to government action overseas." Chicago Council on Global Affairs, "Engaging Religious Communities Abroad: A New Imperative for U.S. Foreign Policy" (report, Task Force on Religion and the Making of U.S. Foreign Policy, Scott Appleby and Richard Cizik, cochairs, Chicago, February 2010), 64, http://www.thechicagocouncil.org/sites/default/files/2010%20 Religion%20Task%20Force_Full%20Report.pdf. For a critique, see the four companion pieces on the *Immanent Frame* including my post, "The Global Securitization of Religion," *Immanent Frame*, March 23, 2010, http://blogs.ssrc.org/tif/2010/03/23/global -securitization/.

83. See Jesse Merriam, "Establishment Clause-Trophobia: Building a Framework for Escaping the Confines of Domestic Church-State Jurisprudence," *Columbia Human Rights Law Review* 41, no. 699 (2010): 699–752. For an interesting earlier discussion of the application of the religion clauses abroad, see John H. Mansfield, "The Religion Clauses of the First Amendment and Foreign Relations," *DePaul Law Review* 36, no. 1 (1986): 1–40.

84. The domestic application of the Establishment Clause is formally regulated by the Lemon Test, which stipulates that a statute must have a secular purpose, the primary effect must neither advance nor inhibit religion, and it must not foster "an excessive government entanglement with religion." *Lemon v. Kurtzman*, 403 U.S. 602 (1971). Over the past four decades since *Lemon* was decided, legal restrictions on government support have become much more relaxed. A harbinger of this shift was the Charitable Choice bill, signed by President Clinton in 1996, which made it easier for FBOs to bid for government contracts without suppressing their religious character and obviating the need to establish separate "non-religious" nonprofits to offer social services. See Robert J. Wineburg, Brian L. Coleman, Stephanie C. Boddie, and Ram A. Cnaan, "Leveling the Playing Field: Epitomizing Devolution through Faith-Based Organizations," *Journal of Sociology and Social Welfare* 35, no. 1 (2008): 31.

85. *Lamont v. Woods*, 948 F.2d 825 (2d Cir. 1991).

86. Jessica Hayden concluded that the "possible foreign policy ramifications of invalidating grants" under the program made it "particularly inappropriate" to adopt the "mechanical approach" of the "pervasively sectarian" test. Hayden, "Mullahs on a Bus," 198–99.

87. Ibid., 198n171.

88. *Hein v. Freedom from Religion Foundation*, 127 S. Ct. 2553 (2007). President Obama later changed the name of the White House Office of Faith-Based and Community Initiatives to the Office of Faith-Based and Neighborhood Partnerships. The White House office is distinct from the more recently established State Department Office of Faith-Based Community Initiatives, now the Office of Religion and Global Affairs, discussed earlier.

89. "The president can promote religion just as he can promote any other social policy, limited only by electoral politics." Sullivan, "After Secularism," 14.

90. Dacey, "Why Is the State Department Opening an Office of 'Religious Engagement?'"

91. Frederick R. Barton, Shannon Hayden, and Karin von Hippel, "Navigating in the Fog: Improving U.S. Government Engagement with Religion," in *Rethinking Religion and World Affairs*, ed. Alfred Stepan, Monica Duffy Toft, and Timothy Shah (New York: Columbia University Press, 2012), 281.

92. Sullivan, Yelle, and Taussig-Rubbo, "Introduction," 13. Alessandro Ferrari argues similarly that "both the separatist and the confessional models, in fact, have lost most of their significance." Alessandro Ferrari, "Religious Education in a Globalized Europe," in *Religion and Democracy in Contemporary Europe*, ed. Gabriel Motzkin and Yochi Fischer (London: Alliance, 2008), 115.

93. Many examples could be cited. For an informed discussion of how in Indonesia "the privileging of religion is made manifest through state support for religious orthodoxy over liminal and heterodox faiths," see Jeremy Menchik, "Productive Intolerance: Godly Nationalism in Indonesia," *Comparative Studies in Society and History* 56, no. 3 (2014): 591–621. On the domestic regulation of religion in Algeria, see Nadia Marzouki, "Conversion as Statelessness: A Study of Contemporary Algerian Conversions to Evangelical

Christianity," *Middle East Law and Governance* 4 (2012), 69–105; see also Vincent Goossaert and David A. Palmer, *The Religious Question in Modern China* (Chicago: University of Chicago Press, 2012); Nandini Chatterjee, *The Making of Indian Secularism: Empire, Law, and Christianity, 1830–1960* (New York: Palgrave Macmillan, 2011); Agrama, *Questioning Secularism*; and Scott, *Politics of the Veil*.

94. Hurd, *Politics of Secularism in International Relations*, chap. 2; Jean Comaroff, "The Politics of Conviction: Faith on the Neo-liberal Frontier," in *Contemporary Religiosities: Emergent Socialities and the Post-Nation-State*, ed. Bruce Kapferer, Kari Tell, and Annelin Eriksen (New York: Berghahn Books, 2010), 17–38.

95. Beaman and Sullivan, *Varieties of Religious Establishment*.

96. Cook, "Religious Tolerance at Home and Abroad."

97. Klassen and Bender, "Introduction," 19. Or, as David Kennedy asks, "which parts of the disaggregated regime of social regularity blossoming across cultures should we think of as 'legal?' Or for that matter, 'religious?'" David Kennedy, "Losing Faith in the Secular: Law, Religion, and the Culture of International Governance," in *Religion and International Law*, ed. Mark W. Janis and Carolyn Evans (The Hague: Martinus Nijhoff, 1999), 310.

98. Stringer, *Discourses on Religious Diversity*, 132–33. Malcolm Evans and Peter Petkoff make a related point, noting that "the entire way in which we approach human rights has the effect of privileging certain forms of religious belief over others. It is clearly more difficult for, let us call them, 'fringe' religions or New Religious Movements to benefit from human rights protections than it is for more mainstream religious traditions to do so." Malcolm Evans and Peter Petkoff, "A Separation of Convenience? The Concept of Neutrality in the Jurisprudence of the European Court of Human Rights," *Religion, State, and Society* 36, no. 3 (September 2008): 214–15.

99. Bender, "Power of Pluralist Thinking," 70. She continues, "contemporary pluralist thinking hides the mechanisms through which we recognize religions as free or many, or why we even find these tallies and their evaluations useful or necessary." Ibid., 73.

100. Barton, Hayden, and von Hippel, "Navigating in the Fog," 281. A February 2008 *Stars and Stripes* headline reads, "Report: U.S. Military Funds Building of Islamic Schools." The same issue reports that in parts of eastern Afghanistan US soldiers distributed copies of the Koran and "mosque refurbishment kits," including prayer rugs and sound systems powered by solar panels. "Report: U.S. Military Funds Building of Islamic Schools," *Stars and Stripes*, February 1, 2008, http://www.stripes.com/article.asp?section=104&article=52094.

101. Quoted in Jon Boone, "US Funds Madrassas in Afghanistan," *Financial Times*, January 29, 2008, http://www.ft.com/intl/cms/s/0/d1b9e546-ceb4-11dc-877a-000077b07658.html. Boone opens his piece by observing that the schools were constructed "in an attempt to stem the tide of young people going to radical religious schools in Pakistan."

102. Barton, Hayden, and von Hippel, "Navigating in the Fog," 281.

103. Peter Mandaville, "Whither U.S. Engagement with Muslims?," *Foreign Policy*, June 4, 2010, http://mideast.foreignpolicy.com/posts/2010/06/04/whither_us_engagement_with_muslims.

104. Sherwood, "On the Freedom of the Concepts," 41.

CHAPTER 5: MINORITIES UNDER LAW

1. For the epigraphs, see Ali Yaman, social anthropologist at Abant İzzet Baysal University, Bolu, quoted in Thomas Grove, "Turkish Alevis Fight Back Against Religion Lessons," *Reuters*, May 5, 2008, http://www.reuters.com/article/2008/05/06/us-turkey-alevi-idUSL2481334820080506; and Hamid Dabashi, "To Protect the Revolution, Overcome the False Secular-Islamist Divide," *Al Jazeera*, December 9, 2012, http://www.aljazeera.com/indepth/opinion/2012/12/2012128153845368495.html.

2. An example is the recommendation in the 2012 report of the US Commission on International Religious Freedom that the president demote Turkey to a "Country of Particular Concern" due to "the Turkish government's systematic and egregious limitations on the freedom of religion or belief that affect all religious communities in Turkey, and particularly threaten the country's non-Muslim religious minorities." US Commission on International Religious Freedom, "2012 Annual Report," http://www.uscirf.gov/sites/default/files/resources/Annual%20Report%20of%20USCIRF%202012(2).pdf. For an informed introduction to the study of minorities in the Middle East and an effort to assess the status of various sociopolitical groups in relation to sites of power, see Joshua Castellino and Kathleen A. Cavanaugh, *Minority Rights in the Middle East* (Oxford: Oxford University Press, 2013). The authors stress the relevance of state practice "both as to how states engage with the international community and related human rights discourse and, domestically, where practices cause a differentiation or social fact of minority status" (379).

3. Roland Dubertrand "Religious Freedom from the Point of View of French Diplomacy" (keynote speech, Protecting the Right to Freedom of Religion or Belief conference, Florence, November 17, 2012).

4. Oren Dorell and Sarah Lynch, "Christians Fear Losing Freedoms in Arab Spring Movement," *USA Today*, January 31, 2012, http://usatoday30.usatoday.com/news/religion/story/2012-01-30/arab-spring-christians/52894182/1.

5. Adelaide Mena, "Senate Bill Would Aid Religious Minorities in Middle East," *Catholic News Agency*, August 22, 2013, http://www.catholicnewsagency.com/news/senate-bill-would-aid-religious-minorities-in-middle-east/.

6. Lauren Markoe, "Global Religious Hot Spots Get Their Own U.S. Envoy," *Religion News Service*, August 20, 2014, http://www.religionnews.com/2014/08/20/new-job-u-s-envoy-religious-freedom-mideast/.

7. Near East and South Central Asia Religious Freedom Act of 2014, S. 653, 113th Congress (2013–14), https://www.govtrack.us/congress/bills/113/s653/text.

8. Ibid.

9. The United States is involved in this activity though to a lesser degree than European institutions due to the integrative impact of ongoing, if faltering, Turkish accession negotiations, economic and historical connections between the EU and Turkey, and geographic proximity.

10. Buket Türkmen, "A Transformed Kemalist Islam or a New Islamic Civic Morality? A Study of 'Religious Culture and Morality' Textbooks in the Turkish High School Curricula," *Comparative Studies of South Asia, Africa and the Middle East* 29, no. 3 (2009): 381–91.

11. See Saba Mahmood, "Religious Freedom, the Minority Question, and Geopolitics in the Middle East," *Comparative Studies in Society and History* 54, no. 2 (2012): 418–46. On

the history of the court in relation to the protection of religious freedom, see Peter G. Danchin and Lisa Forman, "The Evolving Jurisprudence of the European Court of Human Rights and the Protection of Religious Minorities," in *Protecting the Human Rights of Religious Minorities in Eastern Europe*, ed. Peter G. Danchin and Elizabeth Cole (New York: Columbia University Press, 2002), 192–221.

12. Council of the European Union, *EU Guidelines on the Promotion and Protection of Freedom of Religion or Belief* (Luxembourg, June 24, 2013), http://eeas.europa.eu/delegations /fiji/press_corner/all_news/news/2013/eu_guidelines_on_the_promotion_and_protection _of_freedom_of_religion_or_belief_(june_24_2013_fac).pdf. Elise Massicard has remarked on the pressure on Turkey from European institutions to "protect its 'minorities' and treat them equitably." *The Alevis in Turkey and Europe: Identity and Managing Territorial Diversity* (London: Routledge, 2013), 2.

13. Slotte, "Religious and the Secular," 54. Rosen makes a related point: "while analyses of law tend to focus on conflict and resolution, rule-making or rule-applying, one can— without in any way downplaying these aspects—also see law as contributing to the formation of an entire cosmology, a way of envisioning and creating an orderly sense of the universe, one that arranges humanity, society, and ultimate beliefs into a scheme perceived as palpably real." Lawrence Rosen, *Law as Culture* (Princeton: Princeton University Press, 2006), 11.

14. Benjamin L. Berger, "The Aesthetics of Religious Freedom," in Beaman and Sullivan, *Varieties of Religious Establishment*, 33–53; Kahn, *Cultural Study of Law*.

15. Mahmood, "Religious Freedom," 419.

16. Massicard, *Alevis in Turkey and Europe*, 4.

17. Gareth Jenkins, "ECHR Ruling Highlights Discrimination Suffered by Turkey's Alevi Minority," *Eurasia Daily Monitor*, October 12, 2007, http://www.jamestown.org /programs/edm/single/?tx_ttnews%5Btt_news%5D=33075&tx_ttnews%5BbacPid %5D=405&no_cache=1#.UczSehb1hEI.

18. "Alevi Group Demands End to Turkish Mandatory Religious Classes," *Hurriyet Daily News*, November 7, 2010, http://www.hurriyetdailynews.com/default.aspx?pageid=438 &n=alevis-protest-mandatory-religion-classes-by-rally-2010–11–07.

19. Markus Dressler, "The Modern Dede: Changing Parameters for Religious Authority in Contemporary Turkish Alevism," in *Speaking for Islam: Religious Authorities in Muslim Societies*, ed. Gudrun Krämer and Sabine Schmidtke (Leiden: Brill, 2006), 271n6. For an informative discussion of the genealogies of the traditions now assembled under "Alevism," see Markus Dressler, *Writing Religion: The Making of Turkish Alevi Islam* (Oxford: Oxford University Press, 2013), 1–19, 275–87.

20. Markus Dressler, "New Texts Out Now: Markus Dressler, *Writing Religion: The Making of Turkish Alevi Islam*," *Jadaliyya*, June 19, 2013, http://www.jadaliyya.com/pages/index /12302/new-texts-out-now_markus-dressler-writing-religion.

21. Dressler, *Writing Religion*, 17.

22. Asad, *Formations of the Secular*, 175.

23. Contrasting Sunni and Alevi ways of life, David Shankland theorizes that Alevis may be more inclined to resist centralized rule because their myths, rituals, and authority structures undermine the legitimacy of the central government while those of the Sunni majority are incorporated and normalized by the state. Shankland, *The Alevis in Turkey: The Emergence of a Secular Islamic Tradition* (New York: Routledge, 2003), 24.

24. Both traditions honor Ali ibn Abi Talib, the cousin and son-in-law of the Prophet Muhammad. Approximately one-third of the Turkish population of Hatay in southeastern Turkey is of Arab Alawite descent and directly related to Syria's Alawites. Hatay, which was until 1938 part of Syria, has received a large influx of refugees from the Syrian war and has served as a staging ground for anti-Assad forces.

25. Esra Özyürek, "'The Light of the Alevi Fire Was Lit in Germany and Then Spread to Turkey': A Transnational Debate on the Boundaries of Islam," *Turkish Studies* 10 (2009): 238.

26. Associations such as Pir Sultan Abdal Derneği are open to understanding Alevism as a religion outside of Islam, while others, such as Cem Vakfı, counter that Alevism is at the very heart of Islam.

27. Talha Köse, "Alevi Opening and the Democratization Initiative in Turkey" (Ankara: Foundation for Political, Economic and Social Research, March 2010), 12–13, http://arsiv.setav.org/public/HaberDetay.aspx?Dil=tr&hid=28900&q=alevi-opening-and-the-democratization-initiative.

28. See Kabir Tambar, "The Aesthetics of Public Visibility: Alevi *Semah* and the Paradoxes of Pluralism in Turkey," *Comparative Studies in Society and History* 52, no. 3 (2010): 652–59.

29. Markus Dressler, "The Religio-Secular Continuum: Reflections on the Religious Dimensions of Turkish Secularism," in Sullivan, Yelle, and Taussig-Rubbo, *After Secular Law*, 221–41.

30. In a 2005 interview, the Turkish newspaper *Radikal* asked Kazım Genç, former president of Pir Sultan Abdal Derneği, "What do Alevis expect from the EU?" He replied, "We are asking for our individual rights and freedoms without being labelled as a minority. 2004 European Union's Regular Report on Turkey defined Alevis as a minority. Alevis, however, do not consider themselves as a minority." "Alevilik İslamiyet'in içinde değil" [Kazım Genç, interviewed by Neşe Düzel], *Radikal*, October 10, 2005, http://www.radikal.com.tr/haber.php?haberno=166463.

31. Özyürek, "'Light of the Alevi Fire,'" 247.

32. The term *millet* is derived from the Arabic word for "nation" or *millah*, and generally refers to the Ottoman system of social, legal, and religious organization in which different confessional communities under the empire exercised varying degrees of legal autonomy. On Ottoman history in transnational context, see Karen Barkey, *Empire of Difference: The Ottomans in Comparative Perspective* (Cambridge: Cambridge University Press, 2008).

33. B. Ali Soner, "Citizenship and the Minority Question in Turkey," in *Citizenship in a Global World: European Questions and Turkish Experiences*, ed. E. Fuat Keyman and Ahmet İçduygu (New York: Routledge, 2005), 290–93.

34. Özyürek cites a librarian from Cem Vakfı (Foundation): "'There is a difference between having been exposed to injustice and being a minority. [Unlike Kurds] Alevis do not want a separate land or a flag. All they want to do is to be able to practice their worship.'" "'Light of the Alevi Fire,'" 247.

35. Ibid., 245.

36. Benjamin Thomas White, *The Emergence of Minorities in the Middle East: The Politics of Community in French Mandate Syria* (Edinburgh: Edinburgh University Press, 2012).

37. Secil Aslan, "The Ambivalence of Alevi Politic(s): A Comparative Analysis of Cem Vakfi and Pir Sultan Abdal Derneği" (master's thesis, Bogazici University, Istanbul, 2008).

38. The largest Alevi organization in Germany, the Almanya Alevi Birlikleri Federasyonu (AABF), is legally recognized as a religious organization that represents Alevis in Ger-

many, a designation that does not require the group to define its relation to (Sunni) Islam. Among other activities, AABF prepares curricular materials for teaching about Alevism for the ministries of culture and education in several German federal states. Kerstin Rosenow-Williams, *Organizing Muslims and Integrating Islam in Germany: New Developments in the 21st Century* (Leiden: Brill, 2012), 109.

39. See Esra Özyürek, "Beyond Integration and Recognition: Diasporic Constructions of Alevi Identity between Germany and Turkey," in *Transnational Transcendence: Essays on Religion and Globalization*, ed. Thomas J. Csordas (Berkeley: University of California Press, 2009), 121–44; Martin Sökefeld, *Struggling for Recognition: The Alevi Movement in Germany and in Transnational Space* (New York: Berghahn Books, 2008); and Massicard, *Alevis in Turkey and Europe*.

40. Dressler, "Modern Dede," 285.

41. See Ayhan Kaya, "Multicultural Clientelism and Alevi Resurgence in the Turkish Diaspora: Berlin Alevis," *New Perspectives on Turkey* 18 (1998): 23–49.

42. Özyürek, "Beyond Integration and Recognition," 128–31. In 1989 the Hamburg Alevi Association's "Alevi Manifesto" "defined Alevism as a branch of Islam and aimed to make the demands of Alevis publicly known. It asked for recognition of Alevism as a different faith and culture, for equal representation and opportunity in education and in the media, and proportional assistance in religious services." Ibid., 128–29.

43. Kaya, "Multicultural Clientelism," 25.

44. Özyürek, "Beyond Integration and Recognition," 136.

45. "In Turkey's laicist relations, relations understood as separation exist within a set of relations understood as integration, supervision, and control, and the latter relations are understood as part of the larger practice of maintaining the separation of religion from state affairs." Andrew Davison, "Hermeneutics and the Politics of Secularism," in *Comparative Secularisms in a Global Age*, ed. Linell E. Cady and Elizabeth Shakman Hurd (New York: Palgrave Macmillan, 2010), 35–36.

46. Nilüfer Göle, "Manifestations of the Religious-Secular Divide: Self, State, and the Public Sphere," in Cady and Hurd, *Comparative Secularisms in a Global Age*, 45.

47. Act no. 429 reads, "In the Republic of Turkey, the Grand National Assembly of Turkey and the Cabinet which is formed by the Grand National Assembly of Turkey are responsible for the legislation and execution of provisions concerning the affairs of people; and the Presidency of Religious Affairs will be formed as a part of the Republic for the implementation of all provisions concerning faith and prayer of the religion of Islam, and the administration of religious organizations." Quoted in İştar B. Gözaydın, "A Religious Administration to Secure Secularism: The Presidency of Religious Affairs of the Republic of Turkey," *Marburg Journal of Religion* 11, no. 1 (2006): 2, http://archiv .ub.uni-marburg.de/mjr/art_goezaydin_2006.html.

48. Arnold J. Toynbee, *Survey of International Affairs*, vol. 1, *The Islamic World since the Peace Settlement* (London: Oxford University Press, 1927), 573.

49. Murat Somer, "Turkey's New Constitution and Secular Democracy: A Case for Liberty," *E-International Relations*, June 5, 2012, http://www.e-ir.info/2012/06/05/turkeys-new -constitution-secular-democracy-a-case-for-religious-and-non-religious-liberties/.

50. Toynbee, *Survey of International Affairs*, 573. Article 5 of the Law Concerning the Abolition of the Commissariats for the Sheriat and Evqaf and for the General Staff, 3 March, 1340 (1924) reads, "The President of Religious Affairs is charged with the

administration of all mosques of both classes and of all dervish houses within the boundaries of the territories of the Republic of Turkey, as well as with the appointment and dismissal of all rectors of mosques, 'orators,' preachers, abbots of dervish houses, callers to prayer, sacristans, and all other employees [of a religious character]." Quoted in Ibid. Thanks to James Gibbon for the reference.

51. Zana Çitak, "Between 'Turkish Islam' and 'French Islam': The Role of the *Diyanet* in the *Conseil Français du Culte Musulman*," *Journal of Ethnic and Migration Studies* 36, no. 4 (2010). See also Benjamin Bruce, "Gérer l'Islam à l'Etranger: Entre Service Public et Outil de la Politique Étrangère Turque," *Anatoli*, no. 3 (2012): 131–47.

52. Mine Yildirim, "Turkey: The Diyanet—The Elephant in Turkey's Religious Freedom Room?" *Forum 18*, May 4, 2011, http://www.forum18.org/archive.php?article_id=1567.

53. Davison, "Hermeneutics and the Politics of Secularism," 35. The state also provides religious instruction under the education ministry and for cadets and officers in the military.

54. Quoted in Emre Demir-Ahmet Ozay, "For Minority Status, Alevis Bypass Turkey, Appeal to European Court," *Zaman*, November 18, 2006, http://wwrn.org/articles/23423/.

55. Tambar's paradox of pluralism well illustrates how public Alevi social and religious difference has been, and continues to be, domesticated within a singular image of the Turkish nation: "The forms of public visibility attained by Alevi organizations are hinged, paradoxically, to the category of folklore that Alevi movements are seeking to challenge. If the emergence of Alevi religious practice into public view poses a pluralist challenge to the Turkish state's efforts at defining and controlling the religious expressions of its citizenry in singular terms, this very visibility has been justified, legitimated, and sanctioned by discourses that re-inscribe a unitary vision of the nation." Tambar, "Aesthetics of Public Visibility," 658. See also Kabir Tambar, *The Reckoning of Pluralism: Political Belonging and the Demands of History in Turkey* (Stanford: Stanford University Press, 2014).

56. Özyürek, "Beyond Integration and Recognition," 124–25.

57. Although in 2007–8 one chapter on Alevis was added to the textbooks in the "Turkish Sunnite Islam" section, opponents "strongly criticized" the Ministry of Education for representing Alevism as a "mystic interpretation of Sunnism." Türkmen, "Transformed Kemalist Islam," 388, 391.

58. Dressler, "Religio-Secular Continuum," 236.

59. Gözaydın, "Religious Administration to Secure Secularism," 6.

60. Necdet Subaşı, "The Alevi Opening: Concept, Strategy and Process," *Insight Turkey* 12, no. 2 (2010): 170. *Dedes* or "grandfathers" are socioreligious leaders and spiritual guides of the Alevi community that lead the *cem* ceremony (representing Muhammad and Ali), receive confessions at the beginning of the ceremony, and oversee marriages, funerals, and circumcisions. *Dede* is a hereditary position limited to descendants of the Prophet (*ocakzade*).

61. Although the hotel was purchased by the state in 2010, there is disagreement about next steps: "Some Alevi groups have demanded the hotel become a museum to commemorate the massacre, while others such as the Cem Foundation say the building can be put to another use as long as there is a plaque at the door honoring the victims. Some local nongovernmental organizations in Sivas would like to see the building demolished and

a library built on the site, NTV reported. Arif Sağ, an Alevi and prominent folk musician, has meanwhile proposed that the building be torn down and the area used for a flower garden." "Turkish Government Buys Hotel Site of Alevi Massacre," *Hurriyet Daily News*, June 17, 2010, http://www.hurriyetdailynews.com/default.aspx?pageid=438&n=turkish -govt-seizes-hotel-where-many-alevis-intellectuals-were-killed-2010–06–17.

62. Köse, "Alevi Opening," 15. Concerns extend to foreign policy: the head of the Alevi— Bektashi Federation, Selahattin Ozel, has criticized the AKP for attempting to create a "Sunni block" in the region. Ezgi Basaran, "Erdogan's Negative Comments Unite Turk- ish Alevis," *Al-Monitor*, May 9, 2013, http://www.al-monitor.com/pulse/politics/2013/05 /turkey-alevis-erdogan-negative-interview-selahattin-ozel.html.

63. *Hasan and Eylem Zengin v. Turkey* (application no. 1448/04, European Court of Human Rights, Strasbourg, October 9, 2007).

64. See José Luis Martínez López-Muñiz, Jan De Groof, and Gracienne Lauwers, eds., *Reli- gious Education in Public Schools: Study of Comparative Law*, Yearbook of the European Association for Education Law and Policy, vol. 6 (Dordrecht: Springer, 2006); Luce Pépin, *Teaching about Religions in European School Systems: Policy Issues and Trends—NEF Initiative on Religion and Democracy in Europe* (London: Alliance, 2009); Gerhard Rob- bers, ed., *Religion in Public Education* (Germany: European Consortium for Church and State Research, 2011).

65. Religious culture and morality courses were first instituted as electives after the transi- tion to a multiparty system and became a mandatory part of the curriculum only after the 1980 coup. Türkmen, "Transformed Kemalist Islam," 386.

66. Quoted in Ibid., 393.

67. This reflects the authority and precedent of the Treaty of Lausanne in which the term "minorities" referred exclusively to non-Muslim religious communities (Jews, Arme- nians, and Greek Orthodox Christians), as discussed above.

68. "Jewish and Christian students with Turkish nationality, who are not students of mi- nority schools, will not be taught the word of testimony (*kelime-i ̦ sahadet*), the mean- ing of *bismillahirrahmanirrahim*, Koranic verses, suras, prayers, Islamic worship, fasting, hajj." Decision of the Council for Instruction and Education, no. 47 (February 28, 1992), quoted in Türkmen, "Transformed Kemalist Islam," 388. The author explains that "the issuing of these two memorandums has resulted in some inconsistencies: some schools oblige non-Muslim students to take the course, and others do not. The existence of the 1992 decision shows that non-Muslim students are not exempt from the course; the only exemption they can benefit from relates to the content of the course. This decision proves that, contrary to what the Ministry of Education says, this is a course not of general religious culture but of Islamic knowledge, where Muslim students learn Islamic Sunnite rituals and practices." Ibid., 388.

69. Ibid.

70. *Zengin v. Turkey*, 16.

71. Ibid., 18.

72. Ibid., 19.

73. Article 2 of the First Additional Protocol reads, "No person shall be denied the right to education. In the exercise of any functions which it assumes in relation to education and to teaching, the State shall respect the right of parents to ensure such education and

teaching in conformity with their own religious and philosophical convictions." Protocol to the Convention for the Protection of Human Rights and Fundamental Freedoms, art. 2, March 20, 1952, 213 U.N.T.S. 222.

74. *Zengin v. Turkey*, 22.

75. Türkmen, "Transformed Kemalist Islam," 388.

76. Ibid., 396.

77. "Alevi Group Demands End to Turkish Mandatory Religious Classes." Other protestors demanded the abolishment of the Religious Affairs Directorate, the granting of legal status to *cemevis* (Alevi houses of worship), and a halt to mosque construction and the call to prayer in Alevi villages—all perceived as impositions of state-favored Sunni Islam.

78. *Zengin v. Turkey*, 18.

79. On French attempts to formalize and "officialize" identity and community along religious lines in French Mandate Syria, see White, *Emergence of Minorities in the Middle East*, 43–66.

80. Austrian Foreign Ministry, "Vice Chancellor Pressing for Early Adoption of EU Guidelines on Freedom of Religion" (December 10, 2012), http://www.bmeia.gv.at/en /foreign-ministry/news/press-releases/2012/spindelegger-protection-of-religious -minorities-is-a-key-concern-of-austrias-human-rights-policy.html.

81. Pasquale Ferrara, "Reporting on Religious Freedom: The 'Governmental' Approach and the Issue of Legitimacy," quoted in Pasquale Annicchino, "Recent Developments Concerning the Promotion of Freedom of Religion or Belief in Italian Foreign Policy," *Review of Faith and International Affairs* 11, no. 3 (September 2013): 61–68.

82. Council of the European Union, *EU Guidelines*, para. 19, emphasis added, http://www .eu-un.europa.eu/articles/en/article_13685_en.htm.

83. "Even though Alevis in Turkey were reluctant to get help from the European Union, efforts of the Alevi lobby resulted in the European Union's *Regular Report on Turkey*, dated October 6, 2004, which pointed to difficulties Alevis face in Turkey and defined them as a 'non-Sunni Muslim minority.'" Özyürek, "'Light of the Alevi Fire,'" 244. For reasons described above, there was strong opposition to this designation among Turkish Alevis, and the commission dropped it in subsequent reports.

84. On the recommendations of the Venice Commission (an advisory body of the Council of Europe that drafts opinions on freedom of religion and the protection of minorities, among other issues), see Ergun Özbudun, "'Democratic Opening,' the Legal Status of Non-Muslim Religious Communities and the Venice Commission," *Insight Turkey* 12, no. 2 (2010): 213–22.

85. Soner, "Citizenship and the Minority Question," 303.

86. "Overall, there has been limited progress on freedom of thought, conscience and religion. . . . A legal framework in line with the ECHR has yet to be established, so that all non-Muslim religious communities and the Alevi community can function without undue constraints." European Commission, "Commission Staff Working Paper, Turkey 2011 Progress Report" (Brussels, October 12, 2011), 31, http://ec.europa.eu/enlargement /pdf/key_documents/2011/package/tr_rapport_2011_en.pdf.

87. Council of the European Union, *EU Guidelines*.

88. Joe Vella Gauci, "Protection of Religious Freedom: A New Operational Set of Tools," *Europeinfos*, no. 157 (February 2013), http://www.comece.eu/europeinfos/en/archive

/issue157/article/5480.html, emphasis added. This builds on recommendations issued in 2011 by the European Platform on Religious Intolerance and Discrimination calling for the European External Action Service to (1) establish a "Religion Unit" in the Thematic and Multilateral Directorate General to "mainstream the issue of freedom of religion or belief across the geographical directorates and units as well as linking the issue into general human rights promotion within the same DG and advancing the issue in international and multilateral organisations and fora"; (2) appoint a EU Special Envoy for Religious Freedom; (3) order the aforementioned "Religion Unit" to prepare an Annual Report on Progress on Freedom of Religion or Belief in the World ("FoRB"), including a list of countries of particular concern to be revised annually; and (4) incorporate basic understanding of religious dynamics into diplomatic training and consider appointing a "religious freedom officer" in key EU embassies. The European Parliament is urged to get involved in "FoRB" initiatives, be informed about infringements of FoRB, become more active in monitoring other EU institutions with regard to FoRB concerns, and generally "help feature freedom of religion or belief for all higher up the agenda of the European Union." European Platform on Religious Intolerance and Discrimination, "Recommendations of the European Platform on Religious Intolerance and Discrimination to the Institutions of the European Union Concerning the Implementation of Freedom of Religion or Belief" (May 26, 2011), http://www.europarl.europa.eu/meet docs/2009_2014/documents/droi/dv/201/201105/20110526_416recomeprid_en.pdf.

89. See White, *Emergence of Minorities in the Middle East*, 21–66, and Sarah Shields, "The Greek-Turkish Population Exchange: Internationally-Administered Ethnic Cleansing," *Middle East Report* 267 (2013): 2–6.

90. Ussama Makdisi, "Understanding Sectarianism," *ISIM Newsletter*, issue 1, vol. 8, no. 1 (2001): 19.

91. White, *Emergence of Minorities in the Middle East*. See also Saba Mahmood, *The Minority Condition: Religious Difference in the Secular Age* (Princeton: Princeton University Press, forthcoming).

92. Köse, "Alevi Opening," 8.

93. On the reception of the workshops conducted in 2009–10, see Subaşı, "Alevi Opening."

94. Dressler, *Writing Religion*, xiii.

95. Ibid., xiv. Dressler concludes that as of December 2012 the Alevi opening has barely gone beyond publication of a report. Ibid., xv.

96. Gözaydın, "Religious Administration to Secure Secularism," 7.

97. See Cihan Tugal, "Occupy Gezi: The Limits of Turkey's Neoliberal Success," *Jadaliyya*, June 4, 2013, http://www.jadaliyya.com/pages/index/12009/occupy-gezi_the-limits-of -turkey's-neoliberal-suc.

98. Michael Wahid Hanna, "With Friends Like These: Coptic Activism in the Diaspora," *Middle East Report*, no. 267 (2013), http://www.merip.org/mer/mer267/friends-these.

99. Nukhet A. Sandal, "Public Theologies of Human Rights and Citizenship: The Case of Turkey's Christians," *Human Rights Quarterly* 35, no. 33 (2013): 641.

100. Sökefeld observes that the polarization of northern Pakistani society along sectarian lines occurred as a "Shia-Sunni dichotomy became effectively a premise that structured the perception of the social space." Martin Sökefeld, "Selves and Others: Representing Multiplicities of Difference in Gilgit and the Northern Areas of Pakistan," in *Islam and Society in Pakistan: Anthropological Perspectives*, ed. Magnus Marsden (Karachi: Oxford

University Press, 2010), quoted in Aziz Ali Dad, "The Sectarian Ghoul in Gilgit," *News*, December 20, 2012, http://www.thenews.com.pk/Todays-News-9-149434-The-sectarian -ghoul-in-Gilgit.

101. Castelli, "Theologizing Human Rights," 684.

102. Mahmood describes the refusal of the Coptic community at the time of the Revolution of 1919 to accept the designation of "national minority" on the "ground that they were no different than their fellow Egyptians." In drafting a new constitution in 1922, Coptic members of the Wafd Party opposed proportional minority representation while supporting political and civil equality for all Egyptian citizens on the grounds that the former "would create divisions based on religion in the body politic similar to those that divided the Muslims from Hindus in India." Today the Coptic community in Egypt is split, with some (Magdi Khalil) supporting explicit protections for minority rights and others (Samir Murqus) opposing them. Mahmood, "Religious Freedom," 435, 438.

103. Dressler refers to a "trend to religionize Alevism" in the context of a discussion of the changing role of the *dede*, or Alevi spiritual leader, under modern secular regimes of state and transnational authority in which most temporal power has been transferred to secular leaders of Alevi associations and foundations. Dressler, "Modern Dede," 290.

104. Subaşı, "Alevi Opening," 173, emphasis added.

105. "Turkish nationalists tend to be rather intolerant toward interpretations that locate the Kızılbaş-Alevis outside of Islam or rooted in non-Turkish (for example Kurdish or Persian) ethnicity and culture." Dressler, *Writing Religion*, 273.

106. Paul Sedra, "Copts and the Millet Partnership: The Intra-Communal Dynamics Behind Egyptian Sectarianism," in Hurd and Sullivan, "Symposium," *Journal of Law and Religion* 29, 3 (2014): 508.

107. Ibid., 509.

108. Bonnie Honig, *Emergency Politics: Paradox, Law, Democracy* (Princeton: Princeton University Press, 2009), 44.

109. C. S. Adcock illustrates this persuasively with regard to the capacity of the Tolerance critique of religious proselytizing, which, it is argued, subverts and sidelines Untouchables' ability to negotiate their own identities and pursue various forms of anticaste struggle. Adcock, *Limits of Tolerance*, 173.

110. Ayhan Kaya perceptively describes a related dynamic in Germany (and Europe more broadly) in which Alevism has been represented as a secularist "shield" against radical Islam, concluding that this "inevitably contributes to the resurgence of Alevism in a political sense and to the reification of Alevism in a cultural sense vis-à-vis Sunnis." Kaya, "Multicultural Clientelism," 43.

111. For a discussion of a similar dynamic in Sri Lanka, see Benjamin Schonthal, "Constitutionalizing Religion: The Pyrrhic Success of Religious Rights in Postcolonial Sri Lanka," in Hurd and Sullivan, "Symposium," *Journal of Law and Religion* 29, no. 3 (2014): 470–90.

112. Dressler, *Writing Religion*, 287. He concludes that "it is undeniable that this pressure of Sunni Islamic majority discourse ... encouraged Alevis individuals as well as Alevi groups and organizations to move in rhetoric and practice closer to mainstream understandings of Islam." Ibid., 278.

113. William E. Connolly, "Taylor, Foucault, and Otherness," *Political Theory* 13 (1985): 371.

114. Wendy Brown, "'The Most We Can Hope For . . .': Human Rights and the Politics of Fatalism," *South Atlantic Quarterly* 103, nos. 2/3 (2004): 461. See also Moyn, *Last Utopia*.
115. Alexander Livingston, "The Anarchist Vision of William James" (lecture, Northwestern University, October 2012). See also Alexander Livingston, *Damn Great Empires! William James and the Politics of Pragmatism* (Oxford: Oxford University Press, 2015).
116. Asad, "Thinking about Religion, Belief, and Politics," 56–57.

CHAPTER 6: BEYOND RELIGIOUS FREEDOM

1. US Department of State, "Country Reports: Africa Overview" (July 2005), 46, http://www.state.gov/documents/organization/65468.pdf. The program was initially called the Trans-Sahara Counter-Terrorism Initiative: "In 2008, the US created a unified command for Africa, US Africa Command (AFRICOM), splitting responsibility for the continent from EUCOM. As a result, the responsibility for the TSCTI became the responsibility of AFRICOM's Special Operations Command component, Special Operations Command, Africa (SOCAFRICA). The name of the program was also subsequently changed to the Trans-Sahara Counterterrorism Partnership (TSCTP)." "Trans-Sahara Counter-Terrorism Initiative," *GlobalSecurity*, http://www.globalsecurity.org/military/ops/tscti.htm.
2. US Department of State, "Country Reports: Africa Overview," 46.
3. In summer 2014 Villanova University posted a job announcement for an assistant professorship in interfaith and interreligious studies. Other examples are the Humanitas Visiting Professorship in Interfaith Studies at the Universities of Oxford and Cambridge, currently held by Rowan Williams, and Eboo Patel's Interfaith Youth Core.
4. Beaman and Sullivan, "Neighbo(u)rly Misreadings and Misconstruals," 7. Alternatively, as the authors point out, "difference may dissolve such that religious groups are compelled to adopt a universal shape which, in North America and Europe, is decidedly Christian."
5. "In a context in which religion becomes the primary identity marker, getting it 'right' becomes a more pressing matter. Moreover, the ante is upped within religious groups to have this or that version of the religion in question become the benchmark against which others are measured." Lori G. Beaman, "The Will to Religion: Obligatory Religious Citizenship," *Critical Research on Religion* 1, no. 2 (2013): 147.
6. On the cornering of religion in Sri Lankan constitutional law and its sociopolitial consequences, see Benjamin Schonthal's work on "ruling religion" in Sri Lanka. See note 44 of this chapter.
7. Nadia Marzouki, "Engaging Religion at the Department of State," *Immanent Frame*, July 30, 2013, http://blogs.ssrc.org/tif/2013/07/30/engaging-religion-at-the-department-of-state/#Marzouki.
8. Another way of putting this is to say that contemporary materializations of religious freedom fail to address the fragilities that they exacerbate. William E. Connolly, *The Fragility of Things: Self-Organizing Processes, Neoliberal Fantasies, and Democratic Activism* (Durham, NC: Duke University Press, 2013).
9. Melani McAlister, "State Department Finds Religion, but Whose?," *Religion Dispatches*,

December 12, 2013, http://www.religiondispatches.org/archive/politics/7240/state _department_finds_religion__but_whose.

10. Ibid.

11. US Commission on International Religious Freedom, "Special Report: Protecting and Promoting Religious Freedom in Syria" (April 2013), http://www.uscirf.gov/sites/default /files/resources/Syria%20Report%20April%202013(1).pdf.

12. Ibid.

13. Since the rise of Hafez al-Assad in 1970, the Syrian government has been dominated by a regime composed of Syrians of different backgrounds that is overseen by an Alawite family. The Alawites are followers of a branch of Shi'a Islam, and compose roughly 12 percent of the Syrian population. The name Alawite (Arabic: *Alawīyyah*) refers to Ali ibn Abi Talib, cousin of the Prophet Muhammad and considered the first Shi'a imam and the fourth Rightly Guided Caliph of Sunni Islam. Historically subject to social and religious discrimination, the Alawites before 1970 lived principally along the coastal and mountainous regions of northwestern Syria, where under the French mandate they briefly had their own state. Although many retain close ties to that region, today Alawites live in all of Syria's major cities and some rural areas. The Assads have relied on the purported threat of sectarian chaos lurking below the surface of society and politics to justify autocratic rule. Elizabeth Shakman Hurd, "The Dangerous Illusion of an Alawite Regime," *Boston Review*, June 11, 2013, http://bit.ly/16a87wc.

14. Mohja Kahf, "From Grief We Rise: To a Country for All Syrians," *Syrian Sun*, June 9, 2012, accessed on May 15, 2013. This is particularly dangerous because though well absorbed into Assad's authoritarian state project, the Alawis were never well integrated into Syrian society. Clinging to the state in an attempt to hold onto modest gains in social and economic standing, many built their identities under Assad by playing down their origins, even changing their accents. Peter Harling and Sarah Birke, "The Syrian Heartbreak," *Middle East Report*, April 16, 2013, http://www.merip.org/mero/mero041613.

15. An important contribution to this reconsideration is Charles Taylor's *A Secular Age*, a phenomenology of the emergence of "secularity 3," which Taylor describes as a modern context of understanding in which belief and unbelief coexist uneasily, in which one believes or refuses to believe in God, a "cross-pressured" condition in which, "our experience of and search for fullness occurs." Secularity 3 is distinguished from the retreat of religion in public life ("secularity 1") and the falling off of individual religious belief and practice ("secularity 2"). Charles Taylor, *A Secular Age* (Cambridge, MA: Belknap, 2007), 19. On the simultaneous importance and insufficiency of Taylor's approach to the study of religion, law, and politics globally, see Elizabeth Shakman Hurd, "Thinking about Religion, Law, and Politics in Latin America," in "Religions, Post-secularity, and Democracy in Latin America: Reconfigurations of Discourse and Political Action," special issue of *Revista de Estudios Sociales*, no. 51 (January–April 2015).

16. Justin McDaniel, *The Lovelorn Ghost and the Magical Monk: Practicing Buddhism in Modern Thailand* (New York: Columbia University Press, 2011), 9.

17. Yasmine Saleh, "Egyptian Christians Fear Chaos after Wedding Bloodshed," *Aswat Masriya*, October 21, 2013, http://www.reuters.com/article/2013/10/21/us-egypt-christians -idUSBRE99K0KA20131021.

18. Quoted in Hamza Hendawi, "Christians Mourn Cairo Shooting That Killed 4," *Big Story*, October 21, 2013, http://bigstory.ap.org/article/egyptian-pm-condemns-deadly-attack-copts.

19. Quoted in Saleh, "Egyptian Christians Fear Chaos."
20. Kristen Chick, "Sectarian Violence in Cairo Has Egypt on Edge," *Christian Science Monitor*, May 8, 2011, http://www.csmonitor.com/World/Middle-East/2011/0508/Sectarian -violence-in-Cairo-has-Egypt-on-edge.
21. Makdisi, *Culture of Sectarianism*, 174.
22. Ibid., 65. Even in such charged situations, Makdisi shows, it is also often the case that coreligionists refuse to aid one another, subverting the narrative of sectarian unity from another angle.
23. Kaplan, *Divided by Faith*; Evan Haefeli, *New Netherland and the Dutch Origins of American Religious Liberty* (Philadelphia: University of Pennsylvania Press, 2012).
24. Makdisi, *Culture of Sectarianism*, 71.
25. Reidar Visser questions the imposition by the United States and Europe of a master narrative of sectarianism on Iraqi politics. "The Western Imposition of Sectarianism on Iraqi Politics," *Arab Studies Journal* 15/16, nos. 2/1 (2007/ 2008): 83–99.
26. Toby C. Jones, "Bahrain: Human Rights and Political Wrongs" (Washington, DC: Carnegie Endowment for International Peace, September 25, 2012), http://carnegie endowment.org/2012/09/25/bahrain%2Dhuman%2Drights%2Dand%2Dpolitical %2Dwrongs/dwgi.
27. Jonathan Cook, "Onward, Christian Soldiers," *Middle East Report*, May 13, 2014, http:// www.merip.org/mero/mero051314?ip_login_no_cache=519fa174ed39f3c3566446cad b4d3f5b.
28. Cook elaborates, "The main political parties representing Palestinian citizens of Israel have staged protests in the city, including one in April at which youths dressed as soldiers and carried toy rifles. They declared the area a closed military zone, setting up barbed wire and a mock checkpoint. The 'soldiers' then acted out a show in which they harassed other youths as a way to highlight what military service in the Occupied Territories entails. A pamphlet handed out to passersby warned that Israel sought to achieve 'the disintegration of the Palestinian national minority into warring sects.' The Higher Follow-Up Committee, the main political body representing the Palestinian minority, called for a major rally against the enlistment drive and other leaders urged Christian youngsters publicly to burn their call-up papers." Ibid.
29. BBC, "Inside Syria—Syrian Diaries" (Documentary, February 28, 2013), https://www .youtube.com/watch?v=cIke4E1AgsY. The International Crisis Group documented actions by individuals and groups in Syria that defy presumed and ascribed sectarian lines of affiliation and described individuals from differing ethnic and religious backgrounds attempting to meet the everyday humanitarian needs of fellow citizens in difficult circumstances. International Crisis Group, "Syria's Mutating Conflict," *Middle East Report*, no. 128, August 1, 2012, http://www.crisisgroup.org/~/media/Files/Middle%20East%20 North%20Africa/Iraq%20Syria%20Lebanon/Syria/128-syrias-mutating-conflict.pdf.
30. For an attempt to bring some of these individuals and groups back into history, see two books by Orit Bashkin, *The Other Iraq: Pluralism and Culture in Hashemite Iraq* (Stanford: Stanford University Press, 2010) and *New Babylonians: A History of Jews in Modern Iraq* (Stanford: Stanford University Press, 2012).
31. Quoted in Robin McDowell, "Punks Break Myanmar's Silence on Religious Attacks," *Big Story*, August 5, 2013, http://bigstory.ap.org/article/punks-break-myanmars-silence -religious-attacks.

32. Orsi, *Between Heaven and Earth*, 167.

33. We need to "surrender dreams of religious order and singleness or of being able to organize descriptions and interpretations of religious worlds around sets of publicly shared and efficiently summarized meanings and practices." Ibid., 167.

34. Ibid., 7.

35. Ibid., 191.

36. Noah Salomon and Jeremy F. Walton, "Religious Criticism, Secular Criticism, and the 'Critical Study of Religion': Lessons from the Study of Islam," in Orsi, *Cambridge Companion to Religious Studies*, 408.

37. Ibid., 406.

38. Jakob de Roover, "Secular Law and the Realm of False Religion," in Sullivan, Yelle, and Taussig-Rubbo, *After Secular Law*, 43.

39. Winnifred Fallers Sullivan, "The Ambassador of Religious Freedoms," in *The Sunday Edition with Michael Enright* (CBC Radio, February 24, 2013).

40. Taking the argument a bit further than I would, Josephson claims that "the term religion lacks analytic cohesion and is in the process of disintegration." He attributes this to the de-Christianization of the category of religion: "because Christian theological propositions were the only thing holding the category together, this has contributed to its disintegration." *Invention of Religion in Japan*, 257, 249.

41. Michael McCann, "The Unbearable Lightness of Rights: On Sociolegal Inquiry in the Global Era," *Law & Society Review* 48, no. 2 (June 2014): 250.

42. On the history of the construction of the category "Hispanic" in the United States for example, and its varied sociopolitical and economic consequences, see G. Cristina Mora, *Making Hispanics: How Activists, Bureaucrats, and Media Constructed a New American* (Chicago: University of Chicago Press, 2014).

43. Sarah Shortall, "Lost in Translation: Religion and the Writing of History," *Modern Intellectual History* (published electronically December 30, 2014), doi:10.1017/S147924431400081X.

44. Jonathan Young, "Buddhism and Politics in Sri Lanka," a review of *Ruling Religion: Buddhism, Politics and Law in Contemporary Sri Lanka*, by Benjamin Schonthal, *Dissertation Reviews*, March 4, 2014, http://dissertationreviews.org/archives/7815 and Benjamin Schonthal, "The Legal Regulation of Religion: The Case of Buddhism in Post-Colonial Sri Lanka," in *Buddhism and Law: An Introduction*, ed. Rebecca Redwood French and Mark A. Nathan (Cambridge: Cambridge University Press, 2014), 150–66.

45. Anver M. Emon, *Religious Pluralism and Islamic Law: Dhimmis and Others in the Empire of Law* (Oxford: Oxford University Press, 2012), 3.

46. Chatterjee, *Making of Indian Secularism*, 244.

47. Salomon, *People of Sudan Love You*, chap. 1.

48. Benjamin L. Berger, *Law's Religion: Religious Difference and the Claims of Constitutionalism* (Toronto: University of Toronto Press, 2015). While focusing on Canadian constitutional law and religion Berger's argument also has broader application because, as he puts it, Canadian multiculturalism is "one expression of a broader habit of hiding the unruly lived experience of religion and modern constitutionalism under the tidy marquee of principle. It usually reads 'secularism,' and its invocation tells us little of significance." Ibid.

49. Samuli Schielke maintains that "we should take as our starting point the immediate practice of living a life, the existential concerns and the pragmatic considerations that inform this practice, embedded in but not reduced to the traditions, powers and discourses that grant legitimacy to some concerns over others and structure some considerations while leaving others diffuse." Schielke, "Second Thoughts about the Anthropology of Islam," 12.

50. Benjamin L. Berger, "The Legal Unintelligibility of Prayer," *Reverberations: New Directions in the Study of Prayer*, February 13, 2014, http://forums.ssrc.org/ndsp/2014/02/13/the-legal-unintelligibility-of-prayer/.

51. Ibid.

52. AllGov, "Ambassador's Fund for Cultural Preservation" (n.d.), http://www.allgov.com/departments/department-of-state/ambassadors-fund-for-cultural-preservation?agencyid=7203.

53. US Department of State, Bureau of Educational and Cultural Affairs, Ambassadors Fund for Cultural Preservation (n.d.), http://exchanges.state.gov/heritage/afcp.html. Recent projects include conservation of more than two hundred Buddha statues in the Museum of Vietnamese History in Ho Chi Minh City; provision of tools for site management of the ancient city of Busra, in Syria, the northern capital of the Nabataean Empire in the second century BC; restoration of the eighteenth-century Maria Magdalena Church in Managua, Nicaragua; documentation of Romani culture and music passed down through generations for six centuries in Romania; conservation of Pashto, Arabic, and Persian manuscripts dating to the sixteenth century in the Pashto Academy, University of Peshawar, Pakistan; a former GULAG camp in Perm, Russia; a manuscript collection in Kosovo dating from the Ottoman Empire; and a post-Tsunami survey of buildings in the thirteenth-century coastal town of Matara, Sri Lanka.

54. Caroline May, "U.S. Government Funds Mosque Renovation and Rehabilitation Around the World," *Daily Caller*, August 24, 2010, http://dailycaller.com/2010/08/24/u-s-government-funds-mosque-renovation-and-rehabilitation-around-the-world/.

55. "Removing religion from the realm of the religious to the domain of the secular, in particular religion that is sometimes denominated culture or heritage, can re-position majority religion as part of the social fabric and thus as not *really* religion. Removing minority religion from the realm of the religious to the domain of culture can be a way to deny rights, or, on occasion, to claim others. Figuring objects and practices as culture solves some problems while creating others." Beaman and Sullivan, "Neighbo(u)rly Misreadings and Misconstruals," 7.

56. Grants are awarded "based on a combination of the importance of the site, object, or form of expression; the country's need; the impact of the United States' contribution to the preservation; and the anticipated benefit to the advancement of U.S. diplomatic goals as a result of the selection." AllGov, "Ambassador's Fund."

57. Hussein Ali Agrama, "Asecular Revolution," *Immanent Frame*, March 11, 2011, http://blogs.ssrc.org/tif/2011/03/11/asecular-revolution/.

58. Elizabeth A. Pritchard, "Seriously, What Does 'Taking Religion Seriously' Mean?" *Journal of the American Academy of Religion* 78, no. 4 (December 2010): 1093n4. Pritchard has a compelling description of Habermas's domestication and neutralization of religion in his writings on religion in the public sphere: "For Habermas, religion is to be

taken seriously to the extent it can be safely scoured of anything that might trouble the regime of the secular.... Secularism's reach is secured by periodic displays of gracious acknowledgment of that which appears to elude its grasp." Ibid., 1094.

59. Orsi, *Between Heaven and Earth*, 167.

60. Orsi proposes "a disciplined suspension of the impulse to locate the other (with all of her or his discrepant moralities, ways of knowing, and religious impulses) securely in relation to one's own cosmos," and "refuses either to deny or to redeem the other." *Between Heaven and Earth*, 198, 203. Pritchard criticizes this suspensive ethos on the grounds that it "would soften the repugnant, the sexist, the destructive, by locating it in a liminal space and in flourishing compassion for our purportedly underlying humanity." She proposes instead "a 'taking seriously' that does not manage or preempt difference and conflict but risks and even invites them," observing that "to countenance religions with utter seriousness is to regard them as having historical, material, bodily consequences. It is also to consider religions as internally contentious, and to evaluate aspects of them on a case-by-case basis via explicit criteria of interpretation and judgment." Pritchard, "Seriously, What Does 'Taking Religion Seriously' Mean?," 1102, 1104.

61. "Religious idioms that arise within and exist in response to the exigencies of everyday life are not ever completely or securely under the authority either of the persons using them or of religious or political authorities ... everyday religious practice is 'embedded in traditions, relations of power and social dynamics, but it is not determined by them.'" Orsi, "Afterword," 152, quoting Samuli Schielke and Liza Debevec, "Introduction," in Schielke and Debevec, *Ordinary Lives and Grand Schemes*.

62. Winnifred Fallers Sullivan, "Varieties of Legal Secularism," in Cady and Hurd, *Comparative Secularisms in a Global Age*, 117. See, for example, Bethany Moreton, *To Serve God and Wal-Mart: The Making of Christian Free Enterprise* (Cambridge, MA: Harvard University Press, 2010).

63. See, for example, Anna Fedele, *Looking for Mary Magdalene: Alternative Pilgrimage and Ritual Creativity at Catholic Shrines in France* (Oxford: Oxford University Press, 2012).

64. Winnifred Fallers Sullivan, "The Impossibility of Religious Freedom," *Immanent Frame*, July 8, 2014, http://blogs.ssrc.org/tif/2014/07/08/impossibility-of-religious-freedom/.

Bibliography

Abu-Lughod, Lila. "Against Universals: The Dialects of (Women's) Human Rights and Human Capabilities." In *Rethinking the Human*, edited by J. Michelle Molina and Donald K. Swearer, 69–94. Cambridge, MA: Harvard University Press, 2010.

Adams, George. "Chaplains as Liaisons with Religious Leaders: Lessons from Iraq and Afghanistan." *Peaceworks*, no. 56 (2006). http://www.usip.org/publications/chaplains-liaisons-religious-leaders-lessons-iraq-and-afghanistan.

Adcock, C. S. *The Limits of Tolerance: Indian Secularism and the Politics of Religious Freedom*. Oxford: Oxford University Press, 2013.

Agrama, Hussein Ali. "Asecular Revolution." *Immanent Frame*, March 11, 2011. http://blogs.ssrc.org/tif/2011/03/11/asecular-revolution/.

———. *Questioning Secularism: Islam, Sovereignty, and the Rule of Law in Modern Egypt*. Chicago: University of Chicago Press, 2012.

Akram, Sophia. "Cutting Borders: Ethnic Tensions and Burmese Refugees." *Fair Observer*, September 18, 2013. http://www.fairobserver.com/article/cutting-borders-ethnic-tensions-and-burmese-refugees.

"Alevi Group Demands End to Turkish Mandatory Religious Classes." *Hurriyet Daily News*, November 7, 2010. http://www.hurriyetdailynews.com/default.aspx?pageid=438&n=alevis-protest-mandatory-religion-classes-by-rally-2010-11-07.

"Alevilik İslamiyet'in içinde değil" [Kazım Genç, interviewed by Neşe Düzel]. *Radikal*, October 10, 2005. http://www.radikal.com.tr/haber.php?haberno=166463.

Alexander, Ruth. "Are There Really 100,000 New Christian Martyrs Every Year?" *BBC News Magazine*, November 12, 2013. http://www.bbc.com/news/magazine-24864587.

Allen, John L., Jr. *The Global War on Christians: Dispatches from the Front Lines of Anti-Christian Persecution*. New York: Image, 2013.

AllGov. "Ambassador's Fund for Cultural Preservation." n.d. http://www.allgov.com/departments/department-of-state/ambassadors-fund-for-cultural-preservation?agencyid=7203.

Ammerman, Nancy T., ed. *Everyday Religion: Observing Modern Religious Lives*. Oxford: Oxford University Press, 2006.

———. "Waco, Federal Law Enforcement, and Scholars of Religion." In *Armageddon in Waco: Critical Perspectives on the Branch Davidian Conflict*, edited by Stuart A. Wright, 282–96. Chicago: University of Chicago Press, 1995.

Amrieh, Antoine. "Tripoli Mobilizes after Historic Library Torched." *Daily Star*, January 4, 2014. http://www.dailystar.com.lb/News/Lebanon-News/2014/Jan-04/243098 -historic-library-torched-in-n-lebanon.ashx#axzz2pisNlpFu.

Annicchino, Pasquale. "Recent Developments Concerning the Promotion of Freedom of Religion or Belief in Italian Foreign Policy." *Review of Faith and International Affairs* 11, no. 3 (September 2013): 61–68.

Appleby, R. Scott. *The Ambivalence of the Sacred: Religion, Violence, and Reconciliation*. Oxford: Rowman & Littlefield, 2000.

Årsheim, Helge. "Legal Secularism? Differing Notions of Religion in International and Norwegian Law." In *Secular and Sacred? The Scandinavian Case of Religion in Human Rights, Law and Public Space*, edited by Rosemary Van Den Breemer, José Casanova, and Trygve Wyller, 123–51. Göttingen: Vandenhoeck & Ruprecht, 2013.

Asad, Talal. *Formations of the Secular: Christianity, Islam, Modernity*. Stanford: Stanford University Press, 2003.

———. *Genealogies of Religion: Discipline and Reasons of Power in Christianity and Islam*. Baltimore: Johns Hopkins University Press, 1993.

———. "Muhummad Asad between Religion and Politics." *Islam Interactive*, n.d. http://www.islaminteractive.info/content/muhammad-asad-between-religion-and-politics #.T7omUh6JUTM.

———. "Response to Gil Anidjar." *Interventions: International Journal of Postcolonial Studies* 11, no. 3 (2009): 394–99.

———. "Thinking about Religion, Belief, and Politics." In *The Cambridge Companion to Religious Studies*, edited by Robert A. Orsi, 36–57. Cambridge: Cambridge University Press, 2012.

Aslan, Secil. "The Ambivalence of Alevi Politic(s): A Comparative Analysis of Cem Vakfi and Pir Sultan Abdal Derneği." Master's thesis, Bogazici University, Istanbul, 2008.

Austrian Foreign Ministry. "Vice Chancellor Pressing for Early Adoption of EU Guidelines on Freedom of Religion." December 10, 2012. http://www.bmeia.gv.at/en/foreign -ministry/news/press-releases/2012/spindelegger-protection-of-religious-minorities -is-a-key-concern-of-austrias-human-rights-policy.html.

Baker, Peter. "Religious Freedom Is a Tenet of Foreign Policy, Obama Says." *New York Times*, February 6, 2014. http://www.nytimes.com/2014/02/07/us/politics/obama-denounces -religious-repression.html?emc=eta1&_r=0.

Banchoff, Thomas, and Robert Wuthnow. "Introduction." In *Religion and the Global Politics of Human Rights*, edited by Thomas Banchoff and Robert Wuthnow, 1–22. Oxford: Oxford University Press, 2011.

Barkey, Karen. *Empire of Difference: The Ottomans in Comparative Perspective*. Cambridge: Cambridge University Press, 2008.

Bartell, Rich. "U.S. Army Africa Chaplains Teach Resiliency in Africa." March 6, 2012. http://www.army.mil/article/75110/U_S__Army_Africa_chaplains_teach_resiliency_in _Africa/.

Barton, Frederick R., Shannon Hayden, and Karin von Hippel. "Navigating in the Fog: Improving U.S. Government Engagement with Religion." In *Rethinking Religion and World Affairs*, edited by Alfred Stepan, Monica Duffy Toft, and Timothy Shah, 279–90. New York: Columbia University Press, 2012.

Basaran, Ezgi. "Erdogan's Negative Comments Unite Turkish Alevis." *Al-Monitor*, May 9, 2013. http://www.al-monitor.com/pulse/politics/2013/05/turkey-alevis-erdogan-negative -interview-selahattin-ozel.html.

Bashkin, Orit. *New Babylonians: A History of Jews in Modern Iraq*. Stanford: Stanford University Press, 2012.

———. *The Other Iraq: Pluralism and Culture in Hashemite Iraq*. Stanford: Stanford University Press, 2010.

Bauman, Gerd. *Contesting Culture, Discourses of Identity in Multi-ethnic London*. Cambridge: Cambridge University Press, 1996.

Baz v. Walters, 782 F.2d 701 (1986).

BBC. "Inside Syria—Syrian Diaries" (Documentary). February 28, 2013. https://www .youtube.com/watch?v=cIke4E1AgsY.

Beaman, Lori G. "The Will to Religion: Obligatory Religious Citizenship." *Critical Research on Religion* 1, no. 2 (2013): 141–57.

Beaman, Lori G., and Winnifred Fallers Sullivan, "Neighbo(u)rly Misreadings and Misconstruals: A Cross-Border Conversation." In *Varieties of Religious Establishment*, edited by Lori G. Beaman and Winnifred Fallers Sullivan, 1–14. London: Ashgate, 2013.

Bender, Courtney. "The Power of Pluralist Thinking." In *Politics of Religious Freedom*, edited by Winnifred Fallers Sullivan, Elizabeth Shakman Hurd, Saba Mahmood, and Peter G. Danchin, 66–77. Chicago: University of Chicago Press, 2015.

———. "Secularism and Pluralism." Unpublished manuscript, June 2012.

Bennett, Jane. *The Enchantment of Modern Life: Attachments, Crossings, and Ethics*. Princeton: Princeton University Press, 2001.

Berger, Benjamin L. "The Aesthetics of Religious Freedom." In *Varieties of Religious Establishment*, edited by Lori G. Beaman and Winnifred Fallers Sullivan, 33–53. London: Ashgate, 2013.

———. "The Cultural Limits of Legal Tolerance." In *After Pluralism: Reimagining Religious Engagement*, edited by Pamela E. Klassen and Courtney Bender, 98–123. New York: Columbia University Press, 2010.

———. *Law's Religion: Religious Difference and the Claims of Constitutionalism*. Toronto: University of Toronto Press, 2015.

———. "The Legal Unintelligibility of Prayer." *Reverberations: New Directions in the Study of Prayer*, February 13, 2014. http://forums.ssrc.org/ndsp/2014/02/13/the-legal -unintelligibility-of-prayer/.

Beyer, Peter. "Deprivileging Religion in a Post-Westphalian State." In *Varieties of Religious Establishment*, edited by Lori G. Beaman and Winnifred Fallers Sullivan, 75–92. London: Ashgate, 2013.

Bilgrami, Akeel. *Secularism, Identity, and Enchantment*. Cambridge, MA: Harvard University Press, 2014.

———. "Slouching toward Bethlehem: Secularism in the MENA Region." Lecture at the Conference on Crepuscular Secularism, Ann Arbor, MI, March 18, 2013.

Birnbaum, Maria. "Becoming Recognizable: Postcolonial Independence and the Reification of Religion in International Relations." Ph.D. thesis, European University Institute, Florence, 2015.

Bishara, Amahl. "Covering the Christians of the Holy Land." *Middle East Report* 267 (Summer 2013): 7–14.

Blair, Tony. "Taking Faith Seriously." *New Europe Online*, January 2, 2012. http://www
.neurope.eu/blog/taking-faith-seriously.

Boone, Jon. "US Funds Madrassas in Afghanistan." *Financial Times*, January 29, 2008. http://
www.ft.com/intl/cms/s/0/d1b9e546-ceb4–11dc-877a-000077b07658.html#axzz3C
juoONTW.

Bosco, Robert M. "Persistent Orientalisms: The Concept of Religion in International Relations." *Journal of International Relations and Development* 12, no. 1 (2009): 90–111.

———. *Securing the Sacred: Religion, National Security, and the Western State*. Ann Arbor:
University of Michigan Press, 2014.

Brown, Wendy. " 'The Most We Can Hope For . . .': Human Rights and the Politics of Fatalism." *South Atlantic Quarterly* 103, nos. 2/3 (2004): 451–63.

———. *Regulating Aversion: Tolerance in the Age of Identity and Empire*. Princeton: Princeton
University Press, 2008.

Bruce, Benjamin. "Gérer l'Islam à l'Etranger: Entre Service Public et Outil de la Politique
Étrangère Turque." *Anatoli*, no. 3 (2012): 131–47.

Butler, Jon. "Disquieted History in a Secular Age." In *Varieties of Secularism in a Secular Age*,
edited by Michael Warner, Jonathan VanAntwerpen, and Craig Calhoun, 193–216. Cambridge, MA: Harvard University Press, 2010.

Calhoun, Craig, Mark Juergensmeyer, and Jonathan VanAntwerpen, eds. *Rethinking Secularism*. Oxford: Oxford University Press, 2011.

Campbell, David. *National Deconstruction: Violence, Identity, and Justice in Bosnia*. Minneapolis: University of Minnesota Press, 1998.

Campbell, John. "Africa Update." Panel presentation at the Seventh Annual Religion and
Foreign Policy Summer Workshop, New York, June 25, 2013.

Casanova, José. *Public Religions in the Modern World*. Chicago: University of Chicago Press,
1994.

———. "Religion, the New Millennium, and Globalization." *Sociology of Religion* 62, no. 4
(2001): 415–41.

Castelli, Elizabeth A. "Persecution Complexes: Identity Politics and the 'War on Christians.' "
Differences: A Journal of Feminist Cultural Studies 18, no. 3 (2007): 152–80.

———. "Praying for the Persecuted Church: US Christian Activism in the Global Arena."
Journal of Human Rights 4, no. 3 (2005): 321–51.

———. "Theologizing Human Rights: Christian Activism and the Limits of Religious Freedom." In *Non-governmental Politics*, edited by Michel Feher, Gaëlle Krikorian, and Yates
McKee, 673–87. New York: Zone Books, 2007.

Castellino, Joshua, and Kathleen A. Cavanaugh. *Minority Rights in the Middle East*. Oxford:
Oxford University Press, 2013.

Cavanaugh, William. *The Myth of Religious Violence: Secular Ideology and the Roots of Modern
Conflict*. New York: Oxford University Press, 2009.

Chatterjee, Nandini. "English Law, Brahmo Marriage, and the Problem of Religious Difference: Civil Marriage Laws in Britain and India." *Comparative Studies in Society and
History* 52, no. 3 (July 2010): 524–52.

———. *The Making of Indian Secularism: Empire, Law, and Christianity, 1830–1960*. New
York: Palgrave Macmillan, 2011.

Chicago Council on Global Affairs. "Engaging Religious Communities Abroad: A New
Imperative for U.S. Foreign Policy." Report of the Task Force on Religion and the

Making of U.S. Foreign Policy, Scott Appleby and Richard Cizik, cochairs. Chicago, February 2010. http://www.thechicagocouncil.org/sites/default/files/2010%20Religion%20Task%20Force_Full%20Report.pdf.

Chick, Kristen. "Sectarian Violence in Cairo Has Egypt on Edge." *Christian Science Monitor*, May 8, 2011. http://www.csmonitor.com/World/Middle-East/2011/0508/Sectarian-violence-in-Cairo-has-Egypt-on-edge.

Chidester, David. *Savage Systems: Colonialism and Comparative Religion in Southern Africa.* Charlottesville: University of Virginia Press, 1996.

———. *Wild Religion: Tracking the Sacred in South Africa.* Berkeley: University of California Press, 2012.

Çitak, Zana. "Between 'Turkish Islam' and 'French Islam': The Role of the *Diyanet* in the *Conseil Français du Culte Musulman*." *Journal of Ethnic and Migration Studies* 36, no. 4 (2010): 619–34.

Clarke, Gerard. "Agents of Transformation? Donors, Faith-Based Organisations and International Development." *Third World Quarterly* 28, no. 1 (2007): 77–96.

Clarke, Gerard, and Michael Jennings, eds. *Development, Civil Society and Faith-Based Organizations.* New York: Palgrave Macmillan, 2008.

Cloud, Dana L. "To Veil the Threat of Terror: Afghan Women and the 'Clash of Civilizations' in the Imagery of the U.S. War on Terrorism." *Quarterly Journal of Speech* 90, no. 3 (2004): 285–306.

Cloud, David S., and Jeff Gerth, "Muslim Scholars Were Paid to Aid U.S. Propaganda." *New York Times*, January 2, 2006. http://www.nytimes.com/2006/01/02/politics/02propaganda.html?_r=0.

Comaroff, Jean. "The Politics of Conviction: Faith on the Neo-liberal Frontier." In *Contemporary Religiosities: Emergent Socialities and the Post-Nation-State*, edited by Bruce Kapferer, Kari Tell, and Annelin Eriksen, 17–38. New York: Berghahn Books, 2010.

Comaroff, Jean, and John L. Comaroff. *Of Revelation and Revolution: Christianity, Colonialism, and Consciousness in South Africa.* Vol. 1. Chicago: University of Chicago Press, 1991.

Comaroff, John L., and Jean Comaroff. *Ethnicity, Inc.* Chicago: University of Chicago Press, 2009.

Connolly, William E. *The Ethos of Pluralization.* Minneapolis: University of Minnesota Press, 1995.

———. *The Fragility of Things: Self-Organizing Processes, Neoliberal Fantasies, and Democratic Activism.* Durham, NC: Duke University Press, 2013.

———. "Taylor, Foucault, and Otherness." *Political Theory* 13 (1985): 365–76.

Cook, Jonathan. "Onward, Christian Soldiers." *Middle East Report*, May 13, 2014. http://www.merip.org/mero/mero051314?ip_login_no_cache=519fa174ed39f3c3566446cadb4d3f5b.

Cook, Suzan Johnson. "Religious Tolerance at Home and Abroad." Panel presentation at the Seventh Annual Religion and Foreign Policy Summer Workshop, New York, June 25, 2013.

Council of the European Union. *EU Guidelines on the Promotion and Protection of Freedom of Religion or Belief.* Luxembourg, June 24, 2013. http://www.eu-un.europa.eu/articles/en/article_13685_en.htm.

Dabashi, Hamid. "To Protect the Revolution, Overcome the False Secular-Islamist Divide." *Al Jazeera*, December 9, 2012. http://www.aljazeera.com/indepth/opinion/2012/12/2012128153845368495.html.

Dacey, Austin. "Why Is the State Department Opening an Office of 'Religious Engagement?'" *Religion Dispatches*, August 8, 2013. http://religiondispatches.org/why-is-the-state-department-opening-an-office-of-religious-engagement/.

Dad, Aziz Ali. "The Sectarian Ghoul in Gilgit." *News*, December 20, 2012. http://www.the news.com.pk/Todays-News-9-149434-The-sectarian-ghoul-in-Gilgit.

Danan, Liora. "Mixed Blessings: U.S. Government Engagement with Religion in Conflict-Prone Settings." Washington, DC: Center for Strategic and International Studies, August 2007.

Danchin, Peter G., and Louis Blond. "Unlawful Religion? Modern Secular Power and the Legal Reasoning in the *JFS* Case." In "Politics of Religious Freedom: Case Studies,." edited by Peter G. Danchin, Winnifred Fallers Sullivan, Saba Mahmood, and Elizabeth Shakman Hurd. Special issue of *Maryland Journal of International Law* 29 (2015): 414–75.

Danchin, Peter G., and Lisa Forman, "The Evolving Jurisprudence of the European Court of Human Rights and the Protection of Religious Minorities." In *Protecting the Human Rights of Religious Minorities in Eastern Europe*, edited by Peter G. Danchin and Elizabeth Cole, 192–221. New York: Columbia University Press, 2002.

Davison, Andrew. "Hermeneutics and the Politics of Secularism." In *Comparative Secularisms in a Global Age*, edited by Linell E. Cady and Elizabeth Shakman Hurd, 25–39. New York: Palgrave Macmillan, 2010.

de Bernières, Louis. *Birds Without Wings*. New York: Vintage, 2004.

Deneulin, Séverine, and Masooda Bano. *Religion in Development: Rewriting the Secular Script*. London: Zed Books, 2009.

de Roover, Jakob. "Secular Law and the Realm of False Religion." In *After Secular Law*, edited by Winnifred Fallers Sullivan, Robert A. Yelle, and Mateo Taussig-Rubbo, 43–61. Stanford: Stanford University Press, 2011.

Dorell, Oren, and Sarah Lynch. "Christians Fear Losing Freedoms in Arab Spring Movement." *USA Today*, January 31, 2012. http://usatoday30.usatoday.com/news/religion/story/2012-01-30/arab-spring-christians/52894182/1.

Dressler, Markus. "The Modern Dede: Changing Parameters for Religious Authority in Contemporary Turkish Alevism." In *Speaking for Islam: Religious Authorities in Muslim Societies*, edited by Gudrun Krämer and Sabine Schmidtke, 269–94. Leiden: Brill, 2006.

———. "New Texts Out Now: Markus Dressler, *Writing Religion: The Making of Turkish Alevi Islam.*" *Jadaliyya*, June 19, 2013. http://www.jadaliyya.com/pages/index/12302/new-texts-out-now_markus-dressler-writing-religion.

———. "The Religio-Secular Continuum: Reflections on the Religious Dimensions of Turkish Secularism." In *After Secular Law*, edited by Winnifred Fallers Sullivan, Robert A. ·Yelle, and Mateo Taussig-Rubbo, 221–41. Stanford: Stanford University Press, 2011.

———. *Writing Religion: The Making of Turkish Alevi Islam*. Oxford: Oxford University Press, 2013.

Dressler, Markus, and Arvind-Pal S. Mandair. "Introduction: Modernity, Religion-Making, and the Postsecular." In *Secularism and Religion-Making*, edited by Markus Dressler and Arvind Mandair, 3–36. Oxford: Oxford University Press, 2011.

Dubertrand, Roland. "Religious Freedom from the Point of View of French Diplomacy." Keynote speech at the Protecting the Right to Freedom of Religion or Belief conference, Florence, November 17, 2012.

DuBois, Joshua. "The White House, Religion, and Global Affairs." Washington, DC: Office of Faith-based and Neighborhood Partnerships, July 11, 2011. http://www.whitehouse.gov /blog/2011/07/11/white-house-religion-and-global-affairs.

Edge, Peter W. "Hard Law and Soft Power: Counter-Terrorism, the Power of Sacred Places, and the Establishment of an Anglican Islam." *Rutgers Journal of Law & Religion* 12, pt. 2 (Spring 2010): 358–82.

Eichler-Levine, Jodi, and Rosemary Hicks. "As Americans Against Genocide: The Crisis in Darfur and Interreligious Political Activism." *American Quarterly* 59, no. 3 (September 2007): 711–35.

Elshinnawi, Mohamed. "Conflicts Engulf Christians in Mideast." *Voice of America*, August 30, 2014. http://www.voanews.com/content/conflicts-engulf-christians-in-middle -east/2432773.html.

Emon, Anver M. *Religious Pluralism and Islamic Law: Dhimmīs and Others in the Empire of Law*. Oxford: Oxford University Press, 2012.

European Commission. "Commission Staff Working Paper, Turkey 2011 Progress Report." Brussels, October 12, 2011. http://ec.europa.eu/enlargement/pdf/key_documents/2011 /package/tr_rapport_2011_en.pdf.

European Platform on Religious Intolerance and Discrimination. "Recommendations of the European Platform on Religious Intolerance and Discrimination to the Institutions of the European Union Concerning the Implementation of Freedom of Religion or Belief." May 26, 2011. http://www.europarl.europa.eu/meetdocs/2009_2014/documents /droi/dv/201/201105/20110526_416recomeprid_en.pdf.

Evans, Malcolm. "Advancing Freedom of Religion or Belief: Agendas for Change." Lambeth Inter Faith Lecture, London, June 8, 2011.

———. *Religious Liberty and International Law in Europe*. Cambridge: Cambridge University Press, 1997.

Evans, Malcolm, and Peter Petkoff. "A Separation of Convenience? The Concept of Neutrality in the Jurisprudence of the European Court of Human Rights." *Religion, State, and Society* 36, no. 3 (September 2008): 205–23.

Farr, Thomas F. "Cold War Religion," *First Things*, June 2009. http://www.firstthings.com /article/2009/06/cold-war-religion.

———. "Religious Freedom Abroad." *First Things*, March 2012. http://www.firstthings.com /article/2012/03/religious-freedom-abroad.

———. *World of Faith and Freedom: Why International Religious Liberty Is Vital to American National Security*. Oxford: Oxford University Press, 2008.

Fassin, Eric. "National Identities and Transnational Intimacies: Sexual Democracy and the Politics of Immigration in Europe." *Public Culture* 22, no. 3 (2010): 507–29.

Fedele, Anna. *Looking for Mary Magdalene: Alternative Pilgrimage and Ritual Creativity at Catholic Shrines in France*. Oxford: Oxford University Press, 2012.

Ferrari, Alessandro. "Religious Education in a Globalized Europe." In *Religion and Democracy in Contemporary Europe*, edited by Gabriel Motzkin and Yochi Fischer, 113–24. London: Alliance, 2008.

Ferrie, Jared. "Why Myanmar's Rohingya Are Forced to Say They Are Bengali." *Christian Science Monitor*, June 2, 2013. http://www.csmonitor.com/World/Asia-Pacific/2013/0602 /Why-Myanmar-s-Rohingya-are-forced-to-say-they-are-Bengali.

Fessenden, Tracy. *Culture and Redemption: Religion, the Secular, and American Literature.* Princeton: Princeton University Press, 2007.

Fiddian-Qasmiyeh, Elena. *The Ideal Refugees: Gender, Islam, and the Sahrawi Politics of Survival.* Syracuse, NY: Syracuse University Press, 2013.

———. "The Pragmatics of Performance: Putting 'Faith' in Aid in the Sahrawi Refugee Camps." *Journal of Refugee Studies* 24, no. 3 (2011): 533–47.

Furey, Constance M. "Body, Society, and Subjectivity in Religious Studies." *Journal of the American Academy of Religion* 80, no. 1 (March 2012): 7–33.

Gauci, Joe Vella. "Protection of Religious Freedom: A New Operational Set of Tools." *Europeinfos*, no. 157 (February 2013). http://www.comece.eu/europeinfos/en/archive/issue 157/article/5480.html.

Goldfarb, Michael. "Napoleon, the Jews and French Muslims." *New York Times*, March 18, 2007. http://www.nytimes.com/2007/03/18/opinion/18iht-edgoldfarb.4943373.html.

Goldstone, Brian. "Secularism, 'Religious Violence,' and the Liberal Imaginary." In *Secularism and Religion-Making*, edited by Markus Dressler and Arvind-Pal S. Mandair, 104–24. Oxford: Oxford University Press, 2011.

Göle, Nilüfer. "Manifestations of the Religious-Secular Divide: Self, State, and the Public Sphere." In *Comparative Secularisms in a Global Age*, edited by Linell E. Cady and Elizabeth Shakman Hurd, 41–53. New York: Palgrave Macmillan, 2010.

Goossaert, Vincent, and David A. Palmer. *The Religious Question in Modern China.* Chicago: University of Chicago Press, 2012.

Gözaydın, İştar B. "A Religious Administration to Secure Secularism: The Presidency of Religious Affairs of the Republic of Turkey." *Marburg Journal of Religion* 11, no. 1 (2006). http://archiv.ub.uni-marburg.de/mjr/art_goezaydin_2006.html.

Grove, Thomas. "Turkish Alevis Fight Back Against Religion Lessons." Reuters, May 5, 2008. http://www.reuters.com/article/2008/05/06/us-turkey-alevi-idUSL2481334820080506.

Gutkowski, Stacey, and George Wilkes. "Changing Chaplaincy: A Contribution to Debate over the Roles of US and British Military Chaplains in Afghanistan." *Religion, State, and Society* 30, no. 1 (2011): 111–24.

Hackett, Rosalind I. J. "Traditional, African, Religious, Freedom?" In *Politics of Religious Freedom*, edited by Winnifred Fallers Sullivan, Elizabeth Shakman Hurd, Saba Mahmood, and Peter G. Danchin, 89–98. Chicago: University of Chicago Press, 2015.

Haefeli, Evan. *New Netherland and the Dutch Origins of American Religious Liberty.* Philadelphia: University of Pennsylvania Press, 2012.

———. "Toleration and Empire: The Origins of American Religious Pluralism." In *British North America in the Seventeenth and Eighteenth Centuries: Oxford History of the British Empire Companion*, edited by Stephen Foster, 103–35. Oxford: Oxford University Press, 2014.

Hall, David D, ed. *Lived Religion in America: Toward a History of Practice.* Princeton: Princeton University Press, 1997.

Hann, Chris, and Mathijs Pelkmans. "Realigning Religion and Power in Central Asia: Religion, the Nation-State and (Post)socialism." *Europe-Asia Studies* 61, no. 9 (2009): 1517–41.

Hanna, Michael Wahid. "With Friends Like These: Coptic Activism in the Diaspora." *Middle East Report*, no. 267 (2013). http://www.merip.org/mer/mer267/friends-these.

Harling, Peter, and Sarah Birke, "The Syrian Heartbreak." *Middle East Report*, April 16, 2013. http://www.merip.org/mero/mero041613.

Harris, Ian. *Cambodian Buddhism: History and Practice*. Honolulu: University of Hawaii Press, 2005.

Hasan and Eylem Zengin v. Turkey. Application no. 1448/04. European Court of Human Rights. Strasbourg, October 9, 2007.

Hassner, Ron E. *War on Sacred Grounds*. Ithaca, NY: Cornell University Press, 2009.

Hayden, Jessica Powley. "Mullahs on a Bus: The Establishment Clause and U.S. Foreign Aid." *Georgetown Law Journal* 95 (2006): 171–206.

Haynes, Jeffrey. *Religion, Politics and International Relations: Selected Essays*. London: Routledge, 2011.

Head, Jonathan. "The Unending Plight of Burma's Unwanted Rohingyas." *BBC News*, July 1, 2013. http://www.bbc.co.uk/news/world-asia-23077537.

Hefner, Robert W., and Krishna Kumar. "Summary Assessment of the Islam and Civil Society Program in Indonesia: Promoting Democracy and Pluralism in the Muslim World." PPC Evaluation Brief 13. Washington, DC: USAID, Bureau for Policy and Program Coordination, February 2006.

Hein v. Freedom from Religion Foundation. 127 S. Ct. 2553 (2007).

Helm, Toby. "Extremist Religion Is at Root of 21st-Century Wars, Says Tony Blair." *Guardian*, January 25, 2014. http://www.theguardian.com/politics/2014/jan/25/extremist-religion-wars-tony-blair.

Hendawi, Hamza. "Christians Mourn Cairo Shooting That Killed 4." *Big Story*, October 21, 2013. http://bigstory.ap.org/article/egyptian-pm-condemns-deadly-attack-copts.

Herzog, Jonathan P. *The Spiritual-Industrial Complex: America's Religious Battle Against Communism in the Early Cold War*. Oxford: Oxford University Press, 2011.

Hicks, Rosemary R. "Saving Darfur: Enacting Pluralism in Terms of Gender, Genocide, and Militarized Human Rights." In *After Pluralism: Reimagining Religious Engagement*, edited by Pamela E. Klassen and Courtney Bender, 252–76. New York: Columbia University Press, 2010.

Hirschkind, Charles. "Religious Difference and Democratic Pluralism: Some Recent Debates and Frameworks." *Temenos* 44, no. 1 (2008): 67–82.

Hodal, Kate. "Trapped Inside Burma's Refugee Camps, the Rohingya People Call for Recognition." *Guardian*, December 20, 2012. http://www.guardian.co.uk/world/2012/dec/20/burma-rohingya-muslim-refugee-camps.

Hoffner, Anne-Bénédicte, and Frédéric Mounier. "Quand l'Etat Est Amené à Traiter des Questions Religieuses." *La-Croix*, December 16, 2011. http://www.la-croix.com/Religion/Approfondir/Spiritualite/Quand-l-Etat-est-amene-a-traiter-des-questions-religieuses-_NP_-2011-12-16-747748.

Honig, Bonnie. *Emergency Politics: Paradox, Law, Democracy*. Princeton: Princeton University Press, 2009.

Hulsether, Mark. "Review of *Religion and American Foreign Policy, 1945–1960: The Soul of Containment*, by William Inboden." *American Studies* 51, nos. 1–2 (2010): 126–28.

Hurd, Elizabeth Shakman. "Believing in Religious Freedom." In *Politics of Religious Freedom*, edited by Winnifred Fallers Sullivan, Elizabeth Shakman Hurd, Saba Mahmood, and Peter G. Danchin, 45–56. Chicago: University of Chicago Press, 2015.

———. "The Dangerous Illusion of an 'Alawite' Regime." *Boston Review*, June 11, 2013. http://bit.ly/16a87wc.

————. "The Global Securitization of Religion." *Immanent Frame*, March 23, 2010. http:// blogs.ssrc.org/tif/2010/03/23/global-securitization/.

————. *The Politics of Secularism in International Relations*. Princeton: Princeton University Press, 2008.

————. "Religious Freedom, American-Style." *Quaderni di Diritto e Politica Ecclesiastica*, no. 1 (April 2014): 231–42.

————. "Rescued by Law? Gender and the Global Politics of Secularism." In *Religion, the Secular, and the Politics of Sexual Difference*, edited by Linell E. Cady and Tracy Fessenden, 211–28. New York: Columbia University Press, 2014.

————. "Thinking about Religion, Law, and Politics in Latin America." In "Religions, Post-secularity, and Democracy in Latin America: Reconfigurations of Discourse and Political Action." Special issue of *Revista de Estudios Sociales*, no. 51 (2015): 25–35.

Husain, Ed. "A Global Venture to Counter Violent Extremism." Council on Foreign Relations Policy Innovation Memorandum 37 (September 2013). http://www.cfr.org /radicalization-and-extremism/global-venture-counter-violent-extremism/p30494.

Inboden, William. *Religion and American Foreign Policy, 1945–1960: The Soul of Containment.* Cambridge: Cambridge University Press, 2008.

————. "Religious Freedom and National Security." *Hoover Institution Policy Review*, no. 175 (2012). http://www.hoover.org/research/religious-freedom-and-national-security.

International Crisis Group. "Syria's Mutating Conflict." *Middle East Report*, no. 128 (August 1, 2012). http://www.crisisgroup.org/~/media/Files/Middle%20East%20North%20 Africa/Iraq%20Syria%20Lebanon/Syria/128-syrias-mutating-conflict.pdf.

International Religious Freedom Act of 1998, HR 2431, 105th Cong., 2nd Sess. (1998).

"Interview: Nationalist Monk U Wirathu Denies Role in Anti-Muslim Unrest." *Irrawaddy*, April 2, 2013. http://www.irrawaddy.org/interview/nationalist-monk-u-wirathu-denies -role-in-anti-muslim-unrest.html.

Jacobs, Seth. *America's Miracle Man in Vietnam: Ngo Dinh Diem, Religion, Race, and U.S. Intervention in Southeast Asia.* Durham, NC: Duke University Press, 2005.

Jacobson, Matthew Frye. *Barbarian Virtues: The United States Encounters Foreign Peoples at Home and Abroad.* New York: Hill & Wang, 2000.

Jakobsen, Janet R. "Sex + Freedom = Regulation. Why?" *Social Text* 23, nos. 3/4 (2005): 285–308.

Jansen, Yolande. *Secularism, Assimilation and the Crisis of Multiculturalism: French Modernist Legacies.* Amsterdam: Amsterdam University Press, 2013.

Jenkins, Gareth. "ECHR Ruling Highlights Discrimination Suffered by Turkey's Alevi Minority." *Eurasia Daily Monitor*, October 12, 2007. http://www.jamestown.org/programs /edm/single/?tx_ttnews%5Btt_news%5D=33075&tx_ttnews%5BbackPid%5D=405&no _cache=1#.UczSehb1hEI.

Johnson, Greg. *Sacred Claims: Repatriation and Living Tradition.* Charlottesville: University of Virginia Press, 2007.

Johnston, Douglas, and Cynthia Sampson, eds. *Religion, the Missing Dimension of Statecraft.* Oxford: Oxford University Press, 1995.

Jones, Kevin J. "Vatican Urges UN to Help Protect Religious Freedom." *EWTN News*, March 3, 2012. http://www.ewtnnews.com/catholic-news/World.php?id=5006#ixzz20XM0PhXR.

Jones, Toby C. "Bahrain: Human Rights and Political Wrongs." Washington, DC: Carnegie Endowment for International Peace, September 25, 2012. http://carnegieendowment

.org/2012/09/25/bahrain%2Dhuman%2Drights%2Dand%2Dpolitical%2Dwrongs /dwgi.

Josephson, Jason Ānanda. *The Invention of Religion in Japan.* Chicago: University of Chicago Press, 2012.

Joustra, Robert. "Century for Sale." Review of *God's Century: Resurgent Religion and Global Politics* by Monica Duffy Toft, Daniel Philpott, and Timothy Samuel Shah. *Books & Culture: A Christian Review,* September/October 2011. http://www.booksandculture .com/articles/2011/sepoct/centurysale.html?paging=off.

Kahf, Mohja. "From Grief We Rise: To a Country for All Syrians." *Syrian Sun,* June 9, 2012.

Kahn, Paul. *The Cultural Study of Law: Reconstructing Legal Scholarship.* Chicago: University of Chicago Press, 1999.

Kaplan, Benjamin J. *Divided by Faith: Religious Conflict and the Practice of Toleration in Early Modern Europe.* Cambridge, MA: Belknap, 2007.

Kaplan, David E. "Hearts, Minds, and Dollars." *U.S. News & World Report,* April 17, 2005. http://www.globalissues.org/article/584/hearts-minds-and-dollars.

Kaya, Ayhan. "Multicultural Clientelism and Alevi Resurgence in the Turkish Diaspora: Berlin Alevis." *New Perspectives on Turkey* 18 (1998): 23–49.

Keane, Webb. *Christian Moderns: Freedom and Fetish in the Mission Encounter.* Berkeley: University of California Press, 2007.

Kennedy, David. "Losing Faith in the Secular: Law, Religion, and the Culture of International Governance." In *Religion and International Law,* edited by Mark W. Janis and Carolyn Evans, 309–19. The Hague: Martinus Nijhoff, 1999.

Klassen, Pamela E., and Courtney Bender, "Introduction: Habits of Pluralism." In *After Pluralism: Reimagining Religious Engagement,* edited by Pamela E. Klassen and Courtney Bender, 1–30. New York: Columbia University Press, 2010.

Kollantai, Pauline C. H. "Finding a Path to a Common Future: Religion and Cosmopolitanism in the Context of Bosnia-Herzegovina." In *Cosmopolitanism, Religion and the Public Sphere,* edited by Maria Rovisco and Sebastian Kim, 48–67. New York: Routledge, 2014.

Koppelman, Andrew. *Defending American Religious Neutrality.* Cambridge, MA: Harvard University Press, 2013.

Köse, Talha. "Alevi Opening and the Democratization Initiative in Turkey." Ankara: Foundation for Political, Economic and Social Research, March 2010. http://arsiv.setav.org/Ups /dosya/28899.pdf.

Kustusch, Timothy. "Muslim Leaders and Christian Volunteers Host Religious Dialogues in Saharawi Camps." Union de Periodistas y Escritores Saharauis (UPES), April 2, 2009. http://www.upes.org/bodyindex_eng.asp?field=sosio_eng&id=1501.

Laborde, Cécile. "Three Approaches to the Study of Religion." *Immanent Frame,* February 5, 2014. http://blogs.ssrc.org/tif/2014/02/05/three-approaches-to-the-study-of -religion/.

Laliberté, André. "The Communist Party and the Future of Religion in China." *Immanent Frame,* October 4, 2013. http://blogs.ssrc.org/tif/2013/10/04/the-communist-party-and -the-future-of-religion-in-china/.

Lalka, Robert T. "Engaging Faith-Based Communities on Foreign Policy Objectives." *DipNote,* April 1, 2011. http://blogs.state.gov/stories/2011/04/01/engaging-faith-based -communities-foreign-policy-objectives#sthash.Kind5R8c.dpuf.

Lamont v. Woods. 948 F.2d 825 (2d Cir. 1991).

Larsen v. United States Navy. 486 F. Supp. 2d 11, 18 (D.D.C. 2007).

Latour, Bruno. *An Inquiry into Modes of Existence: An Anthropology of the Moderns.* Translated by Catherine Porter. Cambridge, MA: Harvard University Press, 2013.

———. *Rejoicing: Or the Torments of Religious Speech.* Cambridge: Polity, 2013.

———. *We Have Never Been Modern.* Cambridge, MA: Harvard University Press, 1993.

Leiter, Brian. *Why Tolerate Religion?* Princeton: Princeton University Press, 2012.

Lemon v. Kurtzman. 403 U.S. 602 (1971).

Lindkvist, Linde. "The Politics of Article 18: Religious Liberty in the Universal Declaration of Human Rights." *Humanity: An International Journal of Human Rights, Humanitarianism, and Development* 4, no. 3 (2013): 429–47.

Livingston, Alexander. "The Anarchist Vision of William James." Lecture at Northwestern University, Evanston, IL, October 2012.

———. *Damn Great Empires! William James and the Politics of Pragmatism.* Oxford: Oxford University Press, 2015.

Locke, John. *A Letter Concerning Toleration.* Edited by James H. Tully. Indianapolis: Hackett, 1983.

Lopez, Donald S., Jr. "Belief." In *Critical Terms for Religious Studies,* edited by Mark C. Taylor, 21–35. Chicago: University of Chicago Press, 1998.

López-Muñiz, José Luis Martínez, Jan De Groof, and Gracienne Lauwers, eds. *Religious Education in Public Schools: Study of Comparative Law.* Yearbook of the European Association for Education Law and Policy, vol. 6. Dordrecht: Springer, 2006.

Luhrmann, T. M. "Belief Is the Least Part of Faith." *New York Times,* May 29, 2013. http://www.nytimes.com/2013/05/30/opinion/luhrmann-belief-is-the-least-part-of-faith.html?emc=eta1&_r=0.

Lynch, Colum. "In Fighting Radical Islam, Tricky Course for U.S. Aid." *Washington Post,* July 30, 2009. http://www.washingtonpost.com/wp-dyn/content/article/2009/07/29/AR2009072903515.html.

Mahmood, Saba. *The Minority Condition: Religious Difference in the Secular Age.* Princeton: Princeton University Press, 2015.

———. "Religious Freedom, the Minority Question, and Geopolitics in the Middle East." *Comparative Studies in Society and History* 54, no. 2 (2012): 418–46.

———. "Secularism, Hermeneutics, and Empire: The Politics of Islamic Reformation." *Public Culture* 18, no. 2 (Spring 2006): 323–47.

Makdisi, Ussama. *Artillery of Heaven: American Missionaries and the Failed Conversion of the Middle East.* Ithaca, NY: Cornell University Press, 2009.

———. *The Culture of Sectarianism: Community, History, and Violence in Nineteenth-Century Ottoman Lebanon.* Berkeley: University of California Press, 2000.

———. "Understanding Sectarianism." *ISIM Newsletter,* issue 1, vol. 8, no. 1 (2001): 19.

Mandaville, Peter. "Whither U.S. Engagement with Muslims?" *Foreign Policy,* June 4, 2010. http://mideast.foreignpolicy.com/posts/2010/06/04/whither_us_engagement_with_muslims.

Mansfield, John H. "The Religion Clauses of the First Amendment and Foreign Relations." *DePaul Law Review* 36, no. 1 (1986): 1–40.

Markell, Patchen. *Bound by Recognition.* Princeton: Princeton University Press, 2003.

Markoe, Lauren. "Global Religious Hot Spots Get Their Own U.S. Envoy." *Religion News Service*, August 20, 2014. http://www.religionnews.com/2014/08/20/new-job-u-s-envoy-religious-freedom-mideast/.

Marshall, Andrew R. C. "Myanmar Gives Official Blessing to Anti-Muslim Monks." Reuters, June 27, 2013. http://www.reuters.com/article/2013/06/27/us-myanmar-969-special report-idUSBRE95Q04720130627.

Marshall, Katherine. "Journey towards Faith Development Partnerships: The Challenge and the Potential." In *The World Market and Interreligious Dialogue*, edited by Catherine Cornille and Glenn Willis, 190–210. Eugene, OR: Cascade Books, 2011.

Marzouki, Nadia. "Conversion as Statelessness: A Study of Contemporary Algerian Conversions to Evangelical Christianity." *Middle East Law and Governance* 4 (2012): 69–105.

———. "Engaging Religion at the Department of State." *Immanent Frame*, July 30, 2013. http://blogs.ssrc.org/tif/2013/07/30/engaging-religion-at-the-department-of-state/#Marzouki.

Massad, Joseph A. "Re-orienting Desire: The Gay International and the Arab World." *Public Culture* 14, no. 2 (2002): 361–85.

Massicard, Elise. *The Alevis in Turkey and Europe: Identity and Managing Territorial Diversity*. London: Routledge, 2013.

May, Caroline. "U.S. Government Funds Mosque Renovation and Rehabilitation Around the World." *Daily Caller*, August 24, 2010. http://dailycaller.com/2010/08/24/u-s-government-funds-mosque-renovation-and-rehabilitation-around-the-world/.

McAlister, Melani. "State Department Finds Religion, but Whose?" *Religion Dispatches*, December 12, 2013. http://www.religiondispatches.org/archive/politics/7240/state_department_finds_religion__but_whose.

———. "US Evangelicals and the Politics of Slave Redemption as Religious Freedom in Sudan." *South Atlantic Quarterly* 113, no. 1 (2014): 87–108.

McCann, Michael. "The Unbearable Lightness of Rights: On Sociolegal Inquiry in the Global Era." *Law & Society Review* 48, no. 2 (June 2014): 245–73.

McDaniel, Justin. *The Lovelorn Ghost and the Magical Monk: Practicing Buddhism in Modern Thailand*. New York: Columbia University Press, 2011.

McDowell, Robin. "Punks Break Myanmar's Silence on Religious Attacks." *Big Story*, August 5, 2013. http://bigstory.ap.org/article/punks-break-myanmars-silence-religious-attacks.

Mena, Adelaide. "Senate Bill Would Aid Religious Minorities in Middle East." *Catholic News Agency*, August 22, 2013. http://www.catholicnewsagency.com/news/senate-bill-would-aid-religious-minorities-in-middle-east/.

Menchik, Jeremy. "Productive Intolerance: Godly Nationalism in Indonesia." *Comparative Studies in Society and History* 56, no. 3 (2014): 591–621.

Merriam, Jesse. "Establishment Clause-Trophobia: Building a Framework for Escaping the Confines of Domestic Church-State Jurisprudence." *Columbia Human Rights Law Review* 41, no. 699 (2010): 699–752.

Miller, Stuart Creighton. *"Benevolent Assimilation": The American Conquest of the Philippines, 1899–1903*. New Haven: Yale University Press, 1984.

Mitchell, Timothy. "Timothy Mitchell on Infra-Theory, the State Effect, and the Technopolitics of Oil." Theory Talk no. 59. October 25, 2013. http://www.theory-talks.org/2013/10/theory-talk-59.html.

Mockenhaupt, Brian. "Enlisting Allah." *Atlantic*, July 24, 2011. http://www.theatlantic.com/magazine/archive/2011/09/enlisting-allah/308597/.

Moore, Rick. "The Genres of Religious Freedom: Creating Discourses on Religion at the State Department." In *History, Time, Meaning and Memory: Ideas for the Sociology of Religion*, edited by Barbara Jones Denison, 223–53. Leiden: Brill, 2011.

Mora, G. Cristina. *Making Hispanics: How Activists, Bureaucrats, and Media Constructed a New American*. Chicago: University of Chicago Press, 2014.

Moreton, Bethany. *To Serve God and Wal-Mart: The Making of Christian Free Enterprise*. Cambridge, MA: Harvard University Press, 2010.

Moyn, Samuel. "From Communist to Muslim: European Human Rights, the Cold War, and Religious Liberty." *South Atlantic Quarterly* 113, no. 1 (2014): 63–86.

———. *The Last Utopia: Human Rights in History*. Cambridge, MA: Belknap, 2010.

———. "Soft Sells: On Liberal Internationalism." *Nation*, October 3, 2011, 41–43.

Muhanna, Elias. "Letter from Lebanon: A Bookshop Burns." *New Yorker*, January 16, 2014. http://www.newyorker.com/online/blogs/books/2014/01/letter-from-lebanon-a-book shop-burns.html.

Mutua, Makau. *Human Rights: A Political and Cultural Critique*. Philadelphia: University of Pennsylvania Press, 2008.

Near East and South Central Asia Religious Freedom Act of 2014. S. 653, 113th Congress (2013–14). https://www.govtrack.us/congress/bills/113/s653/text.

Nongbri, Brent. *Before Religion: A History of a Modern Concept*. New Haven: Yale University Press, 2013.

O'Neil, Tyler. "Over 50,000 Books Burned in Christian Library in Lebanon over Blasphemy Claim; US Leader Says 'Violent Hysteria' Spreading in Muslim World." *Christian Post*, January 7, 2014. http://www.christianpost.com/news/over-50000-books-burned-in -christian-library-in-lebanon-over-blasphemy-claim-us-leader-says-violent-hysteria -spreading-in-muslim-world-112133/cpt.

Orsi, Robert A. "Afterword: Everyday Religion and the Contemporary World: The Unmodern, or What Was Supposed to Have Disappeared but Did Not." In *Ordinary Lives and Grand Schemes: An Anthropology of Everyday Religion*, edited by Samuli Schielke and Liza Debevec, 146–60. New York: Berghahn Books, 2012.

———. *Between Heaven and Earth: The Religious Worlds People Make and the Scholars Who Study Them*. Princeton: Princeton University Press, 2005.

———. *The Madonna of 115th Street: Faith and Community in Italian Harlem, 1880–1950*. 3rd ed. New Haven: Yale University Press, 2010.

Otis, Pauletta. "An Overview of the U.S. Military Chaplaincy: A Ministry of Presence and Practice." *Review of Faith and International Affairs* 7, no. 4 (2009): 3–15.

Ozay, Emre Demir-Ahmet. "For Minority Status, Alevis Bypass Turkey, Appeal to European Court." *Zaman*, November 18, 2006. http://wwrn.org/articles/23423/.

Özbudun, Ergun. " 'Democratic Opening,' the Legal Status of Non-Muslim Religious Communities and the Venice Commission." *Insight Turkey* 12, no. 2 (2010): 213–22.

Özyürek, Esra. "Beyond Integration and Recognition: Diasporic Constructions of Alevi Identity between Germany and Turkey." In *Transnational Transcendence: Essays on Religion and Globalization*, edited by Thomas J. Csordas, 121–44. Berkeley: University of California Press, 2009.

————. "'The Light of the Alevi Fire Was Lit in Germany and Then Spread to Turkey': A Transnational Debate on the Boundaries of Islam." *Turkish Studies* 10 (2009): 233–53.

Peletz, Michael. "Malaysia's Syariah Judiciary as Global Assemblage: Islamization, Corporatization, and Other Transformations in Context." *Comparative Studies in Society and History* 55, no. 3 (2013): 603–33.

Pépin, Luce. *Teaching about Religions in European School Systems: Policy Issues and Trends—NEF Initiative on Religion and Democracy in Europe.* London: Alliance, 2009.

Pew Forum on Religion and Public Life. "Religious Hostilities Reach Six-Year High." Washington, DC: Pew Research Center, January 14, 2014. http://www.pewforum .org/2014/01/14/religious-hostilities-reach-six-year-high/.

Philpott, Daniel. "What Religion Brings to the Politics of Transitional Justice." *Journal of International Affairs* 61, no. 1 (2007): 93–110.

Post, Dianne. "Land, Life, and Honor: Guatemala's Women in Resistance." *Fair Observer*, October 4, 2013. http://www.fairobserver.com/article/land-life-honor-guatemala -women-resistance.

Povinelli, Elizabeth. *The Cunning of Recognition: Indigenous Alterities and the Making of Australian Multiculturalism.* Durham, NC: Duke University Press, 2002.

Prasse-Freeman, Elliott. "Scapegoating in Burma." *Anthropology Today* 29, no. 4 (2013): 2–3.

President's Advisory Council on Faith-Based and Neighborhood Partnerships. "A New Era of Partnerships: Report of Recommendations to the President." Washington, DC: White House Office of Faith-Based and Neighborhood Partnerships, March 2010. http://www .whitehouse.gov/sites/default/files/microsites/ofbnp-council-final-report.pdf.

Pritchard, Elizabeth A. "Seriously, What Does 'Taking Religion Seriously' Mean?" *Journal of the American Academy of Religion* 78, no. 4 (2010): 1087–1111.

Pritchard, Elizabeth A. *Religion in Public: Locke's Political Theology.* Stanford: Stanford University Press, 2013.

Protocol to the Convention for the Protection of Human Rights and Fundamental Freedoms, art. 2, March 20, 1952, 213 U.N.T.S. 222.

Quiroa, Néstor. "The Popol Vuh and the Dominican Religious Extirpation in Highland Guatemala: Prologues and Annotations of Fr. Francisco Ximénez." *Americas* 67, no. 4 (2011): 467–94.

Rascoff, Samuel J. "Establishing Official Islam: The Law and Strategy of Counter-Radicalization." *Stanford Law Review* 64 (2012): 125–90.

Raustiala, Kal. *Does the Constitution Follow the Flag? The Evolution of Territoriality in American Law.* Oxford: Oxford University Press, 2009.

Rawls, John. *Political Liberalism.* Cambridge, MA: Harvard University Press, 1993.

"Report: U.S. Military Funds Building of Islamic Schools." *Stars and Stripes*, February 1, 2008. http://www.stripes.com/article.asp?section=104&article=52094.

Rifi, Ghassan. "Tripoli Residents Condemn Burning of Saeh Library." Translated by Rani Geha. *Al-Monitor*, January 8, 2014. http://www.al-monitor.com/pulse/security/2014/01 /tripoli-library-burned-islamists-condemned.html#ixzz2tzynmuzU.

Robbers, Gerhard, ed. *Religion in Public Education.* Germany: European Consortium for Church and State Research, 2011.

Rogers, Melissa. "Remarks at the Launch of the Office of Faith-Based Community Initiatives." August 7, 2013. http://www.state.gov/secretary/remarks/2013/08/212781.htm.

Rosen, Lawrence. *Law as Culture*. Princeton: Princeton University Press, 2006.

Rosenow-Williams, Kerstin. *Organizing Muslims and Integrating Islam in Germany: New Developments in the 21st Century*. Leiden: Brill, 2012.

Rubens, Heather Miller. ". . . 'Something Has Gone Wrong:' The JFS Case and Defining Jewish Identity in the Courtroom." In "Politics of Religious Freedom: Case Studies," edited by Peter G. Danchin, Winnifred Fallers Sullivan, Saba Mahmood, and Elizabeth Shakman Hurd. Special issue of *Maryland Journal of International Law* 29 (2015): 361–413.

Ruble, Sarah E. *The Gospel of Freedom and Power: Protestant Missionaries in American Culture after World War II*. Chapel Hill: University of North Carolina Press, 2014.

Saleh, Yasmine. "Egyptian Christians Fear Chaos after Wedding Bloodshed." *Aswat Masriya*, October 21, 2013. http://en.aswatmasriya.com/news/view.aspx?id=2b5d83ba-d465-4a56-9128-4adb73c24d69.

Salomon, Noah. "Freeing Religion at the Birth of South Sudan." *Immanent Frame*, April 12, 2012. http://blogs.ssrc.org/tif/2012/04/12/freeing-religion-at-the-birth-of-south-sudan/.

———. *"The People of Sudan Love You, Oh Messenger of God": An Ethnography of the Islamic State*. Princeton: Princeton University Press, forthcoming, 2016.

Salomon, Noah, and Jeremy F. Walton. "Religious Criticism, Secular Criticism, and the 'Critical Study of Religion': Lessons from the Study of Islam." In *The Cambridge Companion to Religious Studies*, edited by Robert A. Orsi, 403–20. Cambridge: Cambridge University Press, 2012.

Sandal, Nukhet A. "Public Theologies of Human Rights and Citizenship: The Case of Turkey's Christians." *Human Rights Quarterly* 35, no. 33 (2013): 631–50.

Schielke, Samuli. "Second Thoughts about the Anthropology of Islam." *ZMO Working Papers* 2 (2010): 1–16.

Schneible, Ann. "Global Zenit News." June 28, 2012. http://www.catholic.net/index.php?option=zenit&id=35107.

Schonthal, Benjamin. "Constitutionalizing Religion: The Pyrrhic Success of Religious Rights in Postcolonial Sri Lanka." In "Symposium: Re-thinking Religious Freedom," edited by Elizabeth Shakman Hurd and Winnifred Fallers Sullivan. *Journal of Law and Religion* 29, no. 3 (2014): 470–90.

———. "The Legal Regulation of Religion: The Case of Buddhism in Post-Colonial Sri Lanka." In *Buddhism and Law: An Introduction*, edited by Rebecca Redwood French and Mark A. Nathan, 150–66. Cambridge: Cambridge University Press, 2014.

———. "The 'Muslim Other' in Myanmar and Sri Lanka." In *Islam and the State in Myanmar: Muslim-Buddhist Relations and the Politics of Belonging*, edited by Melissa Crouch. Forthcoming.

Schragger, Richard C. "The Relative Irrelevance of the Establishment Clause." *Texas Law Review* 89 (2011): 583–649.

Scott, Joan W. *The Politics of the Veil*. Princeton: Princeton University Press, 2007.

Sedra, Paul. "Copts and the Millet Partnership: The Intra-communal Dynamics Behind Egyptian Sectarianism." In "Symposium: Re-thinking Religious Freedom," edited by Elizabeth Shakman Hurd and Winnifred Fallers Sullivan. *Journal of Law and Religion* 29, no. 3 (2014): 491–509.

Sehat, David. *The Myth of American Religious Freedom*. Oxford: Oxford University Press, 2011.

Shankland, David. *The Alevis in Turkey: The Emergence of a Secular Islamic Tradition.* New York: Routledge, 2003.

Sheftick, Gary. "Chaplain Corps Turns 236 with New Strength." July 28, 2011. http://www .army.mil/article/62568/Chaplain_Corps_turns_236_with_new_strength/.

Sherwood, Yvonne. "On the Freedom of the Concepts of Religion and Belief." In *Politics of Religious Freedom,* edited by Winnifred Fallers Sullivan, Elizabeth Shakman Hurd, Saba Mahmood, and Peter G. Danchin, 29–44. Chicago: University of Chicago Press, 2015.

Shields, Sarah. "The Greek-Turkish Population Exchange: Internationally-Administered Ethnic Cleansing." *Middle East Report* 267 (2013): 2–6.

———. "Mosul, the Ottoman Legacy, and the League of Nations." *International Journal of Contemporary Iraqi Studies* 3, no. 2 (2009): 217–30.

Shortall, Sarah. "Lost in Translation: Religion and the Writing of History." *Modern Intellectual History.* Published electronically December 30, 2014. doi:10.1017/S147924431400081X.

Slotte, Pamela. "The Religious and the Secular in European Human Rights Discourse." *Finnish Yearbook of International Law* 21 (2010): 1–56.

Smith, Huston. *A Seat at the Table: Huston Smith in Conversation with Native Americans on Religious Freedom.* Edited by Phil Cousineau. Berkeley: University of California Press, 2005.

Smith, Martin. "Ethnic Politics in Myanmar: A Year of Tension and Anticipation." *Journal of Southeast Asian Affairs* 2010 (2010): 214–34.

Sökefeld, Martin. "Selves and Others: Representing Multiplicities of Difference in Gilgit and the Northern Areas of Pakistan." In *Islam and Society in Pakistan: Anthropological Perspectives,* edited by Magnus Marsden, 235–58. Karachi: Oxford University Press, 2010.

———. *Struggling for Recognition: The Alevi Movement in Germany and in Transnational Space.* New York: Berghahn Books, 2008.

Somer, Murat. "Turkey's New Constitution and Secular Democracy: A Case for Liberty." *E-International Relations,* June 5, 2012. http://www.e-ir.info/2012/06/05/turkeys-new -constitution-secular-democracy-a-case-for-religious-and-non-religious-liberties/.

Soner, B. Ali. "Citizenship and the Minority Question in Turkey." In *Citizenship in a Global World: European Questions and Turkish Experiences,* edited by E. Fuat Keyman and Ahmet İçduygu, 290–93. New York: Routledge, 2005.

Stamets, Bill. "Anthropologists at War." *In These Times,* June 19, 2008. http://inthesetimes .com/article/3749/anthropologists_at_war/.

Steinberg, David I. "Myanmar: Buddhist-Muslim Tensions." *Sightings,* July 24, 2014. https:// divinity.uchicago.edu/sightings/myanmar-buddhist-muslim-tensions-%E2%80%94 -david-i-steinberg.

Stringer, Martin D. *Discourses on Religious Diversity: Explorations in an Urban Ecology.* Farnham: Ashgate, 2013.

Stuart-Fox, Martin, and Rod Bucknell. "Politicization of the Buddhist Sangha in Laos." *Journal of Southeast Asian Studies* 13, no. 1 (1982): 60–80.

Subaşı, Necdet. "The Alevi Opening: Concept, Strategy and Process." *Insight Turkey* 12, no. 2 (2010): 165–78.

Sullivan, Winnifred Fallers. "After Secularism: Governing through Spiritual Care." Paper presented at the Center for Law and Public Affairs, Princeton University, Princeton, NJ, March 7, 2011.

———. "The Ambassador of Religious Freedoms." In *The Sunday Edition with Michael Enright* (CBC Radio, February 24, 2013).

———. *The Impossibility of Religious Freedom*. Princeton: Princeton University Press, 2005.

———. "The Impossibility of Religious Freedom." *Immanent Frame*, July 8, 2014. http://blogs.ssrc.org/tif/2014/07/08/impossibility-of-religious-freedom/.

———. *A Ministry of Presence: Chaplaincy, Spiritual Care, and the Law*. Chicago: University of Chicago Press, 2014.

———. *Prison Religion: Faith-Based Reform and the Constitution*. Princeton: Princeton University Press, 2009.

———. "Varieties of Legal Secularism." In *Comparative Secularisms in a Global Age*, edited by Linell E. Cady and Elizabeth Shakman Hurd, 107–20. New York: Palgrave Macmillan, 2010.

———. "We Are All Religious Now. Again." *Social Research* 76, no. 4 (2009): 1181–98.

Sullivan, Winnifred Fallers, Robert A. Yelle, and Mateo Taussig-Rubbo. "Introduction." In *After Secular Law*, edited by Winnifred Fallers Sullivan, Robert A. Yelle, and Mateo Taussig-Rubbo, 1–22. Stanford: Stanford University Press, 2011.

Swearer, Donald K. "Center and Periphery: Buddhism and Politics in Modern Thailand." In *Buddhism and Politics in Twentieth Century Asia*, edited by Ian Harris, 194–228. London: Continuum, 2001.

Takase, Hiroi. "Religious Freedom and the New Millennium." Address at the International Coalition for Religious Freedom Conference, Takushoku University, Tokyo, May 23–25, 1998. http://religiousfreedom.com/index.php?option=com_content&view=article&id=375&Itemid=18.

Tambar, Kabir. "The Aesthetics of Public Visibility: Alevi *Semah* and the Paradoxes of Pluralism in Turkey." *Comparative Studies in Society and History* 52, no. 3 (2010): 652–79.

———. *The Reckoning of Pluralism: Political Belonging and the Demands of History in Turkey*. Stanford: Stanford University Press, 2014.

Taylor, Charles. *Multiculturalism and "The Politics of Recognition": An Essay with Commentary*. Edited by Amy Gutmann. Princeton: Princeton University Press, 1992.

———. *A Secular Age*. Cambridge, MA: Belknap, 2007.

Thames, H. Knox, Chris Seiple, and Amy Rowe. *International Religious Freedom Advocacy: A Guide to Organizations, Law, and NGOs*. Waco, TX: Baylor University Press, 2009.

Thomas, Jolyon. "Japan's Preoccupation with Religious Freedom." Ph.D. thesis, Department of Religion, Princeton University, 2014.

Toft, Monica Duffy. "Religion, Rationality and Violence." In *Religion and International Relations Theory*, edited by Jack Snyder, 115–40. New York: Columbia University Press, 2011.

Toft, Monica Duffy, Daniel Philpott, and Timothy Samuel Shah. *God's Century: Resurgent Religion and Global Politics*. New York: Norton, 2011.

Toly, Noah. "Reports Analyzing Issues around the World Oddly Silent on Religion." *Sightings*, March 6, 2014. http://divinity.uchicago.edu/sightings/reports-analyzing-issues-around-world-oddly-silent-religion——noah-toly.

Tønder, Lars. "Ideational Analysis, Political Change and Immanent Causality." In *The Role of Ideas in Political Analysis: A Portrait of Contemporary Debates*, edited by Andreas Gofas and Colin Hay, 56–77. New York: Routledge, 2009.

———. *Tolerance: A Sensorial Orientation to Politics*. Oxford: Oxford University Press, 2013.

Toynbee, Arnold J. *Survey of International Affairs*. Vol. 1, *The Islamic World since the Peace Settlement*. London: Oxford University Press, 1927.

"Trans-Sahara Counter-Terrorism Initiative." *GlobalSecurity*. http://www.globalsecurity.org /military/ops/tscti.htm.

Tugal, Cihan. "Occupy Gezi: The Limits of Turkey's Neoliberal Success." *Jadaliyya*, June 4, 2013. http://www.jadaliyya.com/pages/index/12009/occupy-gezi_the-limits-of-turkey's -neoliberal-suc.

"Turkish Government Buys Hotel Site of Alevi Massacre." *Hurriyet Daily News*, June 17, 2010. http://www.hurriyetdailynews.com/default.aspx?pageid=438&n=turkish-govt-seizes -hotel-where-many-alevis-intellectuals-were-killed-2010-06-17.

Türkmen, Buket. "A Transformed Kemalist Islam or a New Islamic Civic Morality? A Study of 'Religious Culture and Morality' Textbooks in the Turkish High School Curricula." *Comparative Studies of South Asia, Africa and the Middle East* 29, no. 3 (2009): 381–91.

UK Foreign and Commonwealth Office. "Freedom of Religion or Belief—How the FCO Can Help Promote Respect for This Human Right." June 2010. https://www.gov.uk /government/uploads/system/uploads/attachment_data/file/35443/freedom-toolkit.pdf.

US Agency for International Development. "Religion, Conflict and Peacebuilding: An Introductory Program Guide." Washington, DC: Office of Conflict Management and Mitigation, Bureau for Democracy, Conflict, and Humanitarian Assistance: 2009.

US Agency for International Development Bosnia-Herzegovina, World Conference of Religions for Peace, Inter-Religious Action for Tolerance and Co-Existence in the Balkans. "Final Narrative Report, March 1, 2004–March 31, 2005." New York: World Conference of Religions for Peace, June 2005. http://pdf.usaid.gov/pdf_docs/pdacd982.pdf.

US Commission on International Religious Freedom. "Special Report: Protecting and Promoting Religious Freedom in Syria." April 2013. http://www.uscirf.gov/sites/default /files/resources/Syria%20Report%20April%202013(1).pdf.

———. "2012 Annual Report." http://www.uscirf.gov/sites/default/files/resources/Annual %20Report%20of%20USCIRF%202012(2).pdf.

US Conference of Catholic Bishops. "Fortnight for Freedom." 2014. http://www.usccb.org /issues-and-action/religious-liberty/fortnight-for-freedom/.

US Department of Homeland Security. "Faith-Based Security and Communications Advisory Committee." Washington, DC: Homeland Security Advisory Council, 2012. http://www.dhs.gov/xlibrary/assets/hsac/hsac-faith-based-security-and-communications -advisory-committee-final-report-may-2012.pdf.

US Department of State, Bureau of Educational and Cultural Affairs. "Ambassadors Fund for Cultural Preservation." n.d. http://exchanges.state.gov/heritage/afcp.html.

US Department of State. "Country Reports: Africa Overview." July 2005. http://www.state .gov/documents/organization/65468.pdf.

US Department of State. "US Strategy on Religious Leader and Faith Community Engagement." n.d. http://www.state.gov/s/rga/strategy/.

US Government Accountability Office. "Faith-Based and Community Initiative: Improvements in Monitoring Grantees and Measuring Performance Could Enhance Accountability." 2006. http://www.gao.gov/products/GAO-06=616.

Van der Veer, Peter. *Imperial Encounters: Religion and Modernity in India and Britain*. Princeton: Princeton University Press, 2001.

——. *The Modern Spirit of Asia: The Spiritual and the Secular in China and India*. Princeton: Princeton University Press, 2013.

Vásquez, Manuel A. *More Than Belief: A Materialist Theory of Religion*. Oxford: Oxford University Press, 2010.

Visser, Reidar. "The Western Imposition of Sectarianism on Iraqi Politics." *Arab Studies Journal* 15/16, nos. 2/1 (2007/2008): 83–99.

Ward, Olivia. "Meet Canada's Defender of the Faiths." *Toronto Star*, February 14, 2014. http://www.thestar.com/news/world/2014/02/14/meet_canadas_defender_of_the_faiths.html.

Wenger, Tisa. *We Have a Religion: The 1920s Pueblo Indian Dance Controversy and American Religious Freedom*. Chapel Hill: University of North Carolina Press, 2009.

White, Benjamin Thomas. *The Emergence of Minorities in the Middle East: The Politics of Community in French Mandate Syria*. Edinburgh: Edinburgh University Press, 2012.

Wilson, Erin K. *After Secularism: Rethinking Religion in Global Politics*. New York: Palgrave Macmillan, 2012.

Wilton Park. "Conference Report: Promoting Religious Freedom around the World." July 2012. https://www.wiltonpark.org.uk/wp-content/uploads/wp1108-report.pdf.

Wineburg, Robert J., Brian L. Coleman, Stephanie C. Boddie, and Ram A. Cnaan. "Leveling the Playing Field: Epitomizing Devolution through Faith-Based Organizations." *Journal of Sociology and Social Welfare* 35, no. 1 (2008): 17–42.

Woodhead, Linda. "Diversity in Religious Practice: Examples from the UK." Lecture at the India International Centre, Delhi, February 18, 2013.

——. "Tactical and Strategic Religion." In *Everyday Lived Islam in Europe*, edited by Nathal Dessing, Nadia Jeldtoft, Jørgen Nielsen, and Linda Woodhead, 22–36. London: Ashgate, 2013.

World Learning. "Fostering Religious Harmony in Albania: Final Report." June 30, 2007. http://pdf.usaid.gov/pdf_docs/PDACK058.pdf.

Yildirim, Mine. "Turkey: The Diyanet—The Elephant in Turkey's Religious Freedom Room?" *Forum 18*, May 4, 2011. http://www.forum18.org/archive.php?article_id=1567.

Young, Jonathan. "Buddhism and Politics in Sri Lanka." Review of *Ruling Religion: Buddhism, Politics and Law in Contemporary Sri Lanka*, by Benjamin Schonthal. *Dissertation Reviews*, March 4, 2014. http://dissertationreviews.org/archives/7815.

Zaw, Aung. "Are Myanmar's Hopes Fading?" *New York Times*, April 24, 2013. http://www.nytimes.com/2013/04/25/opinion/will-hatred-kill-the-dream-of-a-peaceful-democratic-myanmar.html?pagewanted=2&_r=2&nl=todaysheadlines&emc=edit_th_20130425.

Zunes, Stephen. "The Last Colony: Beyond Dominant Narratives on the Western Sahara Roundtable." *Jadaliyya*, June 3, 2013. http://www.jadaliyya.com/pages/index/11992/the-last-colony_beyond-dominant-narratives-on-the-.

Index